IRISH DANCE

ARTHUR FLYNN

ILLUSTᵣ ... ARRALL

PELICAN PUBLISHING COMPANY

Gretna 1998

Published by The Appletree Press Ltd., 1998
Published by arrangement in North America by
Pelican Publishing Company, Inc., 1998

A catalogue record for this book is available from the U.S.
Library of Congress.

ISBN 1-56554-412-9

Printed in China

Published by Pelican Publishing Company, Inc
P.O. Box 3110, Gretna, Louisiana 70054-3110

Irish Dance 10 9 8 7 6 5 4 3 2 1

CONTENTS

Introduction

Dance is one of the oldest forms of expression known to man. It was a natural part of primitive life. From the moment of his birth, until his death, every important event in man's life had an appropriate dance – dances of joy to celebrate a new birth, elaborate marriage rituals and dances designed to protect the dead from evil spirits.

With primitive man, when a child was born, dancers leaped high to celebrate, hoping some of the strength they were giving out would pass to the child. Boys and girls had to perform various dances when they grew up. Sometimes all the family danced except the girl, who was kept in darkness. Then she danced alone, facing the east. As the sun started a new life each day in the east, so the girl was starting a new life as a woman.

Fertility dances were a mixture of magic and prayer, in the hope of providing a good harvest. It is interesting to note that tribes as far apart as New Zealand and North America performed similar rain dances.

Witch doctors believed that dancing was an integral part of their medicine, helping to drive away illness and evil spirits. Dancing was often used as a show of strength - week long rituals were quite common in the Caribbean. The Pawnee Indian tribe had a gruelling test for warriors and a boy who gave up before his Dance of Admittance was over would never be accepted into the Circle of Braves.

In many countries rain-dances were performed by farming people. In Northwest Australia, they built stone or sand into a mound and placed a magic stone on top, then one man danced round the mound, chanting prayers for rain, until he was so exhausted that he had to stop and someone else would replace him. These dances evolved independently in the different parts of the world, but in more recent times similarity in dance can be attributed to increased travel and communication. Thus it was that such dances as the Minuet spread throughout the courts of Europe. Nearer home it is obvious that the Morris Men of Cornwall and the Mummers of County Wexford perform versions of the same dance carried across the Irish Sea by traders.

Like most cultures, Ireland has a strong tradition of dance. Unfortunately there is little written evidence of the national dances of Ireland in earlier centuries, as Viking invaders in the eighth century destroyed most books of this period. The English authorities introduced stringent laws in an attempt to suppress the Irish people, their customs, language, dance and music, in particular the draconian Statutes of Kilkenny of 1366. These statutes imposed heavy penalties against all those who practised Irish customs. With these repressive measures dance declined for a period but with the strong sense of nationalism and determination of the Irish, dancing continued in secret. Even the Penal Laws of the late seventeenth century, which attempted to suppress the Irish language and native customs, did not kill Irish culture.

From the late seventeenth-century, dance and music were the main forms of entertainment in rural Ireland as neighbours called to each other's houses. According to the accounts of many travellers in the eighteenth and nineteenth centuries, crossroads dancing featured strongly in the social life of rural communities. In winter, or during inclement weather, the dancers

moved into kitchens and barns. There was a growing suspicion by the clergy concerning these "occasions of sin", with many priests condemning the practice from the altar and searching hedges for courting couples. This development was indirectly responsible for bringing about the first *céilí* organised by the Gaelic League in 1897. They saw the potential for having *céilís* with proper tuition in a formal setting. It also enabled dancers to be indoors under supervision.

In the 1930s and 1940s, during periods of emigration and high unemployment, there was a lack of enthusiasm for entertainment. Traditional Irish music and dance were also affected by the Public Dance Halls Act of 1935 that introduced more commercial dance halls with modern dance bands. The Catholic Church used this act to end cross-roads dancing, stating that young people should only attend properly supervised dances; many organised by the Church. Young people deserted the "square" traditional music for the "Ballrooms of Romance". In the early 1960s, groups like the Dubliners, the Clancy Brothers and Seán O'Riada gave an impetus to the revival of Irish music and dance.

Another aspect of Irish dance that has undergone a recent revival is set dancing, with regular sessions in clubs, pubs and hotels throughout the country attracting capacity crowds. In general, set dancing, with its intricate steps, serves as a social outlet and meeting place for adults with a love for Irish culture. They travel long distances to attend dancing sessions and work-shops.

One of the main contributing factors to the revival of Irish dance in recent years has been the world-wide success of the stage shows *Riverdance* and *Lord of the Dance*. Riverdance began as a short interval act during the Eurovision Song Contest in Dublin in 1994. The performances of world dancing champions, Michael Flatley and Jean Butler, received such an enthusiastic reception that the producers developed an entire show which has played to critical acclaim in Ireland, England, Australia and America. Michael Flatley parted from *Riverdance* and created, produced and starred in his own show *Lord of the Dance*. Many dancing teachers today are revising their traditional dancing methods to teach an influx of young pupils all striving to be the next Michael Flatley or Jean Butler.

ORIGINS OF
IRISH DANCE

❖

The early history of Ireland reveals a constant shifting of population through migration and invasions, each group bringing its own music and dance. Little exists in written records of the national dances of Ireland in ancient times. There was a long tradition of music and dance being transferred orally and by teaching methods from parent or teacher to child.

Among the earliest influences were the Druids who danced in religious ritual to the oak and the sun. Traces of their circular dances still survive in the ring dances of today. When the Celts came from central Europe over two thousand years ago, they brought with them their own form of music and folk dances. Around 400 AD when Ireland was converted to Christianity the new priests used the pagan style of ornamentation in illuminating their gospel manuscripts and the peasants retained the same flamboyant qualities in their music and dancing. In the twelfth century, during the Norman Invasion, the *Carol*, a lovesong dance, was popular in Normandy. Originally the

Carol was associated with May Day rituals. Thereafter it was performed in the Irish towns that the Normans had conquered. The leader sang a song and the six couples replied as they danced around him with simple steps.

The art of Mumming in Ireland was started in and has mainly been associated with County Wexford. Mumming has a strong English influence and one of the earliest references would appear to be in *Hanmer's Chronicle* of 1172 when he describes King Henry's celebration of Christmas in Ireland: "...the pastime, the sport, and the mirth, and the continuall musicke, the masking, mumming and strange shewes, the gold, the silver, and plate...". A much later account tells of the shipwreck of an English vessel off the South Wexford coast between Carne and Kilmore Quay early in the nineteenth century. The survivors were brought ashore and when they had

recovered they performed a dance which the locals later copied. Other sources suggest that Mumming came to Ireland in the seventeenth century as a result of trade between Wexford and Cornwall in the days of the old sailing ships.

In 1540 it is reputed that the Lord Deputy of Ireland, Sir Anthony St. Leger, saw the round dance performed and brought it back to England. It was also a form of the English Maypole dance. From the mid-1500s the Irish performed a variety of dances. These included the *Rince Fada*, the *Hey*, jigs, *the Trenchmore* and sword dances. During this period there were repeated attempts by the English to suppress Irish culture including a ban on piping and the arrest of pipers.

In O'Keefe's and O'Brian's *Handbook of Irish Dances*, it is recorded that in Dublin during the reign of King Charles II, "graceful gentlemen were wont to dance with the fair ladies of the Court in the fashion of the Hey and the Fada". In 1569, in a state letter written by Sir Henry Sydney, one of Queen Elizabeth's courtiers in Ireland, he mentioned that he had witnessed in Galway "the dancing of an Irish jig by a number of beautiful Irish girls in magnificent dresses". He then gave a description of this dance, together with the formation of the dancers in two straight lines and this description leads one to believe that the dance was similar to the one known as the *Rince Fada* (Long Dance).

At this time dances began to be performed in the Great Halls of the newly built castles and the sixteenth century English invaders brought some of these dances to the Court of the Queen. One of these was the *Trenchmore*; described as "a big, free form country dance". In 1651 John Playford referred to it as a "long dance for as many as will". Also danced in the Courts was the *Rince Fada* of which the *Rince Mór* (Great Dance) is a modern version. From the mid-eighteenth century, when dances were performed in Court, the services of a dancing master were required.

On Saint John's Eve the dancers would dance in a circle around the bonfire and on occasions cattle would be driven through the fire to purify them. From this period onwards another style of dance, called *The Hey*, was popular. In this dance women wound in around their partners and it is believed that this was a fore-runner of the present day reel.

Records of the origins of solo or step dancing are sketchy but it would appear that these dances came into being around the end of the eighteenth century. In different parts of the country several versions of the same dance could be found. In this way a rich heritage of Irish dance was assembled and modified down through the years. There is also an extensive range of dance tunes and a rough estimate today would put the number at about 6,000, including jigs, hornpipes and hundreds of tunes for sets and half sets and polkas.

HISTORY OF
IRISH DANCE

In 1681, a traveller named Dineley wrote in *A Voyage through the Kingdom of Ireland:* "They [the Irish] are much addicted, on holidays, with the bagpipe, Irish harps, to dance after their country fashion, that in the long dance, one after another, of all conditions, masters, mistresses, and servants".

In 1776, the travel writer Arthur Young wrote in A *Tour of Ireland:*

> "Dancing is so universal among them [the Irish] that there are everywhere itinerant dancing masters, to whom the collars pay sixpence a quarter for teaching their families. Beside the Irish jig, which they can dance with a most luxuriant expression, minuets and country dances are taught, and I even heard some talk of cotillions coming in."

Early descriptions of dancers note that they were barefoot. Soft shoes have only been worn since 1924. In the six-

teenth and seventeenth centuries dancing was a popular pastime, especially in the summer evenings and at weekends. Royalty arriving in Ireland were greeted at the shore by young girls performing native dances. One such occasion was in 1689 when King James landed at Kinsale, County Cork and was greeted by young people dancing the *Rince Fada*. Three people moved abreast, each holding the end of a white handkerchief. They advanced to slow music and were followed by the other dancers in twos, each set holding a white handkerchief between them. The tempo of the music increased and the dancers performed a variety of lively figures. The *Rince Fada* was also performed in Limerick, particularly around May Day. It became a popular dance at the conclusion of balls.

From the late-seventeenth century, the English authorities imposed the Penal Laws which banned the ordination of

Catholic clergy and education of Catholic children. Irish dance and music had to be practised in secret. These laws forced a decline in the Irish language, customs and music. This period of severe repression lasted for over a century until the granting of Catholic Emancipation in 1829 which repealed the draconian legislation.

The dancing master appeared for the first time in rural Ireland in the middle of the eighteenth century. The rural Irish were very poor peasants who created their own form of enjoyment in dancing and music. From this need the dancing master came into existence and travelled around the country from village to village with a blind fiddler. The peasants paid the dancing master to teach their children to dance. The dancing master was a flamboyant figure who wore brightly-coloured clothes.

He had a tall hat known as the *Caroline*, a long-tailed coat and white knee breeches, white stockings and turn pumps. He carried a cane with a silver head and silk tassel – indicating that he was a cut above the normal wandering musicians. He regarded himself as a well mannered and dignified gentleman, and he attempted to instil these attributes into his pupils.

There was great excitement in a village when the dancing master arrived, as it meant that there would be music and dancing for several weeks. Locals were very co-operative with him and would put a room or outhouse at his disposal. On occasions a farmer or landowner would allow him the use of a barn or kitchen. In parts of the country the dancing master would run his classes in conjunction with hedge schools where the different classes would be held at opposite ends of the classroom. In some poor areas a makeshift building, roofed with straw, had to be erected for him. At times the dancing master would stay in a farmer's house and in return for the hospitality he would give free classes to the children of the house. On other occasions he would stay in different houses each night.

In 1776, one of the earliest references to the dancing master is found in *A Tour of Ireland* by Arthur Young. He stated that a fee of sixpence was received by the dancing master from his pupils. The fiddler received about half this fee. The masters were very innovative and worked out the intricate steps of many of the dances themselves. The dances taught were normally jigs and reels.

The basic step the dancing master taught was the rising step, the first step of the jig or the side step when teaching the reel. A major problem for some of the pupils was that they were unable to distinguish between their right and left foot. To overcome this problem the dancing master would tie hay and straw to each foot. He would then instruct them to "lift hay foot" or "straw foot". "Hay rope" and "Straw rope" became familiar terms with dancing masters teaching the basic steps.

To ensure that the weaker pupils were not bored or disheartened the dancing master would organise round or group dances in which all the pupils could employ two basic jig or reel steps. It also gave them an opportunity to enjoy themselves. The standards of these dances was quite high as all the participants had received proper tuition. The solo dancers were held in such esteem that often half-doors were taken off hinges or tables cleared to provide an exceptionally gifted solo dancer with a platform.

The dancing master did not only teach dancing but also taught deportment to children in wealthy families. In the "big houses" of the Anglo-Irish ascendancy, the Lord or Earl would sometimes request that his children were taught waltzes or quadrilles. In the early nineteenth century, in conjunction with dancing classes, cudgel playing was also undertaken, and

sometimes the dancing master gave the instructions. A cudgel was a short stick which was originally used as a weapon by Irish peasants. In cudgel playing, which was a form of fencing, the dancers were taught to hit their opponents but to avoid being struck themselves.

The jurisdiction of the dancing master was well defined and a district would cover about ten square miles. The dancing master would travel from village to village and then begin the circuit over again. A friendly rivalry existed between all dancing masters and each respected the other's territory. When dancing masters met at fairs and social gatherings they would challenge each other to dance in public on upturned barrels. Sometimes they would have an endurance test and would dance until only one still stood. When a parish was in dispute and two dancing masters claimed the same territory, they they would hold a competition to see who would win it. On one occasion before a competition, a dancing master placed oil on the barrel of his rival and when he stepped onto it, fell flat on his face.

When a dancing master instructed his pupils, he discouraged lively movements and insisted more on graceful actions. An important aspect of the solo dancer was control. The body would remain rigid and the dancer would only move from the hips downwards, with the arms flat by the side. The only thing by way of an arm movement that was practised was a threatening gesture with a clenched fist, seen in the jig danced to what was known as a Tune of Occupation.

There were various methods of payment for the dancing master. In some areas he would receive a quarterly fee from his students. They would receive two benefit nights, the first, two weeks into the course and the final, a fortnight later. They would encourage the villagers to attend these events and make a contribution. The dancing master would send his hat among the crowd for a collection for himself and his musician. In poorer villages he would sometimes receive chickens or food in part-payment for his services.

There were three types of dancing master. The most socially respectable was welldressed and carried a stick with a silver top. He would have the pick of the jobs, and would often be assigned to the "big houses". Here he would be treated royally, receiving the best of accommodation, food and clothes. The middle group were less well-dressed and taught all types of dance steps to Irish peasants. The lower range were termed Jig Actors and taught only the basic steps. The Jig Actor would watch others dancing through the window of the big house. He would then return home and imitate the steps. Some dancing masters would bequeath their district to another master upon their death. Other times their best pupil might inherit the district.

Dancing masters survived into the early twentieth century, particularly in Counties Kerry and Clare. Gradually they were replaced by dancing schools run by both male and female dancing teachers.

According to many travellers to Ireland from the mid-eighteenth century, the social life of rural areas included cross-roads dancing. From the mid 1840s, following the famine, there was large scale disease, death and emigration in Ireland. With such a drastic decline in the population the people lost heart, interest waned in Irish culture and the number of music and dance sessions dropped. While the population declined in Ireland over this period, millions of Irish immigrants settled in England and the USA. Irish communities began to develop in London, Manchester, Liverpool, New York, Boston and Chicago. Away from home they had a deeper appreciation of their roots, music and dance. Dancing masters and teachers

began organising classes in the new Irish centres and *céilís* became a regular event in their social lives.

Gradually the position began to improve in Ireland. When revolutionary movements began to develop in the early nineteenth century the attention of all artists was again drawn to their native traditions. This gave rise to the founding of dancing schools in Cork, Limerick and Kerry. While there was high unemployment and poverty, the peasants had to create their own form of entertainment. As there was no cost involved traditional music and dance became popular pastimes. In the small towns and villages, the social life revolved around people gathering in a house for an evening of music, dance and storytelling. In each townland there was a *céilí* house. Ideally it would have a spacious kitchen with a stone-flagged floor. Following a day's fishing or farming the young men and women

26

would mingle with older people. The number of people attending this type of session could vary from six to forty.

These dancing and music sessions normally took place all year round except during Lent. Special events were held in conjunction with weddings, wakes and following the harvest. Word of a session would pass quickly throughout the village and dancers would converge on the appointed house. An assortment of musicians provided the music. Many of the musicians were blind or physically incapacitated, and money from their music gave them a reasonable standard of living.

The word *céilí* originally meant the gathering of people in a house at night to talk and have an enjoyable time together, long before music and dancing became part of the proceedings. The most frequent dances would be sets or half sets, traditional group dances, normally danced by four or eight people. There were numerous regional types and variations of dances. In some areas of the country, the Lancers, the barn-dance and the waltzes were performed. Dancers who perfected their footwork were glad of an opportunity to display their intricate steps and would dance on the flags of the kitchen floor. In the summer months the young dancers would move to the crossroads where there was ample space to dance.

There was a growing hostility by the clergy to these "occasions of sin". Bishop Moylan of Kerry was extremely vocal in his condemnation and even threatened excommunication on those who disobeyed his ruling. Other members of the clergy also condemned cross-roads dancing from the pulpit. The Public Dance Halls Act of 1935 introduced more commercial dance halls with modern dance bands. The Catholic Church used this act to end cross-roads dancing and insisted that young people should only attend dances indoors under supervision.

By the end of the nineteenth century, Ireland experienced a cultural revival and a renewed pride and interest in all aspects of Irish culture. In an effort to halt the decline in the Irish language Douglas Hyde founded the Gaelic League *(Conradh na Gaeilge)* in 1893. Along with preserving and promoting the Irish language the aim of the league was to organise *feiseanna* and *céilís*. The members of the Gaelic League worked enthusiastically to restore dancing to a place of honour in the social life of the nation and organised the first official *céilí*. This *céilí* was not held in Ireland, as would be expected, but in London as the organiser was Fionán Mac Colum, the Scottish secretary of the Gaelic League in London. The date was 30 October 1897 and the venue was the Bloomsbury Hall, near the British Museum. The event was attended by Irish immigrants based in London and Gaelic League members from Dublin who travelled over for the historic event. The ambitious programme included step dancing, sets and waltzes to Irish music. With the introduction of the formal *céilí*, a form of social dancing was devised by having boys and girls face each other in two lines to perform the double jig. Between each step the facing couples changed places by a linking arms and turning so that every second step was performed in the dancers' original positions.

In Wexford Mumming plays composed at the beginning of this century all the characters were drawn from Irish history and included Brian Boru, Wolfe Tone, Robert Emmet, Father Murphy from Wexford, Daniel O'Connell, Patrick Sarsfield and the 1798 rebel leader, Michael Dwyer. The plays were always written in verse and the main theme was a combat between the two heroes, the fall of one of them, and his revival by a doctor. The highlight of each performance was an intricate sword dance.

Mumming plays are still performed today in Wexford. A group or set of Mummers consists of twelve men dressed in white shirts, green and gold sashes, dark pants and tall hats, something similar to bishops' mitres. Sometimes straw masks are worn. Each man carries a wooden sword. The characters the mummers portray vary from place to place and sometimes feature Saint Patrick, Napoleon and King George who all influenced Irish history.

IRISH DANCES

❖

There are two distinctive forms of Irish dancing; solo dances and figure dances. Solo dances are performed nowadays mainly in exhibition or competition and require a great deal of skill and years of practice. Figure dances are simple and easy to perform and require only an elementary knowledge of the most basic steps. They lend themselves well to recreational and social events, as anyone who has been to a *céilí* can confirm. There are three grades for beginners of Irish dance, Grade A, Grade B and Grade C. Grade A is basic steps in dance. A dancer must attain this standard to pass onto Grade B and

do another test before moving onto Grade C. After reaching this standard, a dancer moves upward in age groups to Over 21 where there is no age limit.

The style to be cultivated in the solo dances is one of simplicity and natural grace. The carriage of the body should be natural, upright and relaxed. The arms and hands should be kept flat against the side. The figures and steps should be executed with accuracy and precision, but easily, without any effort. Irish figure or group dancing can be performed in a square, circle or line formation, enjoying only a few simple steps. These dances are essentially the dances of Ireland.

There are several main Irish step dances: reel, light jig, heavy jig, single jig and the hornpipe. There are many variations of these dances and each dancing school has its own version of the steps. A heavy jig is danced in an aggressive manner in heavy shoes, which produce a stamping sound. The heavy jig, *Saint Patrick's Day*, is the only dance all dancing schools have in common. It is a traditional set dance, with eight people in jig time and danced in heavy shoes.

The derivation of the word *jig* has never been satisfactorily explained. Most writers of the last century held the opinion that the term *jig* was of Italian origin. There was indeed a type of musical measure popular in Italy during the eighteenth century termed a *Giga*, and most experts confirm that the Irish jig was derived from this particular type of Italian music popularised by two great Italian musicians, Corelli and Geminani. However, tunes called Irish jigs had previously been published in several editions of Playford's *Dancing Master*, and these booklets were published from 1650 to 1700, many years before the birth of Corelli and Geminani.

The basic music defines the speed of the dance. The time of a tune is shown at the beginning of the music, a jig, for example, is in ⁶⁄₈ time. The first number is the number of beats per "measure" or "bar". The second number is the basic unit for a beat. The tempo of the music determines the speed of the beat: Reel – ⁴⁄₄; Jig – ⁶⁄₈; Slip Jig – ⁹⁄₈; Single Jig – ⁶⁄₈; Hornpipe – ³⁄₄ or ⁴⁄₄ depending on how the music is written.

The lighter jig is a faster dance than the jig, slip jig and heavy jig. The double jig is one of the most popular Irish dances. It commences with the rising step, one of the first steps taught to beginners. The right foot is lifted about 12 inches off the floor, the person hops on the left, while the right is lowered to tap the floor and then each foot in turn is lifted and lowered. This action is repeated three times to one bar of music.

Arm movement is discouraged in Irish dance, as the dancer is taught to demonstrate control and grace. However, there was a time in the early nineteenth century when vigorous arm movements and swinging shillellaghs played a large part in the jig. From the early 1900s arm gestures were removed from the jig, in the same way that all arm movements have been eliminated from the Irish hornpipe. The jig was originally danced by sailors, imitating the motion of the ship. The only thing remaining of its seafaring origin is the rocking movement common to sailor's dances world-wide.

The Irish word for reel is *cor*. In a 1598 book entitled *News from Scotland* there is the following quotation: "Silas Duncan did go before them playing this reill or dance upon a small trump." Both men and women dance the reel. For women, it is a light rapid soft shoe dance which allows for plenty of leaping. The reel is faster than the jig and has a ¾ timing.

One of the earliest references to *Rince Fada* (Long Dance) is in 1549 when a writer stated that there were similarities between the Irish and Scottish versions. There is a strong belief that the dance was brought to Scotland by migrant workers from Donegal and Derry. For the *Rince Fada*, the men stand in a row. The females face them in another row. Dancing begins at one end and gradually works through the line until all are dancing.

The Harvest Time jig is a dance from the west of Ireland, dating from the eighteenth century. It was unusual that it only called for half as many men as women. The man would be in the centre with a woman on each side holding his hand and they would dance a jig. It originated at harvest time when there was a shortage of men, for at that time hundreds of harvesters left home to seek employment in other areas where work was plentiful, returning home when the season was over.

From its title and formation, the jig known as The Piper's Dance would seem to have some associations with an old Irish custom. It is said that at the old country dance gatherings the piper was usually paid by the male dancers. These contributions were put into the piper's hat which was placed on the floor for that purpose after the last dance. The original Piper's Dance was danced by a large number of couples, with the piper seated in the centre. The Haymaker's Jig is for an even number of people, mainly ten. The men form a line facing their partners in another line.

The Sweets of May, originated in County Armagh and dating from the early nineteenth century, is believed to have been inspired by the dancing of the fairies on May Eve (30 April). An old dancing master returning home on May Eve from a house *céilí* passed by a fairy rath and saw "the wee people" perform this dance. When the dancers reached the clapping movement (ringing the bells) all the bell-shaped flowers (butter-

cups, bluebells) shook on their stems, ringing in unison with the tune.

The Cake Dance dating from the early nineteenth century, was not a specific dance but a session of dancing at which a cake was offered to the couple who were the best performers. These gatherings were usually connected with sporting activities. The cake was provided by the wife of the publican or innkeeper. It was placed on top of a pike about ten feet high and a garland of flowers was placed around it. All the dancers began in a large ring and danced around the cake. They fell out as they got tired and the couple to hold out the longest won the cake. This dance is now obsolete.

The Bonfire Dance, danced in reel time, was a delightful and simple old circle dance in which young and old danced around a bonfire. Any number of couples danced but usually no fewer than six. Dancers stood in a ring facing the central bonfire, with the women to the right of their male partners. It had an association with old traditions in that it was supposed to have keen danced originally around the bonfire on Saint John's Eve (20 June). If a real bonfire was not possible then something was placed in the centre of the ring to represent one.

Tory is an island off the coast of Donegal where the sea is particularly rough. The Waves of Tory is a long dance in reel time for an even number of couples. The dancers imitate the motion of the waves. The dance is progressive in sets of four:

two couples in each set. The dance begins with a row of men standing opposite a row of women. The rows advance and retire twice for eight bars. Each person in a set holds right hands in a central wheel and dances in a circle. The action is then repeated from the beginning and in sets, with each person holding left hands in a central wheel and dancing in a circle and each row marching up the centre. The lead couple hold hands and raise their arms to form a bridge and the second couple go under the bridge of the lead couple. The third couple make a bridge and the lead couple pass as waves under a bridge formed by the second couple. Then all couples alternatively form bridges or waves and proceed with this formation until each set returns to its original place.

A set of Mummers is led by a Captain who recites the Captain's rhyme and calls on each to speak his lines. They perform two dances starting with the *claibh* (sword dance) and concluding with the reel. They dance in time with the music and strike perfect time with wooden sticks, or "swords", as they were often called. Each performance has three sections; the presentation, in which they parade on, the drama and a procession in which they march off. Performances take place in local halls, hotels or open spaces. The music for Mumming is performed by a bodhrán, fiddle, uillean pipe or tin whistle and, as County Wexford is rich in traditional music, there is an excellent range of music accompanying each performance of Mummers.

Music

❖

An assortment of instruments has provided the music for dancing throughout the centuries. Formerly the bagpipe was the most popular instrument, but today it is more common to find dancers being accompanied by an accordion, a fiddle or a piano.

In 1601 when pipers were outlawed by the English authorities and their instruments were destroyed, they found a way of overcoming the problem. They made whistles from corn

cobs (the woody centre in a stalk of corn). They cut holes in the improvised whistle to cover with the fingers and made a cornpipe, an instrument similar to today's tin-whistle. It was not until about 1700 that the modern uillean pipes were invented. This new instrument had a much milder and modified tone than that of the war pipes.

During the eighteenth century, harpers wandered the roads of Ireland, playing only when they were certain their music would not alert the English authorities. These notable musicians kept their fingernails very long. With the gradual relaxation of the Penal Laws, the harpers were invited to play their tunes in the Great Halls of princes and lords. Often the lord welcomed the harper to perform and commissioned him to

compose a tune in honour of his family's honour. *Lord Inchiquin* and *Lady Eleanor Brabazon* are examples of two compositions written to honour aristocrats. The harper was a respected man and was welcomed everywhere. In later years, the harpers, were to team up with the dancing masters. Many of the dancing masters were expert musicians themselves, and if a musician was unavailable they could perform on the pipes, fiddle or flute. Quite a number of them composed their own tunes for their newly arranged set dances.

Bagpipers or harpers were the principal musicians – particularly in the seventeenth century but when they were prevented playing in public by legislation, an assortment of other musicians provided the beat. Many of these musicians were blind or had other physical diabilities, and music offered them a reasonable regular income. The most famous of these was the blind harper, Carolan, who delighted the gentry in the "big houses" with his playing. He is best known for his *Carolan's Concerto.*

The music of the harpers was unwritten until 1792 when Edward Bunting made the first attempt to preserve their tunes for posterity at the Great Harp Festival of Belfast with his collection. This was later published as *The Ancient Music of Ireland* (1840).

Music was unwritten and musicians played and learned tunes by ear. Their tunes were passed from one generation to

the next. They must have had excellent memories as a skilled musician could play any one of several hundred tunes on request.

The majority of Irish jigs are native in origin and were composed by pipers and fiddlers such as Leo Rowsome, Séamus Ennis and Micho Russell. Some of the music was adapted from English and Scottish tunes. A good example of adapation is *The Fairy Reel* which was composed in Scotland in 1802 and became popular in Ireland a century later. The titles of many dance tunes had no musical connection with the actual tunes. Most musicians looked around them for inspiration when naming a composition or randomly plucked a name out of the air to give a tune a title, e.g. *Garden of Daisies, Hurry the Jug* and *Stack of Barley*. There were of course some with a political significance, such as *Bonaparte's Retreat*. This was written around 1798 when the United Irishmen expected a French invasion and Napoleon's help to overthrow English rule.

From the end of the eighteenth century dancing at wakes was another familiar sight. The mourners would follow each other in a ring around the coffin to the music of the bagpipe. When no instrument was available the lilter provided the music. Lilting, or *porta beil*, is a unique musical sound produced with the mouth.

Music at *céilís* today is provided by a ceilí band with musicians playing an assortment of instruments including the fiddle, drums, piano and accordion.

DANCING COSTUMES

The costumes of today's dancers reflect the clothing of Ireland from the eighth century. The dresses worn by women are copies of the traditional Irish peasant dress and they are adorned with hand-embroidered Celtic designs based on the *Book of Kells*

and Irish stone crosses. Copies of the famous Tara Brooch are worn on the shoulder holding the flowing shawl which falls down over the back.

In the early 1900s there was a minimum design on the costumes but as dancing schools were established, each one endeavoured to design their own distinctive costumes. The interlocking lines in the design denoted the continuity of life. The favourite colours were green and white. Red was avoided because of its relevance to England. The ancient Irish were fond of bright colours, in fact it was a mark of high social status in the community to be allowed to wear more than one colour. From around the twelfth century gold thread embroidery was an important item on women's clothing. Lace collars came into vogue around the eighteenth century when Carrickmacross and Limerick Lace were first manufactured. These aspects of Irish culture are still visible in today's costumes.

The male's costume is less embellished but no less steeped in history - they wear a plain kilt or pants and jacket and a *brat*, a folded cloak hanging from the shoulder. *Brat* means "cloak" or "mantle" in Irish. The cloak or *brat* was a symbol of rebellion during the suppression since it enabled the rebels to endure the worst weather while holding out in the mountains. There is evidence that the kilt was worn as far back as the fifteenth century. When Shane O'Neill was presented to Queen Elizabeth he wore a kilt and brat, as did his followers.

His appearance is said to have pleased the Queen enormously.

In the early 1800s female dancers wore ordinary peasant dresses and ribbons formed into flowers or crosses. The girl's crimson homespun skirt reached down to her ankles over which she wore a simple black bodice. From the late 1800s pipers wore the kilt, and from about 1910 male dancers began to wear this form of costume. During this period the typical female dance costume consisted of a hooded cloak over a white dress with a sash.

The dress of some of the set dancers of today reminds us of the dance at cross-roads in bygone days. The boy would normally have been a farmer's son dressed in his Sunday best, high-buttoned waistcoat which showed off his cravat, knee breeches and brogues.

Most women in Ireland would have gone barefoot until over a century ago, and this gave them a grace and bearing which today's dancers still strive to achieve. Around 1924 soft shoes were worn for the first time by girls dancing jigs, reels and slip jigs. The men, because they worked on the land, wore home-made raw-hide shoes or brogues which would, of course, have been light on the feet and suitable for dancing. These shoes can still be seen on the Aran Islands where they are called *Broga uirleathair.* Some fishermen on the west coast wore wooden soled taps or clogs, and when it became illegal to teach traditional music, the rhythm of the dance tune was

DANCING COMPETITIONS

From 1890 there was a great revival of all things Irish including the language, theatre, sport, music and dance. The Gaelic Athletic Association (GAA) had been formed in 1884 to promote Gaelic games. The Irish cultural renaissance was further boosted by the efforts of the Gaelic League to bring about a renewed interest in traditional music and dancing.

In 1929 the Gaelic League established an enquiry by dancing teachers into the state of Irish dancing. As a result the Constitution of the Commission of Irish Dancing of Easter 1931 was published. The first year of operation for the commission was 1932/33. They organised examinations for the qualification of teachers and established rules regarding judging and organising dancing competitions. The first examination was for a certificate and the more advanced examination awarded a diploma to candidates. Pupils of unregistered teachers were not permitted to enter for competitions organised by the Commission. The Commission also published a quarterly magazine, *Céim*, which means "step", and covered all aspects of Irish dancing.

Over a period a number of policy differences occurred within the commission resulting in a split in the organisation. The breakaway group of dancing teachers set up their own organisation called *Comhdháil na Muinteoirí Rince Gaelacha* in 1969. The main competition run by this group was the Father Mathew Feis which was named after the temperance priest, Father Theobald Mathew.

The *feis*, which combines competitions in dancing, music and singing, has for a long time been an important part of the cultural life of rural communities. Each dancing school holds its own *feis* and invites other schools in the area to compete. There is an independent adjudicator who awards medals to each group from beginners upwards. At local *feis* level and the national and world championships, there are separate competitions for solo female and male dancers. In group competitions, boys and girls dance in couples.

The major dancing competitions in Ireland are the four provincial competitions of Ulster, Munster, Leinster and Connacht, the Dublin Championship and the All-Ireland Championships. The All-Ireland and World Championships are held at various locations around Ireland, with approximately a thousand competitors entering the All-Ireland Championships. Competitors for the World Championships, held for six days at Easter, come from England, America, Canada, New Zealand, Australia and, of course, Ireland. Any dancer may enter the All-

Ireland and World Championships, where the standard is extremely high but usually dancing teachers will only enter their best pupils.

Entry to the provincial championships is strictly limited to dancers within the catchment area; for example only dancers from schools in the nine counties of Ulster are eligible to enter the Ulster championships.   Only dancers who have entered the Dublin or Provinces Championships can enter the All-Ireland and World Championships.   Competitors from outside Ireland must have entered equivalent competitions in their own countries such as the All-England, All-Amercia and All-Scotland Championships. The competitions are conducted bilingually, in Irish and English.

There are All-Ireland and World Champion titles for each competition category, a male winner for Under 11, a female winner for Under 10 and so on.   Most of the All-Ireland and

World Champion titles are for solo dancers but there are group awards for set dancing and *céilí* dancing for groups. The number of adjudicators varies from one for local *feiseanna* and competitions to seven for the World Championships. This number is divided between members from home and abroad. Most adjudicators are at least thirty before they can sit for the examination to become adjucators.

Competitions in the local *feiseanna* range from Under 5 for beginners to over 21 for adults. Competitions for girls in the All-Ireland and World Championships begin at Under 10 and move upwards by a year per grade to Over 21. Boys competing in the All-Ireland begin at Under 11 and move upwards

by two years as there are less boys competing. To reach this level a dancer must practise two to three hours per day and attend up to five classes per week. In the solo competitions a dancer can choose a reel, jig, slip jig or hornpipe. In the local *feiseanna* the prizes are small trophies and medals. The All-Ireland and World Champions win a gold medal and perpetual trophy on which their name is engraved. Michael Flatley and Jean Butler, who performed in the original *Riverdance* show, are two of the best known World Champion dancers.

In March 1951, a group of musicians which included the master piper, Leo Rowsome and Willie Reynolds, met to discuss holding a Festival of traditional music and dance in Mullingar, County Westmeath. This meeting led to the first *Fleadh Cheoil na hÉireann* being held in Mullingar in June 1951. It attracted only a few hundred patrons – a small but enthusiastic crowd. Eventually *Comhaltas Ceoltóirí Éireann* was to emerge from this event. Within five years this annual gathering had grown to a national festival attended by thousands of traditional musicians, singers and dancers from all parts of Ireland and from overseas. The *Fleadh Cheoil* developed as a mainly competitive event, but with concerts, Irish dancing, parades and street sessions of Irish music.

Throughout the 1960s and 70s the *Fleadh* grew so large that the number of would-be competitors had to attend at qualifying stages at county and provincial level. Branches of

Comhaltas Ceoltóirí Éireann sprang up all over Ireland, organising classes, concerts and sessions at local level. Soon there were County and Provincial *Fleadhanna* and later came the *Fleadh Nua*, (New Festival), the *Tionól Cheoil Seisiún* (Musical Gathering Session) and Scoil Éigse (School of Learning). In recent years the *Fleadh Cheoil na hÉireannn* has been held in Ballina, Listowel, Buncrana, Ennis and Kilkenny, and has been attended by up to 100,000 visitors for the three day event. *Comhaltas Ceoltóirí Éireann* provides a number of cultural facilities at their headquarters at Monkstown County Dublin, from teaching dancing and music to staging regular shows and *céilís* to informal sessions.

The Gaelic Athletic Association, through an organisation called *Scor*, which means "large gathering" in Irish, also runs Irish dancing and music sessions at various venues around the country, particularly during the summer months. The *Scor* competition started in the late 1960s when the GAA initiated cultural activities in the off-season to encourage club members to enjoy other aspects of Irish culture. A programme was devised in north Cork which included figure dancing and later sets. From here it developed into a prestigious competition with All-Ireland finals which were televised.

Also in 1969, *Gael Linn*, believing that a void existed in certain areas of competitive native Irish musical activities, launched *Slógadh*. Its purpose was to give young people an opportunity to develop and display their musical, dancing and dramatic talents through the medium of Irish. Its first National Final was held in Dublin in 1969 with 1,500 participants. This figure has now climbed to over 50,000 competitors from the thirty-two counties.

In the Gael Linn competitions, dancing is covered by three categories - Traditional Sets, Creative Sets and Dance Drama. These categories are group dances for four or eight people. The Traditional Set literally follows the old-style dance with heavy foot banging which was performed in so many house gatherings. The Clare and Kerry sets are representative of this style. Although these sets originated in counties Clare and Kerry respectively, they are now danced throughout Ireland. The Creative or *Cararet* Set gives the dancer more scope and allows for variations, using the lighter Irish dance step. In both sections there are half sets, consisting of four people and full sets with eight people. The Dance Drama consists of one act of twenty minutes duration. It tells a story, mainly with an Irish theme. Dancers portray in a ballet mode an Irish myth, legend or famous event. The life of the patron saint of Ireland, Saint Patrick, and the story of the four Children of Lir are often re-enacted by dancers.

REVIVAL

❖

Siamsa means "having an enjoyable evening with friends" and this is exactly what the members of *Siamsa*, The National Folk Theatre in Tralee, County Kerry attempt to do. The idea for this unique group came from Father Pat Aherne, a Kerry born priest.

Father Aherne was born on a farm and enjoyed the sowing and reaping of hay and corn, all done by hand and primitive implements. His mother played a fiddle in the evenings and friends and neighbours came to listen and enter-

tain. These fond memories remained with him as he grew up and he decided to try and preserve them, or recreate them in an art form. He believed that almost every farmyard activity had an inherent tune. In 1968 he took the jobs, the farmers, the work-hands and the dancers and combined them. The result was named *Siamsa*. It was neither drama, nor concert, nor musical play but a coming together of rural activity that had happened many decades ago.

Through lively music, singing, dance and mime, Siamsa moved from the open air of the fields to the warmth and brightness of a stone flagged lamplit kitchen filled with people enjoying themselves. Here they re-enacted the occupational songs and dances developed over the centuries by the farming communities, with the use of buckets, corn, ropes and scythes as appropriate props to dance. The objects of the farm activity were made the objects of the dances - there was a feeding dance for the chickens, a milking dance for the cows, a sharpening dance for the scythe, a pounding song for the butter churn and a twisting, turning dance for the making of the straw rope.

Siamsa is a series of sketches performed by *Siamsoirí na Ríochta*, which means "Players of the Kingdom", as they became known, in Tralee. Following a television appearance on RTÉ, the reaction was so encouraging that Father Aherne decided to develop an entire show, incorporating all the things

he wanted to remember about the life he remembered as a boy. There is now a cast of about twenty-seven, aged from eleven to seventy all of whom seem able to sing and dance and never tire. The reputation of *Siamsa* spread and they received invitations to appear at various venues around the country. They played in the Abbey Theatre, Dublin, in London, Germany and America.

This nostalgic journey through a forgotten way of life, portrayed in music and dance became a popular form of entertainment. It reflected how the rural Irish lived and worked as a community. They helped with the harvest and the delivery of children. In the evenings they visited each other's homes, talked about mutual interests. Problems solved, the music began and they danced across the flagged floors of the kitchens. The dances of *Siamsa* captured this atmosphere accurately.

During the summer months, *Siamsa* perform their shows nightly in their new Siamsa Tire venue in Tralee. The glamour and innovation of *Riverdance* and *Lord of the Dance* attract international media coverage, *Siamsa* is undiminished by the popularity of these shows and retains the simplistic, nostalgic charm of rural life and the dances of the early twentieth century.

Within the last decade, Irish set dancing has undergone a major revival. There are now regular sessions held in clubs, pubs and hotels throughout the country. Set dancing, with its intricate steps, serves as a social outlet and meeting place, particularly for adults with a love for Irish culture. They travel long distances to attend dancing sessions, workshops and set dancing *céilís*. Set dancing is even performed in group competitions at *Scor* and the *Fleadh Cheoil na na hÉireann*

There is widespread belief that set dancing originated in France in the eighteenth century in the cotillion, a form of country dance. In 1776, the travel writer, Arthur Young, mentions the cotillion being performed in Ireland. In the early nineteenth century, another dance, the quadrille, became popular in Europe. It was danced by four couples in a square formation. The quadrille was brought to Ireland by military officers and was mostly danced in the "big houses" of wealthy Anglo-Irish families. Dancing masters taught the steps and adapted them to Irish music.

Gradually distinctive sets began to develop in Clare, Tipperary and Kerry. To meet the demand for live music at the gatherings *céilí* bands began to form. The most popular names were the Kilfenora and Tulla *Céilí* Bands. Up to two decades ago most sets were unknown outside their own areas. Traditionally, set dancing was confined to rural areas but the recent phenomenal growth has made it equally as popular in rural areas.

From the mid-1970s Connie Ryan, a Tipperary man, did more than anyone else to inspire and encourage the revival of set dancing. He ran regular classes and workshops and his love and enthusiasm for the dance encouraged his hundreds of pupils around the country.

There is a degree of individuality in steps and styles brought to the sessions by the more seasoned dancers. Some dancers beat out the familiar loud rhythm with their feet. Another development in the revival of set dancing was the efforts by the GAA, *Comhaltas Ceoltóirí Éireann* and the *feiseanna* in the 1970s to organise dancing competitions. Teams of dancers from different areas of the country took their own particular styles and dances to the competitions.

At the most established set dancing sessions there is a caller who encourages those less experienced to follow the sets. Prior to the session novices are put through their steps. Classes are held in a range of venues from football and social clubs to pubs and hotels.

Another contributing factor in this great revival is the number of festivals and summer schools featuring set dancing. These include the Willie Clancy Summer School and the Merriman Summer School in Clare and the Joe Mooney Summer School in Drumshanbo, County Leitrim.

RIVERDANCE AND LORD OF THE DANCE

❖

One of the most successful stage shows ever to emerge from Ireland is *Riverdance*. The concept for *Riverdance* began as a seven minute interval act during the Eurovision Song Contest in Dublin in April 1994 when it was transmitted to an estimated

300 million viewers world-wide. Producer Moya Doherty, director John McColgan and composer Bill Whelan created an explosive act of high stepping, short skirted, sensual Irish dancing headed by Michael Flatley and Jean Butler. Jean Butler danced a solo, high stepping slip jig. The tempo changed with a roll of the Lambeg drums heralding Michael Flatley dancing a reel and reinterpreting the traditional dance with his own distinctive tap dancing style. He was joined by Jean Butler and the entire troupe of black clad dancers. The crescendo of the reel and music built to a spectacular climax as the dancers hammered the stage in harmony bringing the show to a rousing finale.

The performance received a standing ovation at the Point Depot and captured the hearts and minds of everyone who witnessed it. The dancing experience was long remembered after the songs of the contest were forgotten.

Fuelled by the enthusiastic reception, the producers developed an entire dance show entitled *Riverdance – The Show*. In February 1995 the show opened at the Point Depot, Dublin and played for a five week run to sell-out houses and critical acclaim. It was an innovative and exciting blend of dance and music, drawing on Irish traditions and featuring an array of talent from Ireland, Spain, Russia and America. The Spanish dancer, Maria Pages, began her *Fire Dance* to the music of a guitar solo. As the sound of the guitar increased, it merged with a drum beat. Michael Flatley joined Maria Pages to the rhythm of Spanish and Irish music, and they danced a duet. The show also featured *From Harlem to Hollywood*, a sequence which merged Irish and Scottish with flamenco and African rhythms to produce an intricate and provocative dance routine. The American tap group began the sequence and were later joined by a group of Irish dancers in a challenge of two tapping traditions. The Moiseyev Dance Company from Russia danced *Marta's Dance*, an energetic and frantic sequence inspired by Russian folk dances. Other groups who appeared in the original full length stage show were the traditional Irish singing group, *Anúna*, and the *Deliverance Ensemble Singers* from the USA. The Irish, high stepping tap show with dramatic lighting, eye-catching costumes and an impressive stage design by Robert

63

Ballagh, travelled to England, America and Australia and received a similar enthusiastic response from each audience.

The critics were unanimous in their verdicts, with the show eliciting enthusiastic reviews and headlines where ever it opened: "Big, bold, exciting!", "Pure genius", "…breathtaking… spectacular new production", "Standing ovation for stunning steps", "Triumphant! A perfect gem!" are some of the press reviews which accompanied the show's performance in London and America.

The original music was released as a single and held the Number 1 position in the Irish charts for eighteen weeks in 1994 and reached Number 9 in the UK charts in 1995. To date over 4 million *Riverdance* videos have been sold. A book, Riverdance – The Story by Sam Smyth, has also been published. The show has been broadcast on television channels throughout the world. The majority of dancers selected for the shows are those who have reached the All-Ireland and World Championship level. Indeed, most of the dancers are either All-Ireland or World Champion winners. These successful shows have for the first time made it possible for champion Irish dancers to pursue a successful a career in Irish dancing. Irish dancing has become full-time occupation with dancers taking leave from their jobs to join the tours. Today there are three *Riverdance* shows on tour, each named after an Irish river: Liffey, Lee and Lagan.

Michael Flatley was born in Chicago of Irish parents. His grandmother had been a Leinster champion dancer. Michael began Irish dancing at eleven years of age. His dancing teacher said he was too late to start but this did not deter Michael. He became the first American to win the World Championships in Irish dancing. He also gained a place in the Guinness Book of Records for his tapping speed and became a concert flautist. For a time he attended Kevin Massey's School of Irish Dancing in Dún Laoghaire, County Dublin. He was also a dancing pupil at the Dennehy School of Irish Dancing in Chicago.

Jean Butler was born in Mineola, Long Island, USA, of Irish parents. She began dancing at the age of four and went on to win several World Irish dancing championships. She attended the Donny Golden School of Irish Dancing in New York. She danced professionally with The Chieftains. At 23 she came to a darkened stage and performed the magic that began the world-wide hit show *Riverdance*. She has now left the show to follow a career in acting.

The lead male dancer, Michael Flatley, who performed in the early productions of *Riverdance*, went on to write, produce and star in another spectacular dance production, *Lord of the Dance*. Set in a timeless Ireland, the theme of the show is the conflict of good versus evil. It combines a number of mythical and modern set pieces performed by masked male dancers dressed in black. Rival gangs confront each other, aggressively challenging the other in a sequence of defiant, thundering steps. There is a dazzling duet when Michael Flatley challenges the dark lord, as good confronts evil. The show merges reels, jigs, hornpipes and tap dancing. *Lord of the Dance* has played to critical acclaim and capacity houses in Ireland, England, America and Australia. Two companies are currently on tour performing *Lord of the Dance*.

FUTURE OF
IRISH DANCE

Irish dance today is at an all-time peak in standard, variety and popularity. Many factors have contributed to this revival, not least the dedication and hard work by competitors and dancing teachers alike, and generally a greater awareness of all forms of native dance and music in recent years.

There are nowadays many opportunities to witness the art and grace of Irish dance. It still forms a regular part of social functions in such places as Achill Island, the Aran Islands, Connemara and many other Gaeltacht areas. Annually many thousands of dedicated competitors attend *céilís*, *feiseanna* and the All-Ireland and World Championships. Irish dancing has spread far and competitors travel from many parts of the world to attend the major events in the Mansion House in Dublin.

From the late 1950s *Radio Telefís Éireann or Radio Éireann* as it was then known, worked with *Comhaltas Ceoltóirí Éireann* to bring a neglected aspect of Irish culture to a wider audience through the medium of the radio. Many people today still cherish fond memories of listening to Din Joe's *Take the Floor*, the first radio programme to feature dancing. Today Irish dancing features prominently on many radio and television programmes, particularly on *Telefís na Gaelige*, the Irish language television channel.

The restoration of Irish dancing began in the late nineteenth century with the successful efforts of the Gaelic League in revitalising all things Irish. During this century, Irish dancing has experienced decline and revival as Ireland struggled with emigration and fluctuating economic fortunes. Irish dance is now an important element of Irish culture with a distinctively high profile.

Abroad there are many dancing schools. In Canada, there are schools in Vancouver, Quebec, Ontario and Toronto. In Australia, there are schools in Sydney, Melbourne and Adelaide. Several British cities are centres of Irish dancing with schools in Manchester, Liverpool, London and Edinburgh. America is also home to Irish dance with schools in Chicago, New York, Arizona, San Francisco, Jersey and Ohio. These schools include Fiona Dore-Buckley School of Dancing in South Jersey, Boland School of Irish Dancing, New York, New Orleans School of Irish Dancing, Francis O'Neill *Céilí* Club, Chicago and Greater Washington *Céilí* Club. In 1964, the Irish Dance Teachers' Association was founded in New York. Today there are over 300 certified Irish dance teachers in America. Ann

Richens from Dublin established the Richens Academy of Irish Dancing in 1972 where hundreds of champion Irish dancers have learned their first steps. Dancers from this school perform at many festivals including the Ohio State Fair, the Columbus Arts Festival and Octoberfest. American dancers compete in *feiseanna* throughout the USA and in the Midwest *Oireachtas*, as well as regional and national championships.

The dance erupts today in a spontaneous form at the *Fleadh Cheoil*. Although dancing does not feature prominently in the *Fleadh* the music of a lone musician can frequently snowball into a full scale *céilí* or set dance. An impromptu outbreak such as this can best express the true love of people for Irish dance.

During the summer months *céilís* are held frequently throughout the country. Visitors are always welcome and will

quickly master the basic steps. The most popular *céilí* dances are *The Walls of Limerick*, *The Bridge of Athlone* and *The Siege of Ennis*. Large crowds including foreign students, attend the Friday night *céilís* in *Comhaltas Ceoltóirí Éireann* in Monkstown, County Dublin.

Another popular feature of night life in Ireland for visitors and locals alike is the number of pubs providing traditional music and set dancing. Many foreign tourists leave the comfort of hotels to seek out pubs with music and dance where they are invited to partake in sets.

Riverdance and *Lord of the Dance* have had an enormous impact on Irish dancing schools. Dancing teachers are agreeable to change and updating the steps to keep abreast of the new trends. With the high profile of the dance shows an increasing number of pupils are joining schools eager to learn the dances. In the past, boys were reluctant to dance in public outside competitions but they are now more prepared to display their skills.

With three *Riverdance* productions and two *Lord of the Dance* shows on world tour, Irish dancing now has world-wide appeal, with audiences clamouring for more shows and extended tours. However, Irish dancing still remains very much part of the heritage of the Irish and the Irish Diaspora abroad. Tourists enjoy the opportunity to sample a few steps at a *céilí* when on holiday but not many have the inclination or determination to master the intricate steps. Instead they are prepared to sit back and watch the talented dancers demonstrate their skills. The evidence from abroad indicates that in the main Irish dance classes are only attended by the Irish and their descendants. However, there is contact between Irish dance and other dance forms. In Australia and North America Irish dancing and ballet sometimes form part of the same class and the result is an unusual, vibrant combination of the two styles.

Mumming began in County Wexford where there are today six active groups of mummers. The Carne set and

Dungier Mummers are perhaps the best known. In 1960, the Carne set performed in the Royal Albert Hall in London for an audience of 9,000. They performed for President John F. Kennedy when he visited New Ross, County Wexford in 1963. The Dungier Mummers in 1966 won the folk section at the International Eisteddfod, a dance and music festival, in Wales. Irish mummers groups are invited to international folk festivals and attract much attention when they perform at Irish festivals. The mumming season was originally confined to autumn but today there are mummers group performing throughout the year all over Ireland.

The dances of *Siasma* delight Irish and international audiences with their portrayal of a nostalgic, rural way of life. *Riverdance* and *Lord of the Dance* remain on tour and play sold out shows to audiences across America, Europe and Australia. Irish dance is now truly on the international stage.

The dances of Ireland do not belong to any one class, generation or region. Grace and beauty of movement on a high level are the main ingredients of Irish dance, and the Irish people, being proud and fortunate possessors of a unique heritage of native dances, have the gifted temperament to combine both.

DANCE STEPS

❖

Seven Steps *Side step in reel*

The seven steps are the basic steps which need to be mastered before dancing a reel. For the beginner, it is important to remember to stand with the weight comfortably balanced on both feet. The routines below incorporates the seven steps and two short threes, where the dancer quickly repeats three steps.

1. Stand centre stage.
2. Hop to knee, raising right foot up to the left knee.
3. Spring onto your right foot

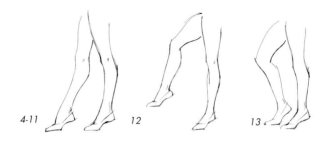

4-11. With right foot pointed out front, move from centre to right side of stage for seven steps. Lead with right foot and follow with left foot.
12. After seventh step, lift right foot with knee bent.
13. Spring onto right foot bringing left foot into rear.
Count one

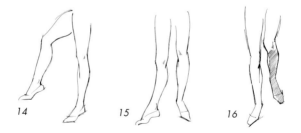

14. Step in place onto ball of left foot. Count two.
15. Step onto ball of right foot, behind left foot. Count three.
16. Lift left foot with knee bent and repeat short three.

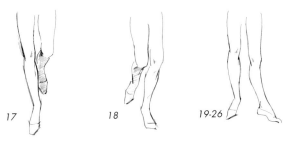

17. Hop to knee, raising left foot up to right knee.
18. Spring onto left foot.
19-26. With left foot pointed out front, move from right side to centre stage for seven steps. Lead with left foot and follow with right foot.

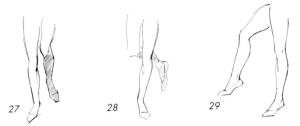

27. After seventh step, lift left foot with knee bent.
28. Spring onto left foot and bring right foot into rear. Count one.
29. Step in place onto ball of left foot. Count two.

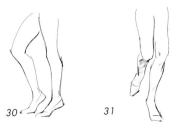

30. Step onto ball of left foot, behind right foot. Count three.
31. Lift right foot with knee bent and repeat short three.

The Rising Step *Side Step in Jig*

1. Hop on left foot while raising right foot in front with toe pointed.
2. Hop again on left foot while bringing right foot to rear.
3. Place right foot behind left foot, transferring weight to left.

4. Hop on right foot while bringing left foot behind.
5. Place left foot behind right while raising right foot.
6. Place right foot down again.

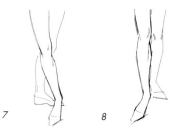

7. Place left foot behind right while raising right foot.
8. Place right foot down again.

76

DATE DUE			
AUG 17 2013			

FJ Voorhees
Voorhees, Coert.
In Too Deep

IN

TOO

DEEP

IN

TOO

DEEP

COERT VOORHEES

HYPERION
NEW YORK

FJ
Voorhees

Printed in the United States of America

First Edition

1 3 5 7 9 10 8 6 4 2

G475-5664-5-13105

Library of Congress Cataloging-in-Publication Data
Voorhees, Coert.
In too deep / Coert Voorhees.—First hardcover edition.
pages cm
Summary: Persuaded by her teacher to seek Cortés's long-lost treasure
during a school trip to Mexico, Annie Fleet, master scuba diver and
history buff, finds that her plans to get Josh to notice her are not the
only thing in danger as rival treasure-hunters try to do away with her.
ISBN 978-1-4231-4035-1 (hardback)
[1. Adventure and adventurers—Fiction. 2. Buried treasure—Fiction.
3. Scuba diving—Fiction. 4. Dating (Social customs)—Fiction.
5. Mexico—Fiction.] I. Title.
PZ7.V943In 2013
[Fic]—dc23   2013002329

Text is set in 11.5-point Sabon LT Standard.

Visit www.un-requiredreading.com

7. 15. 13   JLG 9.95

SUSTAINABLE
FORESTRY
INITIATIVE

Certified Sourcing
www.sfiprogram.org
SFI-00993

THIS LABEL APPLIES TO TEXT STOCK

For my Annie

IN

TOO

DEEP

ONE

It turns out that sunken treasure and an unrequited crush have a lot in common, starting with the fact that it makes no real sense to chase either of them. But even though you're an otherwise reasonably clearheaded and intelligent person, you can't help yourself. The image of your triumph keeps hope alive regardless of the odds, regardless of the disappointment. Because make no mistake: the odds are long, and the disappointment will come.

"What little we do know about the Golden Jaguar," I said as I turned, thankfully, to the last page of my presentation, my voice raspy and my mouth thick with cotton, "came from the journal of a lieutenant on the *Vida Preciosa*, one of Hernán Cortés's ships, which mysteriously appeared in Spain a full three years after it was presumed lost at sea."

As I fought the urge to check if said crush was paying attention, my left kneecap went crazy, twitching up and down like an over-caffeinated Chihuahua. I tried to

3

stop it by straightening my leg, but that only made me light-headed.

"In his journal, Lieutenant Juan de la Torre writes about a gleaming statue of solid gold, twice life-sized, with brilliant emerald fangs and eyes of deep ruby, guarding the entrance to the pyramid of the gods. He tells of a brutal and bloody fight with the native Aztecs, followed by a death march as Cortés's men hauled the Jaguar through a ferocious, impassable jungle."

This was going poorly. For most of the semester-long elective, Mysteries of the Deep, I'd kept my head down and managed to avoid standing in front of the class, but Mr. Alvarez had assigned me the Golden Jaguar, and there was nothing I could do to avoid it.

"But the journal ends there," I said, mercifully close to the grand finale. "Nobody really knows what happened to the Golden Jaguar. Some people think Cortés never got it off the mainland. Others think it was delivered to Charles the Fifth as promised, in secret, and it was scrapped and used to fund what became the Spanish Armada."

"And you?" Mr. Alvarez said with a strange little twinkle in his eye. "What do you think?"

"I think they're both wrong." My throat was raw from clearing it so much. I glanced at the SHOOT FOR THE STARS! poster in the back of the classroom: a little boy lying underneath a tree with his hands behind his head, staring up at a brilliant night sky. "It's probably in the rotting cargo hold of a ship at the bottom of the ocean, covered in centuries of sediment, never to be found."

4

I dropped my eyes down to my presentation as I waited for some reaction from the class—a sarcastic question, a disdainful smirk, anything. But there was only silence.

Mr. Alvarez slapped his hands on his knees. "Any questions for Annie? Anybody?"

I folded my paper in half and finally glanced up at my classmates. I hadn't expected them to be on the edges of their seats, not for the only freshman in their elective, and a faculty kid at that. But I can't say I was prepared for none of them even to be looking at me.

I licked the chap from my bottom lip and headed for my chair. "Okay, I'll—"

"How much is it worth?"

The voice shocked me by belonging to Josh Rebstock. Six-foot-two Josh Rebstock. The Josh Rebstock with the lazy haystack of sandy-blond hair and dimples when he smiled, who up to that point had spoken directly to me only if he'd forgotten to write down a homework assignment. Maybe he was taking pity on me. Maybe he was even thinking forward to the afternoon, to the private scuba diving lesson my mom had railroaded me into giving him, and he didn't want it to be awkward.

"The statue thing," he said. "If someone found it."

I pictured the Jaguar's fierce ruby eyes, the mouth open in a roar, the tail curled around like a whip about to crack. "You can't really put a price on it," I finally said. "It means more than what—"

A voice shouted from the back. Nate Sugar. "Ballpark."

"I don't know," I said. "A hundred million?"

5

There was silence again, but this time everybody was looking right at me.

"Dollars?" Josh said.

"Well, it weighs probably a couple thousand pounds, solid gold—Aztec gold. And that's before you get into its historical significance. Actually, I bet a hundred million is on the low end."

Mr. Alvarez chimed in, "*Extremely* low end."

The bell rang. It took a moment for the dollar-sign glaze to disappear from everyone's eyes, but soon the shuffle started. Books in backpacks, whispers to neighbors, zippers and snaps.

"There's still time to join the Borders Unlimited trip next week," Alvarez said hopelessly. "Change your life. Make a difference."

So far, only four of us had signed up for the field trip to Mexico, a community service/treasure hunting combo platter that Mr. Alvarez had dubbed "Good Deeds and Gold Doubloons." Josh was going, as were the Sugar twins. Nate was built like a pit bull, all shoulders and neck, with brown hair that hid his eyebrows, while Katy had the lean, taut body of a distance runner. They were tae kwon do black belts and ex-gymnasts who performed every weekend in a kind of Cirque du Soleil knockoff show at the Santa Monica Pier. My fellow volunteers. A movie star's kid and a couple of self-proclaimed circus freaks.

"And there'll be more about the Golden Jaguar, too!" Alvarez said, like a salesman desperate to seal the deal. I seemed to be the only one who'd heard him.

6

"There will?" I said.

Mr. Alvarez said, "Annie, hold back a second."

I took my time packing my stuff while the room cleared. My best friend, Gracia Berg, had called Mr. Alvarez a "welcome addition of faculty hotness," which I had to admit was the truth. Sharp jaw, high cheekbones, he looked more like an actor playing a teacher than a real-life one.

"What did you mean, more about the Golden Jaguar?" I said.

He shrugged. "I was hoping your presentation might whet some appetites."

"Didn't work," I said, motioning to the untouched stack of sign-up forms on his desk.

"Not for lack of detail on your part," he said. "I'm impressed. The Golden Jaguar is pretty obscure, as far as these things go."

"It's not obscure if you know what you're talking about."

Over Alvarez's shoulder, I noticed Gracia poking her head into the room, but as soon as she saw me nodding at Mr. Alvarez, she disappeared back into the hallway like she'd been yanked back by a giant fishhook.

"Cortés had a wife here, you know," he said.

"What?"

Mr. Alvarez wandered behind his desk and began to fill his old leather satchel with stacks of our essays. "Your presentation could have used a bit more primary research. There's an archive room in the Iglesia de la Virgen Madre, down in San Juan Capistrano. The archivist is Father

Rubén Gonzales." His smile was a challenge as he zipped the satchel and pointed to the door. "In case you *really* want to know what you're talking about."

Gracia snagged me as soon as I stepped into the hall. She is shorter than I am, with blonder hair and a bigger chest she never misses an opportunity to feature. She glanced back as she pulled me away from Alvarez's door. "How'd it go in there?"

"Did you know that Cortés spent his final years—"

"Blah, blah, blah, priceless gold, blah, beautiful treasure, blah. I was afraid of that. How about Josh?" Her accent is Atlanta Southern, but she speaks too fast for it to be anything close to a drawl. She bit her bottom lip and nodded. "Maybe he looked a little embarrassed for you?"

The walk from the north hall to the lunch pavilion took us across the quadrangle and past a marble statue, a replica of *The Thinker*. The Pinedale Academy is Los Angeles's foremost preparatory school; its students are children of movie stars and talent agents and entertainment lawyers. Gracia's dad, for example, is the producer of *Return to the Stone Age*, a new reality show where two teams of contestants are supposed to mimic a Neanderthal clan and use only rocks and sticks and words with a maximum of two syllables. Everyone is expecting a huge hit.

My dad, however, is a Pinedale faculty member, famous only for his refusal to offer extra credit. He chairs the History department and teaches AP World and sophomore Euro, and, thanks to his years of dedicated service to the advancement of the Pinedale Academy's mission, I received a faculty-offspring scholarship.

"I'll have you know," I said, "that Josh was extremely interested. He asked not one but two questions."

Gracia laughed, but when I kept walking, her smile disappeared. "You're lying."

I winked at her as we stood at the pavilion doorway. Enough of the students had spent most of their time on movie sets—either visiting their parents or as actors themselves—that lunch was referred to as craft service. Today's craft service was different from usual, with trays of food arranged on two long tables on either side of the room. Gracia spotted Mimi Soto at a center table, gazing into the distance and *mm-hmm*-ing into the phone at her ear.

"What's with the buffet?" Gracia said as she sat.

Mimi covered the receiver and whispered, "One of the sophomores complained about no vegan options, so the school is auditioning new cooks. The gluten-free flautas are amazing."

Then she put her finger to her bright red lips. "Sure," she said into the phone, and her eyes lit up. "Really?"

America had literally seen Mimi grow up before its eyes. As the child of a single-parent bar owner on the sitcom *Daddy's Little Girl*, which dominated its time slot for eight of its ten seasons, she'd evolved from a spunky toddler into a saucy and confident teenager with long black hair she used as a weapon.

9

Now that the show was over, she swore she just wanted to be normal.

Mimi snapped her phone shut and pressed it between her palms as if in prayer. "Okay, guys, that was our house manager. Apparently, the gala my parents were planning to throw next week has been canceled. The governor of Hawaii's not available or whatever. Point is, the villa in Malibu is free now, so we should take advantage."

"Enjoy," I said. "I'll be in Mexico, remember?"

"That's right. Such a noble thing you're doing."

"Shut up," Gracia said.

"I'm serious." Mimi looked shocked. "Hurricane victims are people too."

Katy Sugar ambled past the table. "That was a fascinating presentation, Annie," she said, nibbling on a flauta. "Really."

"I am not a fan of yours," Gracia called out, but Katy ignored her.

I put my hands on the table and leaned in to my friends. "Can you both sign up? I can't handle her by myself."

"Didn't you hear what I said about the villa?" Mimi said. "It's free next week."

"Please? It will be fun with you guys. Right now it's just me, Josh, and the Sugars."

"At least you have Josh," Mimi said.

"Or not," Gracia said. She elbowed me and winked. "Annie went all Dorka the Explorer again."

Mimi laughed into her sparkling water. "What was it this time? The Confederate gold or the lost Incan totems—"

"Is there a sign on my forehead that says 'Give me crap'?" I said.

Gracia cupped my chin in her hands. "Perpetually."

I brushed her away. "The Incans didn't have totems."

A huge roar came from the corner, where Josh and some of his friends were pounding on the table. Last year, his mom won an Academy Award for her leading role as an out-of-work truck driver in *The Long and Winding Road*. Her career—not to mention Josh's status—was exploding because of it.

"What, exactly, are you guys going to be doing there, again?" Mimi said.

"Apparently we're studying Cortés's lost—"

"Here we go—"

"And cleaning up after the hurricane," I said.

"Ooh, so Josh'll probably be outside, shirt off, all sweaty and golden." Mimi held out both hands as if weighing her options. "Golden Rebstock, Malibu villa. Golden Rebstock, Malibu villa."

Josh picked up his backpack, but instead of moving toward the exit, he turned to us. He was looking at me.

Mimi froze. "Is he coming this way?" she said without moving her lips. "I think he's—"

"Don't be weird," Gracia whispered back.

"Shh. Don't tell me I'm being—"

"He's like ten feet away—"

"Shut up—"

"You shut—"

"Ladies," Josh said.

11

We all shut up. Mimi flipped her hair behind her shoulder and leaned one arm on the back of her chair. Josh glanced at my friends before settling his green eyes on me.

"What's going on, Annie?"

I tried to say something, but there was too much pressure with everyone staring at me. Just be yourself, I thought.

"Just being myself," I said.

Mimi let out a groan.

Josh laughed. "That's the way to go, I guess."

Why was he talking to me? In public, in front of Mimi and Gracia and Gracia's boobs? I stole a glance behind him to see if his friends were watching, if they'd sent him over here on a dare, but the table was emptying out; nobody was paying any attention.

Josh shrugged, running his thumb under the backpack's shoulder strap. "So, I'll see you at three thirty?"

"On the dot," I said. I didn't need to look at my friends to know what they were thinking; I could feel the disbelief oozing from their pores.

He laughed at me again. "Right. On the dot."

I watched him go—we all did, all three of us, heads tracking him slowly. As soon as he turned the corner, my friends whipped around and stared at me.

"What the hell was that?" Gracia said.

"What?"

Mimi pointed. "That. The 'see you at three thirty.' See you where?"

"I'm hurt." Gracia blinked. "We both are."

"You don't shut up about him all year," Mimi said, "and all of a sudden you have an 'on the dot'?"

"And we don't know about it?" Gracia said.

I dismissed them with a little head shake. "His mom hired my mom to give him a private lesson. They're going to Fiji next month, and how can Josh possibly experience the breathtaking majesty of the open water if he's not certified, et cetera, et cetera."

"And you come in, how?"

"None of our instructors were available for a private, and my mom wasn't interested. As a general rule, she can't stand anybody who's graced the pages of *Us Weekly.*" I turned to Mimi. "No offense."

"Oh, please. *In Touch* is way worse."

"You didn't tell us," Gracia said.

I shrugged. "Maybe I didn't want you to make it a bigger deal than it is."

"Maybe you're worried you're going to be a disaster," Mimi said.

Gracia shot her a look. "Not helpful, Mimi. The real question"—she rested the prongs of her fork on the edge of her plate and leaned forward—"is, what are you wearing?"

"What do you mean, what am I wearing? My suit."

"Not the sensible one-piece," Gracia said.

Mimi shook her head. "The lesson-giving suit?"

A familiar sense of exasperation crept up my spine. My friends looked at me with the twinkle of challenge in their eyes, as though I were a native they couldn't wait to civilize.

"But I *am* giving a lesson," I said weakly.

Gracia's twang took on the lilt of a patient school-teacher. "That doesn't mean you have to act like it. Look at Mimi here. Hard-nosed, driven . . . but does she dress like she's on the ethics committee?"

Mimi turned and posed with one hand behind her head and the other on her hip. Her tight white T-shirt rose enough to show the three inches of midriff she could easily cover up if a teacher wandered by in search of dress code violations.

"Rhetorical question," Gracia said. "The point is that you've already established yourself as the dorky girl who likes the ocean." She reached over and unpinned the blue-and-green Marine Park Conservancy Fund button from my collar. "Which means you don't need to wear this, or hit anybody up for donations, or talk about sunken treasure. Mix it up a little bit, why don't you."

"And get a new suit," Mimi said. "Seriously."

A hand clamped on my shoulder. Gracia's eyes widened, and my button clattered to the table.

Mimi tugged down the bottom of her shirt. "Hi, Mr. Fleet," she said, all melodious.

"Young ladies," my dad said as he sat next to me.

"Bye, Mr. Fleet." Gracia patted me on the leg and spun away. Mimi hopped up. Then they were gone, and my dad waved after them. If he was aware that he'd caused their sudden departure, he wasn't letting on.

14

"What's with the bird's nest up there?" I said, motioning to his hair. "You've gone full 'scatterbrained professor' on us."

"It gives me gravitas, don't you think?" He skimmed his fingers over the uncombed brown mane and adjusted his striped yellow tie. "I ran into Mr. Alvarez on the way over. He said your report was solid. A bit lacking in—"

"Primary sources, I know."

The worst thing about being a faculty brat—aside from the wonderful lunchroom encounters with my dad—was the complete lack of privacy. A normal kid could get away with lying to her parents about what was going on at school, but my dad had essentially taken to streaming the events of my school day in real time.

"Have you eaten yet?" Dad rapped his knuckles on the table and stood. "Come on, I heard the baba ghanoush is organic."

When I was little, we would take a metal detector to the beach and spend hours walking through the sand. Sometimes we'd find a watch or a set of keys. Once, we found a silver bracelet, which I gave my mom for her birthday. On the days we struck out, Dad would bury something for me, but I had to create a search grid before he'd let me look for it. Blaming your parents for how you turned out is a cheap way to handle things, but really, my whole treasure obsession is all my dad's fault.

TWO

The bitter scent of chlorine was thick in the air even though I'd propped the side door open with an empty oxygen tank. We stood next to the pool in the back of my mom's dive shop with an array of diving equipment at our feet. The grumble of the pool's filter pump wasn't nearly loud enough to cover the sound of my heartbeat in my ears.

There was no reason for Josh to be shirtless just yet—I still had on shorts and a tank top over my lesson suit—but it was probably a reflex. *Grr, me see pool. Me take shirt off.* And I guess he'd been working out, because he kept glancing down at his arms and his chest, probably hoping I'd follow his gaze. Which, of course, I did.

"Let's review a couple things first," I said as I sat on a folding metal chair.

Josh pulled his chair three feet from me. He collapsed into it. He stretched out his legs and crossed his ankles and leaned back. "I bet your dad is totally freaking out, huh? Teacher's kid busted for cheating."

"What are you talking about?"

"Oh, right, of course," he said, waving at me with both hands. "It's like in those movies, where the convicts are sitting in the prison yard, swearing that they're all innocent—"

"Seriously. What are you talking about?"

"The trip to Mexico? Good Deeds and whatever. Alvarez making us all do his stupid volunteer stuff because he says we cheated?"

I scrambled to make sense of what he was saying. Josh smiled at me like I was in on it, so what was I supposed to do—admit that I'd signed up for the trip because I *wanted* to go?

"Yeah," I finally said. "My dad's totally freaking out. You want to get started?"

"Okay, fine." Josh cracked open his *PADI Open Water Diver Manual* and hunched over it, his fingers tracing the words of a random page. "Nitrogen narcosis. Ooh, sounds bad."

My mom's voice percolated in from the adjacent retail room, a conversation with a customer about dive knives. "How about something with a four-inch blade? You're a sport diver, not a Navy SEAL."

The PADI manual landed on my lap, and I flinched. "Wake up, Annie. It's time to get a-certifyin'."

A high-pitched buzz sounded when the door opened and the customer left.

"I want you to walk me through the equipment here,"

I said. If there was one thing I could focus on, it was this. "Step number one?"

It's not that difficult. The tank is strapped to the buoyancy compensator, or BC, which is pretty much like an inflatable vest that you use to control your buoyancy depending on your depth. The regulator is what you breathe from, and it connects to the tank, along with other hoses for the BC, the pressure gauge, and the secondary air source known as the octopus.

"When you put the regulator on the tank," I said, "you have to make sure the O-ring is flush with the valve."

"Ooh." Josh bounced his eyebrows. "You said *O-ring*."

"That's sexual harassment," I said. I wanted to throw him into the pool, but then, of course, he would have glistened.

My phone rang, and I groped at it like it was a lifeline.

"You're not alone with him, are you?" Gracia twanged at me.

"Mmm-hmm."

"Shut up," she squealed. "Are you guys gonna go in the pool? Gonna get-ah wet-ah?"

"Okay, then. Sounds good." I covered the mouthpiece and whispered to Josh, "It's my dad."

Gracia lowered her voice. "Seriously, though, is he hitting on you? Are you hitting on him? You have to talk to me, here. How's it going?"

"We should be fine as long as he doesn't drown," I said, loud enough for Josh to hear. "Okay, gotta go."

"Annie—"

I hung up and tossed the phone into my backpack. "Sorry about that. Let's get back to it, okay?"

Josh reached for the regulator and laid it in his lap. He gave me one of those sincere looks, as though the narrowness of his squint would prove how interested he was. *Don't say anything stupid,* I reminded myself. *Let him fill the space. Let him bring the conversation to you. Wait.*

He said, "You really like treasure hunting, huh?"

"It's awesome," I said. More of a yelp, really, as if I'd sat on a thumbtack. I tried to recover with a laugh, but that just made things worse. I looked away. "Yeah. It's cool."

The front door buzzed right on cue, like I was a losing contestant on some game show. *Annie, for two hundred dollars, please try* not *to make an ass out of yourself in front of Josh Rebstock. . . . BZZZZZZ! Wrong answer, thanks for playing!*

I cleared my throat. "What's this called?" I said, holding up the octopus.

"You're sure I have to know all this stuff?"

"That depends. If your regulator hose malfunctions at eighty feet, maybe you might want to reach for your backup. Or you could just die. I guess that's up to you."

"You're more of a smart-ass than you are at school," he said. "I like that."

Oh, boy.

My mom poked her head into the small room. "Annie, can I borrow you for a second?"

I sighed for her benefit. Then I held up Josh's regulator and pointed to a nearby tank. "When I get back, I want to see this put on correctly. No leaks."

"Yes ma'am," he said with a smile. "And don't forget about the O-ring, right?"

I shook my head and laughed in spite of myself.

"It's going okay?" my mom said as we entered the retail area. Wetsuits and BCs hung from circular stands in the center, while masks, fins, and snorkels lined the entire wall to the right.

"Maybe you should finish up in there." I didn't think I could trust myself with him.

Mom gave me one of those annoying motherly pats on the back as we reached the customer. "This gentleman and I were having a discussion about fins."

"Your mother tells me she's a traditionalist." The man's skin had the tanned and pockmarked look of an old leather couch. He was all muscle and bulk, and his massive shoulders slumped forward. "But she says you're a fan of the hybrid fins."

"Do you use a typewriter instead of a computer?" I said.

The customer flashed me a bewildered smile. "I'm sorry?"

"Do you ski with leather boots? Play golf with wooden woods? Shy away from Gore-Tex?"

"I'm afraid I don't see where you're going—"

"The hybrid fin is the best of both worlds. You get the power of the paddle fin with the comfort and maneuverability of the split fin. Deliberately avoiding technologically superior equipment isn't being a traditionalist; it's just dumb."

Mom clamped a hand down on my shoulder. The way things were going with the shop, we couldn't afford to lose even a tiny sale like this one, and we were far enough in that I knew she couldn't just bounce me from the conversation.

"Unless, of course," she said, "you'll be doing a lot of current diving, in which case the paddle fins might be better suited—"

"Come on," I said while still looking at Mr. Pockmarks. "Big guy like him? I bet he could power through—"

"Jesus, oops!" Josh's voice carried from the pool room. "Which way do I turn this?"

"Righty tighty, lefty loosey!" I yelled over my shoulder. "Sorry," I said to the customer. "He's just learning."

"No prob—"

"I did it!" Josh yelled. There was a loud crash, and then, "Turdballs!"

I suppressed a smile. "Language!"

"Sorry!"

My mom glanced at me, and her eyebrows shot skyward. She nodded toward the pool, all the while showing us how white her teeth were.

"I should probably get back in there."

Mr. Pockmarks gave me a slight bow as I stepped away. "Thanks for your help."

"Yes, Annie," my mom said. "Thank you so much."

21

Josh was sitting on the edge of the pool, dangling his feet in the water and breathing air from the tank at his side. He removed the regulator from his mouth and smiled.

"Guess whose O-rings aren't leaking?"

"It's a miracle," I said after a quick check, just to be sure. "So, are you ready to go under?"

"Ready as I'll ever be."

I rolled my eyes. "I hope not, for your sake."

He took a deep breath from the mouthpiece, holding it in and letting his cheeks puff out. "This is high-quality O-two," he squeaked. He breathed out and doubled over, coughing.

"Easy, there. Compressed air makes your throat dry," I said.

He got up to lean against the wall for support while he hacked violently, and he had tears in his eyes when he finally looked up at me. "Do we get wetsuits?"

"It's just twelve feet, all right? It's for you to get comfortable, to get a sense of how the water feels around you. We'll hang out at the bottom for a few minutes and come back up."

He strapped on his weight belt, and I lifted his tank so that he could put his arms through the BC. He snapped the buckle around his waist and shrugged the vest until he seemed satisfied. Then he turned around and reached for my tank.

I slapped his wrist away. "Nobody touches my gear but me."

"That's what *he* said. Come on, Annie, you can't just lob them up there like that."

I could feel his eyes on me as I kicked off my shorts and pulled my tank top over my head. My ideal swim date with Josh would have included a midnight hot tub and a new bikini, not this over-chlorinated cinder-block room and my old black, boxy, lesson-giving one-piece. My friends were right: the suit was definitely function over form. Plus, the fluorescent lighting made my freckles practically leap off my skin.

"You should wear your hair pulled back more often," Josh said.

My hand instinctively went to the back of my head, where I'd wrapped a quick rubber band around hair that was just a shade too light to be legitimately brunette.

"Seriously. Maybe you could come by my mom's set sometime. Her stylist might be able to take a look?"

It seemed as though he'd just asked me out on a date, and to a movie set, no less. My bosom should have swelled, right? He looked pleased with himself, apparently unaware that telling a girl she needed to see a stylist might, you know, give her the impression that he thought she needed to see a stylist.

I lifted my vest by the shoulder straps, propped the tank on my thigh, and stuck my right arm underneath the strap as I spun quickly to my left. One more nimble motion, and the BC was on.

The door buzzed again. Josh stared at me. "You know

what I think?" he said, those undeniably fantastic green eyes of his magnified by the mask's plastic lens. "I think this whole I-can-do-it-myself thing you've got going is just an act."

"Enough small talk, Aquaman," I said, positioning him near the edge.

I showed him the proper way to enter the water—one big step off the edge with a hand over my face so the mask and regulator stayed in place—and then I watched him do it. We gave each other the "okay" sign, then emptied the air from our BCs and began to descend. Beginners tend to have trouble with the first ten feet, filling their lungs with gulps of air, so I'd put an extra ten pounds on Josh's weight belt. He sank like a stone, and I joined him at the bottom.

We sat cross-legged, and my ears squeaked as the pressure equalized. Our tanks rested against the concrete, angling our upper bodies slightly toward each other. I pointed to the pressure gauge to show him how much air he had left. Thank god my dork-tastic smile was covered by the gear.

We'd been down for two minutes when Josh pulled out his regulator and pointed to his lips, where he tried to make smoke rings with his air bubbles.

I shook my head and gestured that he should put the freaking mouthpiece back in right now, but he just grinned at me like a moron. Little bubbles escaped from the edges of his mouth and danced along his cheeks as they rose to the surface.

And that's when Josh coughed again.

He let go of the regulator as he flailed forward, and it writhed like a snake in the water, free-flowing a torrent of air bubbles that momentarily obscured his face. I motioned for him to take it easy, to calm down and put the regulator back in, but I could tell that full-blown panic had already gripped him. He opened his mouth as if to cough once more, and his legs shot out.

I vaulted toward him and tried to help him to the surface, only to find that the weight belt and equipment had made him too heavy for me to get any leverage. I reached for the belt's clasp, but Josh flailed and an open palm caught me on the cheek and knocked me to the side. I tried to jam the regulator back into his mouth, but by that time he was thrashing and terrified, and he pushed me back again.

I took a deep breath and ditched my weight belt and BC in two quick movements. A dull thud echoed as my tank hit the bottom. I ducked under Josh's whirling arms, swam around behind him, and clutched at the buckle of his weight belt. Panic was surging through me, but I inflated his BC and pushed off the bottom of the pool, kicking straight up.

We broke the surface, and I gasped for air. I slid his mask off, letting it drop to the bottom of the pool. Josh wasn't breathing and his eyes were closed. He was dead weight.

I tore off my mask and threw it against the wall. I undid the clips on his BC as I gave him two rescue breaths before I kicked frantically for the edge.

"Mom! Call nine-one-one!"

I reached the edge and pushed Josh's BC away; then I climbed out, keeping one arm under his. You hear the stories about mothers lifting cars off their babies, and that's pretty much the only way to explain how I got him out. The fear of being on the cover of the *Enquirer* gave me superhuman strength, and I pulled Josh onto the wet concrete.

"Mom!"

Think! I'd been certified in CPR since I was eight, but this was the first time I'd ever had to use it. I tilted his head back to get his airway clear. I put my ear to his mouth and listened for breathing, praying that I'd see his chest rise.

Out of the corner of my eye, I saw my mom come running, but she stopped in the doorway. "Annie!"

"Nine-one-one! Nine-one-one!"

She disappeared again, and Josh wasn't moving and his face was turning pale. I put my lips on his and breathed twice, then moved to his chest and pumped down with my arms locked. Thirty times, to get the circulation going, and then back up to his mouth. A rhythm, a cycle to keep my mind off of what was actually happening.

Mom ran back in, clutching the phone against her chest. "They're on their way."

Again, the cycle. And again. Finally, Josh coughed. He spit up water, and I turned his head to the side so that he wouldn't choke on it. He coughed again, spit up, and pushed himself slowly to his hands and knees.

My mom rushed over to Josh and put her hand on his shoulder as if assuring herself that he was actually alive there.

She moved to me, but I was too exhausted to stand up, so she just huddled over me while I panted. "My god, Annie, I don't even know what to say."

She looked from Josh to me, and then she leaned against the wall and slid down. We stayed like that for a while, the three of us saying nothing, listening only to the whining rumble of the pump.

Josh lolled his head toward me. "Did you slip me the tongue?"

I slapped him on the shoulder hard enough to leave a red handprint on his skin. "I should have let you die."

THREE

If this had been a movie, Josh would have felt a sense of gratitude so profound that he'd have begged me to ride in the ambulance with him, to hold his hand and assure him that he would be okay. Though his energy was weak, he would have found the strength to brush a strand of hair from my forehead as we held each other's gaze, the wail of the siren blending into the background. We would have known—*known*—that no matter what happened from that point forward, we would always be linked together.

Unfortunately, this wasn't a movie. After the paramedics did the whole vital signs check—blood pressure, blood oxygen level, heart and lung check with the stethoscope—they stuck a little electrode on Josh's chest and hooked him up to a portable monitor. He made a big stink about it, but they loaded him onto a stretcher and wheeled him from the pool room into the shop.

My adrenaline rush ebbed slowly, robbing me of the

ability to control my legs like a normal person, so I had to stay seated against the wall. My stomach hurt, my head pounded, and my fingers shook so badly that I stuck my hands under my arms so they wouldn't freak me out.

Gracia had called again to check up on me, and when she heard the news she had her driver bring her right over. We hadn't been able to get in touch with Josh's mom, but her assistant, Violet, was adamant that we not let Josh go anywhere.

"I don't think that's up to me," my mom said icily.

The paramedics were a medical odd couple: one tall and bald, the other short with a belly and a black mustache. While they monitored Josh over near the wetsuits, I mustered up the energy to change into shorts and a T-shirt. Physically, I was better, but now that the action was over, my mind was filled with thoughts of what could have happened. Josh dead. My parents sued. The shop gone. Me responsible.

"Did you really save him?" Gracia said, enveloping me in her Southern embrace as I came out of the small dressing room. "As in, mouth-to-mouth?"

"We call it cardiopulmonary resuscitation," I said with a wink. At least she'd gotten me to joke about it.

"So you put your lips to his *and* pumped his chest? You vixen!"

It's not like I'm the kind of girl who needs her best friend by her at all times, but it was nice to have Gracia there.

The paramedics were just about to wheel Josh out of

the shop when the door buzzed, and in stepped a short man in a shiny, expensive-looking suit. His hair was a blond, slicked-back number, and he was talking into a headset.

"Yeah, I'm here now," he said, pressing a button on his earpiece. He scanned the room quickly and took a decisive step toward my mom. "Larry Schuster," he said, extending his hand. My mom shook it warily, but Larry moved to Josh's side before she could say anything.

My mom shot me a worried glance, and I knew what she was thinking: lawyer.

"You okay, buddy?" Larry said, putting an awkward hand under Josh's chin.

Josh just nodded and turned away. "Hi, Larry."

"He looks good, right?" Larry said to the paramedics. "Real good. Nothing to worry about, right? Thanks for your help."

The paramedics seemed confused. "We've got to take him for observation," the bald one said.

"Observation." Larry tilted his head back and laughed at the absurdity of it all. "I'm observing him right now. Looks fine." Then he motioned for the paramedics to join him over by the ladies' wetsuit rack, where the three men engaged in a discussion straight out of a silent movie. Nodding, shrugging, lots of fast hand gestures from Larry.

Gracia looked at me all bug-eyed. "Say something," she mouthed.

"Is that your dad?" I said.

Josh's laugh was as unexpected as it was genuine. He

winced as he pulled the electrode from his chest, and the heart line on the monitor went flat. He swung his legs around and dangled them off the side of the stretcher. I waited for the paramedics to tell him to stop. But if they noticed, they didn't say anything.

"Is he a lawyer?"

"Don't you know? That man right there is Jessica Rebstock's agent." Josh hopped off the stretcher and rolled his head from side to side. He bent over as if loosening up his back or his hamstrings.

"Are you late for a track meet?" Gracia said.

I took a tentative step toward him. "Maybe you should—"

Larry Schuster slapped the round paramedic on his back. He retrieved a pen from within his suit coat and scrawled a signature on some kind of form. And just like that, the meeting was over. The paramedics shrugged one last time, nodded at each other, and moved back to Josh. They reminded him to take it easy, then they packed up their stretcher and left.

"Nice work, young lady," the bald one said to me on the way out.

Larry went to my mom. "We're going to get him checked out by our guy. Thanks for everything you've done."

My mom nodded like a robot, clearly just as lost as I was, and Larry put his hand on Josh's shoulder. "Your mom will see you at home. Okay, bud?"

"Okay, Larry," Josh said without making eye contact. He wandered toward the fins and sat on the old yellow surfboard we use as a bench. He put his elbows on his knees and drooped his head forward.

Larry Schuster took out his phone and dialed as he turned back to me. "We've already made sure the police will keep the whole thing out of the blogs and the tabloids, so you won't get any recognition for saving him, I'm sorry, but if there's anything you need—anything at all—please let me know."

He shook my hand once, quickly and firmly, before pressing a button on his headset. "Yeah, I'm back."

The buzzer sounded, and he was gone.

Josh stood up but quickly staggered back, knocking into the surfboard bench. A masked mannequin was the only reason he didn't crash all the way to the floor.

"You should probably take it easy," Gracia said.

"Yeah," I said. "Even though—"

"I'm fine," he said—barked would be more accurate—while looking at the floor. One arm was wrapped around the mannequin's neck, and the other was held out to us as if stopping traffic. When he spoke next, I could hardly hear him. "I'm fine. Don't worry about me."

Gracia and I said nothing more. Josh was silent as he stepped tentatively across the room. He paused at the front door as if gathering himself, and then he was gone.

"Thanks for saving my life, Annie," Gracia said. "Now go to hell."

It was my turn to sit on the surfboard bench. "Spring break in Cozumel. Should be a blast."

FOUR

The wheels yelped at landing, and the plane fishtailed for a moment before the brakes engaged and we began to slow. I'd hardly peeked out the window as we approached—choosing to ignore the turquoise water, the beaches, and the inevitable dive boats just offshore, drifting gently with the current.

"Mmm, those peanuts were sure something," Katy said, smiling at me. "I don't even need dinner."

We'd taken a commercial flight because my parents had balked at a trip on Josh's mom's private jet, and the whole way down, Katy had offered variations on the theme: *Who knew a layover in Houston could be so much fun? The seats on United are* much *more comfortable than on a Gulfstream. I love flying with so many people!* And on and on.

That morning, my parents had walked in on me at the exact moment that I was tucking my dive mask and regulator into my suitcase. My enthusiasm about the trip had been dampened, to say the least, by the knowledge that the only other people going were doing so against their will. I'd been at least hoping to squeeze in a dive or two.

"This isn't a vacation," Dad said.

"Just in case?" I said meekly, though I knew it was no use.

"It's a chance for you to broaden your horizons, to experience the world through the eyes of others. Your friends might have these kinds of opportunities all the time, but you don't. It's important for you to take advantage. No messing around."

"What he means, Annie," my mom had said as she removed the regulator from my suitcase and draped it over her shoulder, "is that we want you to stay focused on what matters."

Now, on the plane, I snagged the brochure from the seat pocket in front of me. Borders Unlimited was a volunteer relief organization geared specifically toward high school students, with offices in Asia, Africa, and all over Latin America. The brochure's propaganda included stats on college acceptances and quotations from former volunteers about how meaningful their experiences had been. *I thought I would be coming down to help these people,* said one, *but what I learned from them was far more than I could offer. Thanks, Borders Unlimited!*

A gust of humid air blew through the cabin when the airplane door opened. I gathered my stuff and waited for the passengers in front of us to deplane, avoiding Katy's "I can't believe I'm flying commercial" smirk as much as

I could. I followed Josh down the aisle to the doorway, where there were stairs instead of a ramp. I'd never gotten off a plane that way before.

Josh stepped out onto the top landing and waved to an imaginary crowd like a visiting dignitary. "I do that every time," he said, winking at me over his shoulder.

I had no idea where I stood with him. It was as though the whole saving-his-life incident had never happened. He wasn't unfriendly; he just never brought any of it up. And because I wasn't going to bring it up, either, it was just *there*. Uncomfortable for me, but maybe not for him. Maybe my saving his life was just another in a long line of serendipitous things that happened to him all the time, as momentous as a sunny day or a good parking space.

I looked out over the island. The sun sat low in the sky, the humidity making it seem bigger, more orange even than what we see on smog-alert days in Los Angeles. A low canopy of trees lined the horizon. I'd always wanted to come to Cozumel, but not like this. Not with the incredible dive sites I'd heard so much about—Palancar Gardens, Santa Rosa Wall, Punta Sur—close enough to smell, and me not being able to take advantage of them.

Katy cleared her throat, so I sped down the stairs, hustling to catch up with Josh, and followed the other passengers along a white line painted on the asphalt.

I hadn't expected instant poverty, but the airport was surprisingly modern for an island supposedly in need of disaster relief. Three orderly lines at the passport check led to a spacious baggage area. Everything was concrete and recently painted, with huge color posters on every wall: divers emerging from a coral cavern; a close-up of a brilliant queen angelfish nibbling at a sea sponge; an aerial view of the island, complete with turquoise water and a sandy beach. Good thing I hadn't looked out the window on the way in.

We waited at the carousel with the other passengers. I barely heard Katy say, "I just *love* public baggage claim," because as each bag of dive gear passed by on the conveyor belt, I felt more and more like the one little kid at lunch whose parents packed a dessert of carrots and celery while everyone else got cupcakes.

Josh put his arm around me like a buddy, and for a moment I forgot everything except the warmth of his forearm against the side of my neck. "This must be killing you."

A pasty balding guy with a baggy muscle shirt and a tattoo of a shark on his right calf grabbed a mesh equipment bag and high-fived his doughy companion. "Maracaibo Reef, here we come!" he said. Then he actually whooped.

"At least I don't have to be in the water with that guy," I said.

As soon as we passed through customs and onto the sidewalk, we were accosted by offers of taxi rides to the *centro*, tours of the island, hotels, diving, and more. "Cheaper than Walmart!" one guy said, pointing to a poorly laminated picture of an ocean-side villa.

Mr. Alvarez shook his head at the offers and pointed to

a driver holding a piece of paper with ALVAREZ scrawled on it. The taxi drivers and tour operators backed away from us, only to converge on the shark-tattoo guy behind us. "Tay-nay-mos hotel!" he screamed, waving his finger at them like an angry kindergarten teacher.

Our driver, clad in flip-flops, shorts, and an old orange tank top, motioned around the corner to a beat-up Datsun pickup truck. Alvarez sat in the front cab while the rest of us followed our bags into the bed of the truck.

"The best thing about being out of LA?" Josh said as he hopped over the side. "No paparazzi here to take pictures."

Katy's brother, Nate, turned to me. "I'm sure he hates the attention."

A two-lane highway took us parallel to the ocean and into San Miguel, past condos and hotels and the occasional mega-resort. Cruise ships dotted the horizon like giant bath toys.

"Have you ever been on a cruise?" Josh asked me.

I shook my head. "What's it like?"

"We did a show on the *Carnival Conquest* in the Bahamas last summer," Katy said. She stood with her hands on the roof of the truck, letting the wind blow through her hair. "Two performances a night, six nights a week. We basically vegged out by the pool the rest of the time. Trust me, cruises are nothing special."

The sun was almost at the horizon when we pulled to a stop in front of a small brick building with a sign out front that read, TANGO DIVERS! WE ARE YOUR DIVE SHOP!

How awesome for me. As if a diveless trip to Cozumel wasn't enough, we had to stop at a freaking dive shop.

A short man with a penguin shuffle appeared from around the corner of the building. He waved at us and increased the speed of his waddle.

Alvarez jumped out of the cab and threw up his hands. "Eduardo!"

"*¡Amigo!*" the man said, grabbing Alvarez in a warm embrace. "*¿Cómo estás, mi cuate? ¿Cómo fue el viaje?*"

"Trip was good," Alvarez said. "You look great."

Eduardo rubbed his belly. The thin wisp of black hair sprouting from the top of his head danced in the breeze. "I think am now just a little bigger."

Alvarez stepped aside and motioned to us, making the introductions. Eduardo had a pleasant way about him; the crow's-feet that clawed at his eyes seemed to reveal a friendly wisdom. "Come, come. I am so happy to see you, *amigos*. We very much look forward to have you here."

"It's nice to meet you, Eduardo," I said as I hopped onto the concrete.

"Please," he said, waving his hand at me, "call me Wayo. Is the *sobrenombre* for Eduardo, the nickname."

Katy elbowed her brother. "Like Nate for Nathaniel."

"*Exactamente!*"

We unloaded one by one, following Wayo along a cracked sidewalk. "You are staying at the hotel there," he said, pointing to a sign hanging out over the street a block away. "My friend, he owns the place. But first, I will show you Tango Divers."

Josh glanced at the hotel and shrugged. "It ain't the Presidente."

"The what?"

"The Presidente InterContinental," he said. "Down the road a couple of miles. It's the best hotel on the island by far."

"You've been here before?"

"My mom shot a commercial for Spectacle Shampoo a couple of years ago, so she brought down the whole family. We got to snorkel right off the dock. It was great. Housekeeping made little swans out of the hand towels and put them on our beds."

The disappointment was as surprising as it was instantaneous. I guess I'd been hoping—as unromantic as volunteer work was bound to be—that we'd at least share the experience together. But he already had a memory of this place, and I doubted that hurricane relief could compare to little swan towels in a fancy hotel room.

The day before, I'd found Gracia down in her basement, sitting at the edge of a deep brown leather recliner and yelling at a TV that stretched at least five feet across. I plopped on the couch behind her and let out a sigh.

"Island vacay tomorrow," she'd said without looking at me. Her fingers hammered the buttons of a video game controller, and she wore a headset with one ear covered by a headphone and a microphone coming out to the side. A werewolf-looking thing exploded on-screen, the furry head rolling away in slow motion. "Are you excited? I'm thinking sundresses. Guys love that. You let the light shine through the fabric so they can see the shadows of your legs—damn, reload, reload!—so you're showing them some leg without actually doing it. It's very Puritan."

"You're better at those kinds of games than I am."

She flipped the microphone so it was pointing straight up like an antenna. "Elaborate, please."

"You put too much effort into pretending," I said. "NoobKilla321—"

"Indeed, I am a noob killa!" She leaned to the side, holding the game controller above her head, her fingers working the buttons furiously.

"Down here in the basement like you have something to hide."

"There's nothing wrong with presenting an illusion of myself. So I let guys think they know everything about me—so what? If one of them ever cared, I might let him in on the rest of the iceberg, eventually. But it's just too much trouble if a guy feels insecure around you. Then you have to deal with all his issues." Another explosion on the screen. This time a life-size zombie head melted to gold sludge.

"What about Baldwin Forneau? Does he feel insecure around you?"

Gracia hesitated, and the screen flashed red as one of the zombies took a bite out of her arm. The life-force level at the top-right corner started to dwindle. "You know about that?"

"Seriously?" I said. "You think I don't notice the

furtive glances? The wistful yearnings of hot nerd-on-nerd action?"

"Your lips are sealed, Annie. There's nothing there yet. And there won't be if you tell him I'm NoobKilla."

"You could find a guy who isn't so insecure."

"I'm going to go after college graduates now? We're in high school. *Nobody* isn't so insecure." She glanced over at me and must have noticed something in my eyes, because she took off her headset, hit a button to kill the monitor, and hopped over the chair. "Look at you! Except for Josh, right? That's what you're thinking, isn't it?"

"No," I said, glancing away, which wasn't exactly the most convincing maneuver of my life. "It's just that—"

"I love it. I *love* it! You spend all week playing it cool, pretending there's nothing going on between you even though you *saved his life*—"

"There is nothing going on—"

"Not yet, at least." She clasped me by the shoulders and gave me a gentle shake. "Get back to me after a week in the warm Caribbean sun."

But now, as I watched Josh roll his bag through the low doorway of Wayo's shop, it became clear that we wouldn't be having our moment together after all, whether I'd saved his life or not.

"You know, his last girlfriend was a princess." Katy had appeared behind me like a ghost. Her voice was pleasant—even helpful. "A real one, from Monaco or something. They met last summer."

I pretended not to hear. "Huh?"

"I'm just saying. I wouldn't get your hopes up."

"I don't know what you're talking about."

Katy brushed past me. "Of course you do."

Tango Divers was about half the size of our shop's front room. One side held a desk with a map of the island underneath a glass surface, a small refrigerator, and a wide paper calendar. Well-used wetsuits and BCs covered the entire back wall.

Wayo shepherded us toward a small round table in a corner of the shop and lifted plastic chairs from a stack near the wall. A bowl of tortilla chips sat on the table next to a pile of paper plates. The legs of our chairs rubbed against the linoleum as we pulled them up to the table. Wayo emerged from behind the refrigerator door with a large ceramic bowl, which he placed next to the chips.

"Conch ceviche," he said as he sat down. "Is pull fresh from the sea this morning."

"Isn't the island a protected national park?" I said.

Nate rolled his eyes. "As if on cue."

"From here to the south, yes. But very few people dive the northern reefs. The current is too strong for most. If one minute you lose your concentration, you are halfway to Cuba." He smiled and made a zooming motion with his hand.

Alvarez came through the door holding a huge plate piled high with steaming tamales in one hand and a bowl of black beans in the other. "Don't believe anything he says about me. Or about anything, really."

Wayo thumbed at Alvarez. "The crew called him El Payaso, because he jokes like a clown."

"What crew was that?" Josh said.

Alvarez pulled up a chair and helped himself to a tamale. "You might say we used to search for ships that had become lost." He gave me a knowing smile. I couldn't tell if he meant it or if he was just messing with me.

"Lost a long time ago." Wayo bounced his eyebrows. "With gold on them."

"You never talked about it in class," Katy said, suddenly interested.

Mr. Alvarez used a tortilla chip to slice a piece of tamale and scoop it up. "Nobody wants to hear about unsuccessful treasure hunters. I might have told you guys if I'd actually found something."

I laughed. "You wouldn't be teaching if you'd actually found something."

"Fair enough."

"So Wayo is the 'Gold Doubloons' part of the trip?" I said.

"I am the what?" Wayo said.

"Nobody's really sure what Wayo is anymore." Alvarez smiled and backhanded his friend gently on the belly. "The slow pace of island life seems to agree with him."

"You should know," Wayo said, leaning in and whispering to the rest of us, "that you are being led by a man who leaves his gear on top of a taxicab. Twice."

"The second time wasn't my fault."

43

Seeing the two of them together was both strange and comforting. Strange because of the unfamiliarity with running into a teacher out of school, the odd surprise of that teacher's life away from the classroom. The comfort came from their ease with each other, the banter, the genuine friendship. It made me wonder what Gracia and I would be like in twenty years.

Nate snorted a little. "Good Deeds and Gold Doubloons. Dumbest name ever."

Alvarez ate another tamale tortilla chip and nodded through the crunch. "I'm so bad with names that if I had a boat, I'd just name it *My Boat*. Pinedale loved it, though. The administration ate that up."

"You guys never found anything?" Katy said.

Mr. Alvarez and Wayo glanced quickly at each other before turning their attention back to their meals. Finally, Mr. Alvarez looked back at us and said, "Nope."

That seemed to put a damper on the evening. We ate quickly, the conversation never again venturing past mumbled small talk. From time to time, Wayo reminded us how happy he was for us to be there, and how excited he was that we were working hard for his island. Eventually, we left Alvarez and Wayo together in the dive shop and went down the street to the hotel, where Katy and I were sharing a room. Oh, joy.

FIVE

The kids in the Borders Unlimited brochure had built roads and houses, had dug latrines and water wells, had cleaned up after mudslides and tsunamis and tropical storms. We were painting the inside of a school. *Re*painting the school, to be exact. A school that apparently hadn't even been damaged in the hurricane nine months before. I sincerely doubted that it was what my parents had had in mind when they'd encouraged me to take advantage of this opportunity.

Alvarez was supposed to be our chaperone, but two days into the trip he had spent a grand total of about an hour at the job site. The first day, he looked around, pointed to some paint buckets, and reminded us how meaningful the experience would be. Three minutes later he told us he was confident that we'd be able to handle the rest of it ourselves, and then, leaving us in the care of an ancient woman he said was Wayo's aunt, he disappeared.

But if the Good Deeds portion of the trip was less

than advertised, the Gold Doubloons part was virtually nonexistent. Regardless of what Alvarez had promised in class, there was no mention of Cortés or the Jaguar. In fact, the word *treasure* hadn't even crossed his lips since that first dinner with Wayo.

When Nate confronted him about it, Alvarez just laughed. "I'm just the chaperone. Remember why you're here."

"Because I got caught cheating—I know."

"No, young man," Alvarez said. "Because you want to give back."

After Alvarez dropped us off the second day, Katy, who by then had gone and gotten herself the ridiculous spring-break-tourist hair braids, decided she'd had enough of the work and spent the morning sunbathing, her shorts rolled up and her tank top pulled all the way to her chest.

By midday we were almost finished with the walls. It was hot, and we were sweating. Josh hadn't taken his shirt off yet, but no doubt Mimi's vision of a Golden Rebstock was going to come true at any moment. I hadn't brought a towel, and because I was wearing a tank top, there were no sleeves to help me deal with the beads forming on my forehead.

The concrete floors were splattered with white paint, but at least we hadn't gotten any of it on the desks in the center of the room. The paint was all over my hands and clothes. Josh and I worked while Katy lay in the courtyard just outside the door and her brother started exercising, alternating from sit-ups to push-ups and back again.

"Does anyone else get the feeling that we're just going through the motions?" I said.

Katy laughed from the other side of the door. "Maybe you could get your dad on the phone. Ask him to make it harder."

My defensiveness was a reflex. "What does my dad have to do with this?"

Nate paused in the middle of some push-ups. "He gave her a B-minus last year."

Katy said, "Not that you even need to worry about grades, right? You're probably on scholarship."

"Which I have to get straight A's just to keep," I barked, instead of pointing out that she wasn't making any sense.

Katy noticed my desperation and pounced on it with her own brand of contempt. She didn't look at me, didn't even open her eyes. Just lay in the sun and said, "Like anyone's going to give a teacher's kid a B."

I kept painting. Up. Down. At least Josh was still painting, too.

Nate finished his push-ups and went straight into some weird tae kwon do kind of maneuver: choreographed kicks and punches, punctuated by the occasional scream.

"What are you doing?" Josh said, as mystified as I was.

"I have a belt test coming up. Second-degree black belt," Nate said, kicking his leg straight out and doing a double punch. "It's a big deal."

Wayo's aunt brought us a late lunch, a pot of fish soup with corn tortillas and black beans. She still hadn't said anything to us, just pantomimed like we were idiots.

47

Which we were, clearly, because one man could have done a better job painting in half the time it was taking us. The soup was wonderful, though. A thick broth with onions, lime wedges, and big chunks of whitefish.

Out of nowhere, Nate screamed, "God, I'm so bored!"

"Tell yourself a story." The words were out of my mouth before I could think.

Nate dropped his tortilla in his bowl and looked at me with a mocking little grin. "Excuse me?"

When you blurt out something that makes you look like a jackass, you really only have two options. The first is to say nothing, not even if prompted. Your only goal is to not make it worse, no matter how bad you sounded or how tempting it might be to clarify. You shut your mouth and let the whole thing blow over. The second is to try to explain the original blurt, because you figure that your jackassery will disappear if only people knew a little more. The second option never works.

Guess which one I went with anyway.

"My dad says there's no such thing as bored," I said, ignoring the flashing red STOP signs spinning in my brain. "He used to tell stories or have me make them up."

Katy snickered. "Don't you and your dad have something special."

"Damn, Katy," Josh said.

"What?"

That terrible sense of impending tears appeared. I felt it creep up from the pit of my stomach to my throat. I hated myself for wanting to cry, and I hated myself for hating myself. I dropped my spoon into the bowl, sending a healthy wave of soup over the rim, and tried my hardest not to run out of the room.

I made it as far as the curb outside the school and sat on the concrete. The ferry horn sounded in the distance. Only a sliver of ocean was visible between the buildings, but it was enough to taunt me even further. The cruise ships drifting by on the horizon, the dive boats returning from their afternoon tours. And me, on the curb, surrounded by leaves and trash and three juniors who thought everything I cared about was stupid.

I sat there long enough to feel good and sorry for myself, but now I had to deal with the sticky issue of reentry.

"It's nice to get some fresh air, isn't it? I think I might be high from the paint." Josh eased down next to me, but not too close. His pity made me feel even worse.

"You didn't have to come out here," I said.

"My dad and I used to be that way, too," he said.

"Come on, Josh—"

"I still remember the first time we went upside down on a roller coaster together. The Cyclone. I was six. I freaked when they buckled me in, and I begged him to let me off, but somehow he convinced me to go through with it. The whole rest of the day, every time we passed the Cyclone, he pointed at it and said, 'You did that.'"

"'Used to be that way'?"

Josh snapped pieces off a small twig and threw them into the street. "My mom started to get good parts, and all of a sudden she wasn't around anymore. They hung on for as long as they could, but the end was inevitable. Dad moved, I stayed, and Larry Schuster the wonder-agent made sure the whole thing was handled discreetly."

"I'm sorry."

"Aah, you know how it is. Life. Things happen. By the way," he said, looking off toward the ocean, "thanks for the whole CPR deal."

"You mean saving your life?"

"Well, when you put it that way . . ." His laugh was so genuine, so surprisingly humble, that I turned to look right at him just to be sure it wasn't coming from someone else.

Unfortunately, he happened to be looking right at me at that exact moment. I tried not to think of the paint splattered all over my fingers and probably my face; tried not to worry about how nasty my hair was, stuck against the back of my neck in the humidity.

A light breeze saved us, breaking my mute spell before it had the chance to cross over into something truly disastrous. A torn Chupa Chups wrapper blew down the street, and I watched it go. I could tell Josh was still looking at me.

"What's the best shipwreck story you know?"

I kept it light, meeting his gaze with a big ol' smile on my face. "Teasing is a form of bullying. Did you know that?"

"I'm serious; let's have a story. What else are we going to do? Repaint the room? Again?"

Who knows why I didn't run away right then. Maybe

because I wanted to believe he was really interested. Maybe because he was bored, and I, potentially, had the cure. Probably because things couldn't really get any worse than they already were.

I nodded and took a deep breath and went for it. I told him about Alfonso de Corralao's bold seaside attack on the city of Melaka in 1501, the subsequent plunder of gold and jewels, and the *Flor do Amelia*, an unsinkable ship built entirely for the purpose of bringing the impossibly large treasure back to Portugal in one fell swoop.

"Her holds were constructed to transport most of Corralao's spoils. Over twenty-four tons of gold, a fourth of which came from the sultan's palace alone. Golden Buddhas, birds, animals, coins—even the sultan's throne. Over two hundred chests of precious stones: diamonds, rubies, sapphires, emeralds. She took three years to build, but she was a masterpiece. The engineering marvel of her day."

"Like the *Titanic*," Josh said.

"Pretty much." I nodded. "But a month after unfurling her sails for Lisbon, she vanished. In a year with no major recorded storms, following a route protected by the Portuguese Armada, the *Flor do Amelia* disappeared without a trace. Over three hundred souls, and a treasure worth more than any in recorded history, gone. The current theory is that she was a myth, a complex misdirection to draw pirates' attention from a fleet of smaller treasure ships."

"I take it not *everybody* believes that."

"Some people think she's real." I looked at him and smiled. "And that she's still out there, waiting patiently for someone to find her."

There was a nice long pause as the mystery of the *Flor do Amelia* hung suspended between us. Josh finally pointed at me. "You really, really like this stuff, huh?"

Alvarez appeared just then, munching on french fries from a paper cone. A pink folder was tucked snugly under one arm. "You guys eat lunch yet?"

Josh groaned. "Why do I get the feeling that you're not just here to check up on us?"

Alvarez smiled. He fished out the last of the fries, crumpled up the cone, and tossed it to the ground.

I shook my head. "You'd fit right in with all the Good Deeds going on in there."

"Glad to hear it." He winked as he handed me the folder. "Time for the Gold Doubloons part."

I pushed myself to my feet and took the folder from him. Attached to the cover was a teacher's standard worksheet with fill-in-the-blank questions. Cozumel, the Mayans, the ruins, Spanish conquistadors. There were some short-answer questions at the bottom. "This is going to be so awesome," I said, my sarcasm on overload.

Alvarez kept smiling at me. He wiped something from the corner of his mouth with his thumb, inspected it quickly, and rubbed his hands together.

I opened the folder, and all my follow-up sarcasm vanished instantly. With each successive page, my heartbeat grew louder in my ears. There were printed scans of documents in elaborate Spanish calligraphy. Some were as clean and elegant as if they'd been written that morning, and some were photocopies of photocopies, hardly legible at all. I flipped through drawings of ships and their corresponding manifests. In the center of the stack was a picture I had never seen before but recognized instantly. A color sketch, brilliant gold, of a jaguar with piercing red eyes and sharp green teeth.

"You're kidding," I said.

"You were right about de la Torre's journal."

"Is this it? The original pages—"

"Primary sources, remember?" he said. "Father Rubén Gonzales?"

Josh peeked over my shoulder and pulled out the worksheet. "We have homework?" he said, scanning the questions.

Alvarez chuckled. "This is a school trip, Josh. You want to get the others?"

"They're still working in there," Josh said. "Working hard."

"The museum closes at five o'clock. You'd better get to it."

"Can we just not learn anything?" Josh said. "Just for this week? I promise I'll learn stuff when we get back."

I turned back to the picture of the Jaguar and ran my fingertips across its open mouth. "This is going to be so awesome," I said, and this time I meant it.

SIX

"This is going to be so stupid," Katy said, but I surprised myself by not caring. I held the folder securely in both hands; it was all I could do not to pore through the information on our way to the museum.

By now it was midafternoon. The sun inched down the cloudless sky, and a thick layer of humidity settled over everything. We walked up the main street, Avenida Rafael Melgar, past jewelry stores and day-tour operators and nightclubs filled with enthusiastic spring-breakers who were neither willing nor able to wait for the night.

A woman and her little boy sold silver pendants in the main square, mostly sea creatures and Mayan designs. I squatted down and ran my finger across the top of a small sea turtle pendant about the size of my thumbnail. It was classy and understated, a piece of jewelry that said, "Why, yes, I care about the ocean, but I don't need a button as evidence." Gracia and Mimi would approve.

"Come on, Annie," Nate said, waving at me like an

exasperated parent as I paid the little boy with some of the pesos my dad had given me. I quickly fastened the thin silver chain around my neck and hustled back to the group.

The museum was two blocks inland, overlooking a small dirt park with a single soccer goal. We trudged up a short flight of old stone steps, and Nate picked a flake of dark green paint from the wooden door as we pushed through.

"I bet we could hit this place when we're done with the school," he mumbled with a snort.

"*Veinte pesos*," said a girl at the front desk who couldn't have been more than ten years old.

"*Estudiantes*," Josh said, turning on the charm as he patted his pockets to explain that he hadn't brought his wallet. "Students, *sí*?"

The little girl smiled and held out her hand. "Twenty pesos. Special student price."

Josh and the Sugars looked at me. Katy shrugged. "I only carry plastic."

"Of course you do." I dug into my pocket.

The museum was essentially a single hallway winding around a small courtyard with a flagpole in the center. We sat on the floor against the wall outside, and I laid the contents of the folder on the dusty brick in front of us.

"Divide and conquer," I said, handing Josh the worksheet. "You and Nate go answer as many of the fill-in-the-blanks as you can, and Katy and I will try to figure out what this all has to do with the Golden Jaguar."

Josh stared at the worksheet as if trying to will the answers into existence. "Why do we even have to do this?"

"It's just a stupid exercise," Nate said. "Fake treasure hunt or a scavenger hunt or whatever."

I motioned for them to get moving. "The sooner we finish, the sooner we can get back to doing nothing."

"Uh-oh," Nate said. "Looks like we got ourselves a teacher's kid in here."

"Just go," I said.

"Yes, ma'am," Nate said with a salute.

"That's kind of cool," Katy said when they'd left, pointing at the picture of the Golden Jaguar. "What is it?"

"The Golden Jaguar," I said. "Cortés's Golden Jaguar? I did a presentation on it last week?"

"Hmm," she said, but there was no recognition on her face.

"Really?" I said.

Most of the documents were in Spanish, and that's where being a freshman really worked against me. Apparently they didn't cover original Spanish nautical logs until junior year, so I had to depend on Katy.

She squinted at the old calligraphy and read slowly. "Okay, it says the *Vida Preciosa*?"

"The name of the ship," I said.

"Approached the land of the *golondrinas* during a storm. Looking for *refugio*—refuge, maybe? Shelter?— and dropped anchor on the side *de sotavento*—beats me—where the waters were more calm."

"Does it say where the land of the *golondrinas* is?" I said.

Katy shrugged. "I don't even know what *golondrinas* means."

"What does it say after that?"

"You know what would be awesome?" Katy said, and by the tone of her voice I could already tell she didn't mean continuing to translate. "If you sat there and obsessed over your treasure, and I sat way over here and didn't, and we waited for the boys to come back so we could get out of this place."

While not technically "awesome," per se, her plan did have the benefit of the two of us not working together.

I sat with the folder in my lap, staring at the color picture of the Golden Jaguar with questions bouncing around my head like Ping-Pong balls in a lottery machine. Why did Alvarez give me the folder? What did that have to do with the museum? What is the land of *golondrinas*? What if this wasn't just a scavenger hunt? What if it wasn't just an exercise?

A giggle came from the open doorway, and I looked up to see the front-desk girl whispering to a friend and pointing. I followed her gaze to Katy at the flagpole in the center of the courtyard. She'd wrapped her arms around it so that her body was parallel to the ground, and she was inching up slowly. Even I had to admit that it was impressive.

Josh bounded into the courtyard with Nate trailing behind. "We're done here," Nate said.

"Show me how to do that!" Josh said to Katy as he folded the worksheet and put it into his pocket.

"You guys," I said, "I don't think we're supposed—"

"It'll be quick," Josh said.

Katy wrapped her arms around him from behind, showing him how to position his hands. She whispered something in his ear before stepping away. Josh braced one elbow at his waist and lifted, but before he could get his legs parallel to the ground, he came crashing down in a heap.

He groaned and rolled over onto his back. "I think I broke my kidney."

Katy covered her giggle with both hands. Weren't they so cute together.

A uniformed security guard stepped toward them, and Josh jumped to his feet. The guard removed his baton from its holster and pointed at the door, but he was laughing too much to do any real intimidating.

"If that was the Gold Doubloons part of the trip," Nate said as we were walking out, "it sucked as much as the Good Deeds."

I waved to the girl behind the desk, and Josh said, "Pretty cool that Cortés came here, though, right?"

I stopped halfway down the steps. "What did you say?"

"Cortés landed in Cozumel. What, you didn't know that? I thought you knew everything about him."

"I spent most of my time on what happened after he got the Jaguar," I said, more defensively than I wanted.

"It said in there that Cortés came to the island in something like—"

"Show me." I grabbed his hand—I'm not sure which one of us was more surprised—and pulled him back up the stairs and into the museum.

"Why are you so—"

"Just show me where you saw it."

Josh saluted the security guard as we rushed through the hallway, and he led me to a large panel filled with drawings of conquistadors and ships and accompanying text in Spanish and English.

"Right here," he said. The image in the center showed a Mayan contingent spread out on the shore like a welcome party, with the Spanish galleons bearing down on them from the ocean. "Cortés landed in 1519, and there wasn't any resistance from the native Mayans. He used the island as a staging ground for the conquest of Mexico. Looks like the Mayans should have resisted, though. Smallpox practically wiped them out a few years later."

"Cortés was here," I said to myself.

"Can we go now?"

"Wait." The panel before the one on Cortés caught my eye. It was all about the original settling of the island, the Mayans, and their multitiered temples.

"'The Land of Swallows,'" I read.

"So?"

"From the Mayan words *cuzam*, meaning 'swallows,' and *lumil*, meaning 'land of.' *Cuzam lumil* . . . Cozumel!"

"I get it." Josh chuckled. "Why are you shouting?"

"Do you have a dictionary? Or a phone or something?"

"In the hotel," he said. "Why?"

I raced back to the girl at the front desk and dropped the folder on the counter. My hands shook as I opened it and flipped frantically through the pages. There it was. "*Golondrina?*" I said. The girl looked at me like I was crazy. Damn you, Spanish!

"*Golondrina*," I said again, speaking as slowly as I could make myself. I put my trembling thumbs together and flapped my hands in the worst finger-puppet bird ever made. "What does it mean? *En* English? *Es un* bird?"

Josh put his hand on my shoulder. "Are you okay?"

The girl behind the counter recovered enough from her shock to answer me. "*Sí, es un pájaro pequeño.* A small bird. It means a swallow. Cozumel is called the land of swallows. The name comes—"

"Thank you," I said. "*Muchas gracias.*"

"Annie?" Josh said.

I held the photocopy of de la Torre's journal in his face as if it were a winning lottery ticket. "The *Vida Preciosa* approached the land of the *golondrinas*—the Land of Swallows—during a storm! They dropped anchor on the side where seas were more calm."

"What's the *Vida Preciosa* again?"

"The leeward side of the island! Where seas were calm," I said again, pointing to the gentle waves only two blocks away. "De la Torre was *here*, Josh. And that means the Jaguar was here, too."

SEVEN

My mind was on overdrive. I felt like a character in one of Gracia's video games, as if my entire life force had been transferred to my brain, rendering the rest of my body almost completely unresponsive. I could hardly put one foot in front of the other. Eventually, the others got tired of telling me to hurry up, and they let me wander on the wide concrete sidewalk that ran between Avenida Melgar and the seawall.

I remembered a conversation I'd had with my dad after the last of our metal detector trips to the beach. I was twelve. I'd found an old silver pocket watch and was twirling it in circles as we walked back to the car. The sun had been low in the sky, just like tonight. And like tonight, my mind had been filled with the excitement of treasure.

"Did you ever think of actually being a treasure hunter?" I'd said. "A real one?"

"That's what drew me to your mother in the first place. She was smart, of course. And good-looking. But she was the first female diver I had ever met, and I had this dream that we could get famous together. The dynamic duo."

"So, why—"

"We got married. Then you came along." He stopped walking and dragged his toes through the sand. "The truth is that I probably didn't have what it took anyway. I know it probably seems romantic to you, but it's dangerous. Pirates are still out there, but not with swords and cannons. Now everybody has guns."

"So you decided it was better to study history than to make it?"

He'd let a short burst of air escape through his teeth as though I'd punched him. It hadn't been what I'd meant, and I'd apologized, but the damage had been done. He gave me a quick little squeeze on the shoulder and hauled his metal detector back.

Now, though, I had to wonder. If he'd ever held in his hands what I was holding in mine—actual evidence, a clue to something more—would he still have walked away?

I didn't know what any of it meant yet, but there had to be something there. De la Torre's journal said that the *Vida Preciosa* had anchored off of Cozumel during a storm. What if he'd unloaded it? What if the Jaguar was here, on the island? Did Cozumel just happen to be a safe harbor, or was it the destination all along?

I was so lost in thought, I didn't notice that the others had stopped walking until I almost hit my head on Nate's shoulder. They were standing on the seawall, glaring down at the ocean below.

"What's going on?" I said.

Alvarez was standing in the water, waist-deep, on the other side of the seawall, his T-shirt drenched, hefting an enormous mahimahi onto the sidewalk.

"Looks like they were biting," Nate said.

Alvarez smiled at Nate's tone. "Wait here."

He waded to a small boat anchored about fifty feet offshore, where Wayo loaded him up with what looked like a marlin. Alvarez slogged back through the water with one hand clutching the body of the fish and the other holding a washcloth around the spearlike nose.

"White marlin," Alvarez said when he got back to the seawall. He tried to lift it up. "A little help?"

"I'm not touching that," Nate said.

Josh reached over and grabbed the washcloth-covered spear, but not the body of the fish. Alvarez pushed while Josh pulled, and the marlin slid across the concrete, clear scales sprinkling into the ocean like snowflakes.

"Careful with the beautiful fish, *amigos*!" Wayo laughed, sloshing through the water as he carried two huge silver wahoos by the tails. His two fish smacked to the sidewalk when he deposited them.

Katy scoffed. "Having a nice vacation?"

"It was a tournament," Alvarez said. "Wayo needed an extra hand."

There were now seven fish lying in a row like torpedoes: a white marlin, the two wahoos, a silver barracuda sporting the telltale underbite, and three emerald-green mahimahi.

Alvarez dumped two buckets of seawater on the fish and pointed down the shore to the main pier, where another marlin was hanging by its tail from some sort of crane. A line of boats waited just offshore. "You get to weigh one of each species you catch. Greatest combined weight wins."

"Wins what?" Josh said.

Wayo pulled himself up on the seawall. "*Dinero*," he said. "*Mucho, mucho dinero.*"

"So you get to go fishing and make money, and we have to paint all day?" Nate said.

Alvarez hefted himself onto the sidewalk. "You got to see the museum, didn't you?"

An old woman pedaled by with a snack cart on her bicycle, stopping when Wayo waved her down. "*Lo que quieren*," Wayo said to the woman. He motioned for us to help ourselves from the cart.

There didn't seem to be much else to do, so I stuffed the folder into my back pocket and chose a paper cone of jicama sticks sprinkled with red chile salt. Josh got a pack of gum, and the Sugars ignored the offer altogether.

Wayo knelt down next to the marlin and began to clean it. A small crowd was gathering around us. Some were cruise ship tourists, the men with lobster sunburns, the women in island-themed T-shirts at least a size too big. More locals appeared as word seemed to spread.

"Wayo and I used to fish quite a bit," Alvarez said to me. "Back when we were young and he was skinny."

"I hear you just fine from here," Wayo said with a laugh. He filleted the marlin and cut the meat into massive chunks. He gave the first big piece to the old woman with the cart.

"It's not about the money," Alvarez said. "He's donating all his winnings to the school. It's about the ocean, about beating the fish. He's very competitive. Hates to lose."

The crowd swelled, the locals overtaking the tourists, and as more people came over, Alvarez and I stepped back to give them space. Wayo would cut a big piece off the marlin, point to someone in the crowd, and that person would walk away with the night's dinner.

There was something so peaceful about it. We stood only a few feet from the ocean, with the sun dipping toward the horizon, and golden light sparkled off the waves. My lips tingled from the chile on the jicama. For a moment I actually felt like I was on vacation.

I noticed a dive boat coming back to town, wetsuits tied to the canopy frame and flapping in the wind. That made me remember the paint on my fingers. And the folder in my back pocket.

"Why would you wait two days to show me that stuff?" I said so that only Alvarez could hear.

He stared straight ahead, but his face broke into a huge smile. "I knew you'd figure it out."

"Cortés was really here?" I said.

"Now you understand the importance of those primary

sources." He turned to me and smiled again. There was so much more I wanted to ask him, but the crowd was still growing.

Katy and Nate dangled their feet above the ocean, and suddenly Josh went over and sat on the seawall with them. He could have sat next to Nate, but he didn't. He chose Katy. They shared a laugh, and she elbowed him. How wonderful for them.

I did my best to look away from that disaster, and since I didn't feel like contemplating the beauty of the open seas, I turned my attention to the crowd. One of the assembled witnesses looked just like the guy with the pockmarks who my mom had tried to persuade to buy the paddle fins.

"Hey!" I said, waving at him. The man didn't say anything, looking over his shoulder and apparently deciding that I wasn't talking to him, so I tried again. "You were at my mom's dive shop a couple of days ago? In California?"

"Right," he said as he wandered over. He wore an aggressively Hawaiian shirt and was gnawing on a piece of sugarcane. "Of course."

"I hope you went with the hybrid fins."

"You were quite persuasive. How's the diving so far?"

"I wish I knew," I said, wiggling my paint-splattered fingertips. "Volunteer work."

"Building up the résumé already, am I right? I have a niece about your age." His laugh was warm and good-natured. He winked at me and nodded politely to Alvarez and then continued on down the street.

"Small world, huh?" I said to Alvarez. "I met that guy at our dive shop."

"Mmm," he said, nodding as he watched Mr. Pockmarks disappear into the evening crowd.

Josh was still talking to Katy, and now they actually seemed to be deep in conversation. She pointed toward the central plaza, and I could have sworn that she let her hand rest on his shoulder as she brought it back down.

Wayo turned the marlin over, bringing it up and slapping it on the concrete. A dull sound rang out, as though he'd hit the ground with a hammer.

"Where did you meet this guy?" My question was both genuine and rhetorical.

"Have you ever heard of the *Santa Lucia*? Small ship, nothing huge like the *Atocha*, for example. Just one of the many Spanish ships that didn't make it back home."

I turned to Alvarez. "Near the Keys? In the Spanish Main?"

He must have noticed the eagerness in my voice, and it seemed to make him happy. "We worked that crew for over a year together."

I waited for more, but he had nothing else to add. "And?"

"That's it," he said with a shrug. "We never found it. Mel Fisher looked—"

"For twenty years for the *Atocha*—I know. My mom and I got my dad one of the silver pieces of eight from that wreck."

"Shipwrecks are amazing that way. The treasure can

be right under your nose for years, and you have no idea if you're hot or cold. That's what makes it so frustrating, and so addictive. You think that if you can just stay in the game long enough, you'll find what you're looking for."

"So you didn't find the *Santa Lucia*, and that was it?"

"That was it. The investors ran out of money, and we all went on our way. Treasure hunting is expensive."

The kernel of a thought began to sprout in my mind, an explanation for what had been bothering me ever since our arrival. "There's nothing wrong with this island, you know. The Good Deeds. They don't need us here."

Alvarez turned and grinned like an idiot. "The locals worked hard to clean it up."

When it hit me, I laughed, and a piece of jicama snagged in my throat. "This is a sham?"

"*Sham* is such a negative word," Alvarez said. "The Pinedale Academy prides itself on providing a wide range of opportunities for its motivated student body. I was just doing my part. Besides, I tend to get sick of being in one place too long."

"You just wanted to see your friend," I said.

The crowd had thinned out by now. The sun was well below the horizon, and the air held a slight chill. Wayo had distributed nearly all of his catch.

"And you're going to have Borders Unlimited on your college application. That's what I call a win-win."

A wheelbarrow had appeared, and Wayo filled it with the skeletal remains of his fish. He lifted the white marlin by the tail, and as he moved it to the wheelbarrow, something fell from its mouth and hit the concrete with a thud. I stepped closer for a better look.

It was a five-pound dive weight.

Wayo sheepishly picked it up and tossed it into the wheelbarrow as he said something in Spanish.

"Combined weight wins, huh?" I said.

Alvarez shrugged as if to say, *What can you do?* Then he clapped and rounded up our little crew. "Let's go eat some fish!"

EIGHT

The hotel room I shared with Katy was simple, with a thin carpet and twin beds on either side of a small bedside table. As with the previous nights, Katy and I had nothing much to say to each other. When we came back from dinner, she disappeared immediately into the bathroom. The springs in my mattress squeaked a protest when I dropped onto the bed.

I sat cross-legged, the pages of de la Torre's journal spread out in front of me, and a Spanish–English dictionary at the ready. There had to be something more in those pages—an account of what happened after the storm, or clues about whether the Jaguar made it onto the island—and if Katy wasn't going to help out anymore, I'd have to handle it myself. The going was incredibly slow, given the combination of the calligraphy, the antiquated Spanish, and my utter inability to say anything other than *"Dónde está el baño?"*

"What do you think, Annie?" Katy said. She stood in

the bathroom doorway wearing a bright red bikini top and an expensive-looking sarong that didn't even come close to her knees. "Too first-world slutty?"

I rested the dictionary in my lap and rubbed my eyes to make sure I was seeing clearly. "What are you talking about? Why are you—"

"You didn't think we were staying in, did you?"

There was a knock at the door. Katy opened it to reveal Nate wearing a white muscle shirt and a gold chain necklace and looking a lot like a third-rate mobster. Behind him, Josh had wrapped his freshly showered hotness in a bright blue vintage T-shirt with something like a phoenix on it.

Nate rubbed his hands together as if to warm them. "You guys ready?"

"You don't want to change?" Josh said.

My voice didn't seem to work. I looked down at my outfit: dirty pink tank top, paint-splattered shorts. "I can't," I said eventually.

"Come on," Josh said. "Just for a bit."

Nate rocked impatiently from side to side. "I didn't come down to Mexico for spring break so I could lock myself in a hotel room."

"There's a brand-new club," Katy said. "It's supposed to be hot."

"You checked out a club?"

"Try to keep up."

"But Alvarez—"

"And Wayo will be telling war stories in that dive shop

71

for the next four hours, and you know it," she said.

Josh pulled a wad of American cash from his pocket. "This'll be fun," he said with a wink. "Trust me."

I opted to give de la Torre a rest and changed into something less comfortable. The thought occurred to me, as I slid into my flip-flops and hustled after the others, that the thing they'd never admit in health class is that peer pressure is almost impossible to resist. And Josh was the ultimate gateway drug: harmless at first, all green eyes and aw-shucks grin, but once you got a taste, you wanted more and more until you found yourself doing things you'd never have believed were possible.

NINE

The smell of sweat and spilled alcohol hit me like a wave the moment we stepped onto the second level of Club Starzz. Black lights ignited white clothes and set teeth aglow. Framed movie posters papered the walls, and cardboard cutouts of famous actors and actresses stood sentry at various points around the room. A seven-foot Jessica Rebstock—brandishing an old rifle and dressed as a straight-shootin' prairie mama from *No Home for Cowards*—hovered eerily next to the packed dance floor.

"I was getting homesick," I said as we lucked upon an empty table, but Josh either didn't hear me or didn't grasp the absurdity of us going to a Hollywood-themed club.

"Margaritas!" Nate said, and we all clinked our glasses together. A techno remix of last year's Top 40 rattled the drink in my hand. I put it down on the table after the tiniest of sips. Sneaking out of the hotel was one thing, but getting drunk would take it to a whole different level.

A level where the *least* horrible thing that could happen would be losing my scholarship.

Nate took his drink with him as he stalked around the dance floor, leaving me and Katy at the table with Josh.

"So, is it weird to see that poster of your mom?" Katy put her elbows on the table and pressed her boobs between her arms as she leaned toward Josh. "Is it like she's . . . watching you?"

I hoped he'd see right through her, but it was obvious that the only thing he saw was exactly what she wanted him to see. Her chest shook when she giggled, and I thought smoke was going to come out of his ears.

"You get used to it," he said.

"Don't you think someone might recognize you?" I said.

"Nah, I'm nobody."

Nate returned with half his drink already empty and motioned to a pair of blondes dressed in outfits that made Katy's look Amish.

"Those chicks are college girls, bro. Down here from Idaho." He snorted a laugh. "Ida-ho."

"Shouldn't we be getting back?" I knew how it sounded, but I couldn't help it.

Josh pulled his phone from his pocket. "It's only ten fifteen," he said.

"I told them we went to UCLA," Nate said, and then, nodding to me, "and that she was your little sister."

"Sis!" Josh said, elbowing me and laughing.

I gritted my teeth into a smile I hoped would mask my shame.

"I can definitely see the resemblance," Katy said.

After not nearly enough urging, Josh got up and followed Nate to the dance floor. Katy stayed at the table for about a millisecond longer. Then she gulped her drink and headed into the throng directly behind Josh, where the two of them proceeded to, as they say, ignore their inhibitions.

Josh had forgotten his cell phone on the table. I figured it had an international plan, and besides, he wouldn't mind if his sister made a phone call, right?

I snatched it up and pushed my way downstairs through the crowd and across the street. I hopped onto the seawall and dialed a number and let my legs dangle over the gentle lapping of the waves. I should have borrowed a mask and fins for a peaceful night snorkel instead of letting myself get dragged along like a little girl.

"Gracia, it's me," I said when she answered.

"Annie?" she said uncertainly. "Whose phone is this? Is that techno in the background?"

"They made me sneak out! We've been here for two days and—"

"Slow down. What do you mean, sneak out? What's Cozumel like? How's Josh?"

"Katy said his last girlfriend was a princess."

"Okay, first of all, that totally didn't take."

A cluster of drunk spring-breakers spilled out of the

Hard Rock Cafe and onto the street. Someone told some-one else to shut up. A beer bottle shattered. Then another. Then they all laughed and disappeared.

"You knew?" I said.

"Duh, and I didn't tell you because I knew you'd get all, 'Boo-hoo, I'm not a princess, I don't stand a chance,' on me."

"I can't do this for a whole week," I said. "Katy just now practically assaulted Josh with her bikini, and—"

"I don't want to hear any more of this 'can't do it,' sol-dier. Make him jealous. Dance with the hottest guy you can find, and be sure to glance at Josh from time to time. Give him a look that says, 'All this could be yours.' "

I rolled my eyes even though she couldn't see. "Good-bye, Gracia."

"You're in Mexico, sweet pea. Now get back in there and hook up with a native."

Josh and Nate were getting busy with the Idahos on the dance floor when I went back inside. I couldn't find Katy, but three fresh drinks had been added to the collec-tion of empties at our table.

A black-haired guy wandered tentatively up next to me and nodded. His sleeveless white T-shirt glowed under the black lights, revealing well-built arms and the broad shoulders of a swimmer. "What's up?"

I smiled and used my margarita like a crutch, taking a tiny sip before pushing it away.

"Something wrong with your beverage?" His jaw was strong, and his eyes were dark brown and sultry. Except for the traces of a unibrow, he was far too good-looking for me to talk to. Maybe he had me confused with someone else.

"Nope," I said. "It's fine."

He opened his mouth, then closed it. He looked confused. Then he shook his head and walked away. I reached for my drink again but thought better of it.

Nate appeared over my shoulder, his hips still bumping with the beat. "Want me to kick that dude's ass for you? I could, you know. I could kick it."

"You're such a gentleman."

"The offer stands," he said, moving back to the dance floor, the margaritas clearly having their intended effect. "If you want me to kick it."

"No offense, but you need to work on your moves," Josh said, startling me as he collapsed into the chair. His cheeks were flushed, and he was sweaty and out of breath. "That guy was totally hitting on you."

"He was not." Besides, it didn't matter. How was I supposed to tell Josh I didn't want *that* guy hitting on me?

"Why are you surprised? I'd totally hit on you," he said, and my own breath disappeared. A few strands of his hair were caked sexily against his forehead. "You know, if we weren't related."

The DJ slowed the bumping and grinding on the dance floor. Unibrow had found a new target in Katy, and he held her waist and went to work as she laughed and threw her hands into the air.

Josh placed his glass in the center of the table and

pointed to mine. "You going to drink that?"

I pushed my drink across to him. Condensation on the glass made it slide faster than I'd expected, and I might have shoved it harder than necessary. He caught it, but not before a hefty splash of margarita cleared the rim.

"Oooh," he said, wiping the liquid from the meat of his hand. "Cut her off!"

It was midnight by the time we finally took a taxi back to the hotel. Katy was drunk enough that she didn't talk to me, which was fine. I collapsed into bed. It might not have been the Presidente InterContinental, but the sheets were clean, and I fell into a deep sleep almost the moment my head touched the pillow.

Less than an hour later, I awoke to a fierce pounding at the door.

TEN

"Annie and Katy!" Alvarez yelled between knocks. "Wake up and get dressed. I need everyone at Tango Divers in five minutes."

He moved on to the boys' room and pounded some more. He knew everything—I was sure of it. He'd probably already called my parents, who were probably already on their way down here.

"Katy," I said, shaking her. "Wake up!"

I heard Nate's groggy voice through the walls. "Go to hell!"

"No thanks," Alvarez said with a laugh. "Be at the dive shop in five minutes—no, make that four."

"What's going on?" Katy said, rubbing her eyes.

"He must have followed us," I whispered. "He must have known exactly what we were doing."

Katy waved me away as if I had BO, which I totally didn't.

"Please shut up. Please." She shuffled to her drawer and threw on a pair of shorts and a T-shirt. I did the same. We met up with Nate and Josh outside our room and trundled silently across the street like a quartet on death row.

Just as we reached the door of the dive shop, I leaned over and whispered, "Josh, what—"

"You need to keep your mouth shut, Annie," Nate said.

Alvarez and Wayo sat with their arms crossed in the plastic chairs next to the corner table, which was now covered with a gray beach towel. The only lighting came from two exposed bulbs in the middle of the ceiling. We stood before them in a police lineup.

Say nothing, say nothing, say nothing, I reminded myself. I pretended to look around the shop, but my eyes were tracking Alvarez the whole time. He pushed himself to his feet and walked toward us with his arms dangling at his sides.

He was doing one of those torture scenes where the interrogator rolls out a tray of rusty instruments, the wheels squeaking on the stained linoleum floor, and lets his silence make the pitiful victim crack.

"We have to get some things out in the open." Now he was pacing in front of us like a drill sergeant.

All I could think about was my mom and dad. The disappointment on their faces. *Where did we go wrong?* they'd say to each other. Tears were welling up in my eyes so that I almost couldn't see Alvarez as he turned back toward the table. A single drop broke free and rolled down my cheek.

"Get a hold of yourself," Katy whispered through clenched teeth.

Alvarez grabbed the towel and yanked it off the table with a flourish. His change in mood was so unexpected that it gave me an excuse to rub the tears from my eyes. I waited for the lecture, but it didn't come. For some reason, we'd been given a stay of execution. I stepped closer.

"I may not have been completely honest with you guys about why I wanted to come down here," Alvarez said.

The table was covered with maps and charts, some of which were new color printouts while others were clearly hundreds of years old. In addition to the documents I recognized as de la Torre's journal, there were others. Photocopies of the Spanish calligraphy with corresponding translations.

"You had the English version already?" I said, picking up a page of the journal to reveal an ancient map of the Yucatán Peninsula. "You could have saved us a lot of time."

I tore my eyes away from the table just long enough to see that everyone was either drunk and tired, or as confused as I was, or a combination of all three.

"This was not part of my plan," Alvarez said. "You were supposed to do your volunteer work, get your credit. Those of you who cheated would have your slates wiped clean. But when you're flying by the seat of your pants, the plan has to change from time to time."

"This isn't for real?" Josh said. He squinted at Alvarez. "We can't put this on our résumés?"

"Borders Unlimited is real. Your résumé will be fine." Alvarez laughed. "But treasure hunting is expensive. Plenty of dead ends, and even dead ends cost money, so I've learned to get creative." He leaned back and gestured to the room as if it proved his point. "Here we are, down in Mexico on Pinedale's nickel!"

I couldn't tell if this made sense or was the most ridiculous thing I'd ever heard—or if it was both. "Good Deeds for us, Gold Doubloons for you?"

Katy said, "You're still a treasure hunter?"

"Part time," Alvarez said modestly. "Only part time. Treasure hunting isn't a real dependable source of income, hence the day job."

"How do you know we won't tell the administration about this?" Nate said.

"My word against yours, of course." Alvarez slapped his hand on his forehead as if remembering something. "Oh, and a statement I've already written to the ethics committee about how uncooperative you were. And the tests you cheated on, which I still have. I'm sure you've heard of the concept of mutually assured destruction."

"I'm still telling," Katy said.

"Teaching jobs are a dime a dozen, no offense, but there's only one Golden Jaguar."

There was silence. Then Nate said, "You're insane."

Alvarez ignored him and focused on me as though I were the only other person in the room. "We had plans. Things fell through. And, Annie, it just so happens that we need you to be our Plan B."

"What happened to Plan A?" I said.

"We had another diver and a crew all lined up, but they had to cancel at the last minute." Alvarez glanced at Wayo before saying, "Don't worry about that right now."

"Why can't you just hire someone else?" I said.

"Is no time," Wayo said.

"Wait, wait." Katy stepped forward and shook her head as if to clear it of the tequila haze. She walked toward the table. "Why does Annie get to be Plan B? We have skills."

"If he needs a cartwheel, he'll give you a call," I said.

Katy shot me an icy look and leaned an inch in my direction. "I could kill you with my bare hands—how's that for a cartwheel?"

"Easy, now." Alvarez smiled, trying to defuse the tension.

"I don't have any skills," Josh said matter-of-factly.

Nate hit him on the shoulder with the back of his hand. "Sure you do. You're famous, almost. You can be a distraction."

"Look," Alvarez said. "I like history and everything, but at the end of the day, isn't there something pathetic about studying it? About teaching it? No offense to your dad, Annie. But we're stuck in classrooms reading about people who were out there actually *making* history. So why not do something worthy of reading about?"

I had to admit that he had me there. I thought of Gracia and Mimi, of the way they rolled their eyes at me whenever the subject of treasure—or even the ocean— happened to come up. The eye rolls said I was different, that I would never quite get it, whatever "it" was.

"So I'm your Plan B," I said. "What does that mean?"

Alvarez nodded at Wayo before leaning in to me, and the corners of his mouth ticked up in mischief.

ELEVEN

"Do you know La Garganta del Diablo?" Wayo said.

"The Devil's Throat? As in the dive site off Punta Sur?" I nodded, feeling the warmth of excitement begin to build deep inside me but not quite ready to embrace it. Basically a narrow coral shaft starting at 100 feet deep and going all the way down to 130, the Devil's Throat is one of the most famous dives in the world, ranking up there with the Blue Hole in Belize and Bloody Bay Wall in the Caymans. It's deep, technical, and dangerous.

Alvarez came around to my side of the table, suddenly more animated than I'd ever seen him. His fingers were shaking like he'd overdosed on caffeine. He shuffled through the photocopied pages until he came up with the right one.

"Here's what de la Torre wrote: 'The *Vida Preciosa*, under full sail ten days due north, approached the land of swallows during a storm. Looking for shelter, she dropped anchor on the leeward side, where—'"

"Where the waters were calm," Katy said. "We know that already."

I glared at her. "But that's as far as we got. Unfortunately."

Alvarez continued, "'Three days later, *VP* set sail for the mainland, her holds lighter of cargo the captain is sure to retrieve under more agreeable conditions.'"

"But they never came back to get it, did they?" I felt giddy. "Whatever it was. De la Torre never left Spain again."

"I know what you're thinking. The Devil's Throat doesn't even start until a hundred feet. There's no way they could have gotten the cargo down that far. To say nothing of gear, fins, masks—"

"Not necessarily," I said. "Leonardo da Vinci had a design for scuba gear in 1500. It was supposed to be something like a leather bag over the diver's head, connected to a cane tube to replenish the air."

Silence. I swear I could hear the waves lapping at the shore two blocks away.

"I'm a dork, I know." More silence. "Anyway, he never did anything with it because he decided to concentrate on the diving bell."

"What's a diving bell?" Josh said, and I felt a little better. If he wanted to know, maybe I wasn't such a dork after all.

Mr. Alvarez jumped in. "Like an upside-down jar

that traps the air so divers can breathe. If you build a big-enough one, you can fit a couple of people inside—"

"Alexander the Great got down to about eighty feet in one," I said. "And that was around 300 BC."

Alvarez instantly morphed back into a high school teacher again. "Even Aristotle wrote about divers going a hundred feet deep to collect sea sponges."

Nate laughed. "Looks like dork is contagious."

"Okay, so it was possible to go down that deep," I said.

"Right." Alvarez went back to the journal. "This comes much later, after a reference to that other entry: 'A narrow shaft leading to a fissure accessible by only the slightest of men reveals a hidden compartment. In this compartment the key was concealed, its location revealed by the Southern Cross.'"

"The constellation?" I said. "Can you even see the Southern Cross from Mexico?"

Alvarez shook his head impatiently. He searched the pile for another paper and pointed to a crude drawing of what looked to be a cross attached to an uneven rock wall. "Here's a sketch, from the same diary."

I could feel my pulse in my temples.

He continued, "The *Vida Preciosa* never traveled remotely close to a latitude where the Southern Cross constellation would have been visible. This cross has got to be in that compartment, off Punta Sur."

"Punta Sur," I said. "Southern Point. You're saying—"

"At that point, Cortés was losing power, facing upheaval in Mexico City, under investigation for not paying his fair share back to the Spanish crown. Not to mention he'd been accused of murdering his wife. He had a lot going on. He needed to fund the expansion of his army, and the Jaguar was worth enough, but there were too many people who knew about it. He had to hide it somewhere for safekeeping."

"So why not come back to familiar territory, right?" I said. "The first place he landed in Mexico."

"But there was too much scrutiny for him to ever retrieve the Jaguar. Mexico was in a state of near anarchy, and Cortés returned to Spain in 1541 to restore his reputation. To his great shock, the king refused to see him, and Cortés died before ever setting foot in Mexico again."

"Many people search in vain for El Jaguar Dorado," Wayo said. "For hundreds of years."

"The Golden Jaguar is at the bottom of the Devil's Throat?" I said.

"Probably not the Jaguar itself, no," Alvarez admitted. "But a clue. Maybe *the* clue."

My head was spinning so fast I could hardly see the documents in front of me. Only moments before, I was about to get busted for drinking on my community service spring break trip. A community service trip that was a farce, engineered so my teacher could go fishing with an old friend. But now it turned out that there was more to the trip after all. Much more. And Alvarez needed me to make it happen. Whatever Plan A had been, I was Plan B.

"Want to go for a dive?" Alvarez patted the table and leaned back.

"Yes, please."

I felt the strangest sense of calm wash over me, a feeling as invigorating as it was unexpected. It didn't matter what had happened up to this point. I was here. With treasure nearby. Not some rumor I'd read in a book, but real treasure. And I was here because of who I was, *really*. Everything in my life had been leading me toward this moment, and Mr. Alvarez had recognized it and had chosen me, and I felt—I hate to say—special.

"You like a small wetsuit or medium?" Wayo said, and it was only then that I noticed the two piles of gear he was assembling by the door.

"What, now? At *night*?"

Alvarez said, "If we do it during the day, we may run into someone else—other divers, like those idiots at the airport who just *have* to hit the Devil's Throat before downing a six-pack of Coronas underneath the beachside *palapa*."

"You can no touch the coral," Wayo explained, holding up a bright yellow wristband. "The Parque Nacional is protected by the government."

"We can't risk being seen and reported," Alvarez said.

"Tonight, though?" I would have preferred a practice dive first, during the day, so I could get a sense of the current, or the feel of the cavern itself, especially if I was going to be using unfamiliar equipment.

"There's no moon, the seas are calm. Conditions will never be better," Alvarez said. And then a little more forcefully, "It has to be tonight."

"How do you know it's still there," I said, "whatever it is?"

"I don't. Not for sure, at least. But the only people who know about it"—Alvarez pointed to the research— "are in this room."

I shook my head. "Unless someone else came to the same conclusion as you did."

"My god," Katy said. "Little Miss Rain Cloud over here. How about some optimism?"

I tried to ignore her. "Isn't that dive spot hard enough to find in the daytime?"

Wayo shook his head. "Right after the fishing tournament today, I attach a . . . how do you say . . . glow stick? A glow stick at the bottom, fifty meters south of the entrance to La Garganta."

I took a deep breath and blew it out slowly. "The Devil's Throat at night," I said, this time to myself. "I don't know."

"Just think what you and your family could do with the money," Alvarez said.

"Don't bring my parents into this." I had to defend our honor, and I think I actually pulled off the indignation pretty well, but the truth was that I'd already begun to think about the money.

"The way your dad talks about you in the teacher's lounge, I would have thought you'd go crazy for this chance." Mr. Alvarez crossed his arms, disappointed. "I guess I was wrong."

"It's not safe," I said, choosing to ignore for the moment the fact that my dad talked about me in the teacher's lounge. "It sounds hurried and poorly planned, and—"

"I'll do it," Katy said.

Alvarez whipped his head around. "What?"

"I'll do it. You need another diver, someone who can fit through the opening—who better than a circus freak?"

"She *can* touch her toes to the back of her neck," Nate said.

Alvarez squinted at her. "You really think you can handle the dive?"

"I'm certified," Katy said. "We did that resort course in the Bahamas. Nate, remember? On the cruise?"

Things were getting out of hand. Never mind that a resort course doesn't actually give an open-water certification, I wouldn't trust a resort course graduate on a routine daylight dive, and this was hardly a routine dive, no matter how you sliced it. Even if she were sober, she'd have to conserve her air while controlling her buoyancy with pinpoint accuracy; otherwise she'd bounce off the walls or get her hoses caught on the coral.

Josh stared at me. Everyone else was looking at Katy, even Alvarez, who seemed to nod slightly as though trying to talk himself into it. But Josh had his eyes—those ridiculous green eyes—on me.

"Katy," I said.

"I can do it," she said. "Besides, Wayo will be right there in case anything goes wrong."

"She can't dive," I pleaded. "She's—"

Katy narrowed her eyes and shook her head almost imperceptibly. The message was clear.

I was trapped. Alcohol puts even an expert diver at a higher risk for nitrogen narcosis, decompression sickness, or just plain doing something stupid. But I couldn't spill the beans about the margarita adventure, or Katy would kill me with her bare hands.

Alvarez stood and paced in front of her, scratching the nape of his neck and frowning. "You're small enough to fit."

"I'm going," I said.

Katy started to protest. "But—"

"Just stop. You got certified on a cruise ship."

"You don't have to do it, Annie." The concern in Josh's eyes was genuine, and surprising, and I wanted to kiss him for it, even though those same eyes were part of the reason I found myself in that position.

"Katy's going to kill herself if I don't."

"You're sure?"

Katy took a step forward and threw a hand on her hip. "I'm not a *complete* jackass, you know."

I ignored her. "I'm sure, Josh."

I was surprisingly sure, actually, in the midst of it all. And once I'd said it out loud, I realized that my sudden conviction had nothing to do with saving Katy from certain doom. One thought overpowered all others. It was crazy—I *knew* it was crazy—but it still made sense: this was exactly what I'd been put on this earth to do.

TWELVE

The small boat skipped across the glassy midnight sea. I felt triumphant and light-headed at the same time, as though I'd just shoplifted a balloon and sucked the helium out. There was no way this was actually happening to *me*! I looked up at the bright ivory sash of the Milky Way and couldn't help but think of the poster in Mr. Alvarez's room.

"What's funny?" Alvarez said.

"Shoot for the stars."

"You're going to do great. Wayo's the best diver on the island."

The boat was a fourteen-foot fiberglass runabout with bench seats lining the sides and a canopy frame without the canopy. A single outboard motor whined against the water. "It's a cute boat," Wayo had said when we sneaked out onto the dock in San Miguel.

I sat on the bench next to Alvarez and Nate, while Josh and Katy sat across from us. There was just enough starlight to see the tension on everybody's face; it looked like the impending adventure had sobered them right up.

I was wearing a shorty wetsuit, only 2mm because even at night the water was in the low eighties. I was used to the fifties water of the Pacific, so I probably didn't need a wetsuit at all. But since I hadn't packed a swimsuit of my own, I had to wear one of Wayo's store samples, which fit me even more ridiculously than my sensible one-piece.

Josh nodded to Alvarez. "You arranged this whole trip just for this?"

"You heard Annie's presentation. There's over a hundred million dollars at stake here. I'm a known treasure hunter; I couldn't just come down here by myself. People might have noticed, might have become suspicious. But a teacher? On a humanitarian mission? It's the ultimate misdirection."

Katy said, "Josh is a movie star's kid."

"Maybe," Alvarez said. "But let's call that hiding in plain sight."

"Why did you really assign me the Golden Jaguar?" I said. "It's not like you didn't already know everything."

"As I said before, if you're going to treasure hunt on the cheap, you have to use all the tricks in your toolbox. I was hoping you might come up with something I'd missed."

"You said people might have noticed?" Nate said. "What people?"

Alvarez shrugged. "I've been looking for the Golden Jaguar, on and off, for a while now. You meet people. Sometimes they want the same thing you do."

The only way I could deal with the flicker of dread about to engulf my courage was to stick to my predive routine. Wayo didn't seem to have any antifogging drops on board, so I spit into my mask and spread the saliva around so the lens wouldn't fog up.

Alvarez craned his neck over the side of the boat to scan the now-charcoal water but said nothing. The motor's whir became lower, and we slowed. Waves lapped at the boat as the engine puffed at a near idle. Wayo also leaned over the edge, steering the wheel with one hand. The upper body of his wetsuit dangled from his waist like a half-peeled banana.

Nate tried again. "So are you going to tell us what people, or are you going to let that hang out there, all ominous?"

"Ominous is way more interesting, don't you think?" Alvarez chuckled and slapped his palm against the old neoprene of my wetsuit. Then he winked at me. *Winked* at me!

"You're having too much fun with this," I said.

"Thrill of the hunt, Annie!"

"We are close," Wayo called out.

I pulled the mask over my head, now confident that the lens wouldn't fog. I situated a waterproof headlamp just above the mask and turned it on.

"Careful of the light," Wayo said without looking at me, so I cupped my hand over the front and opened my fingers just a sliver.

I imagined Gracia on the boat, smoothing down the shoulders of my wetsuit and looking at me the way my mom checked my outfits on Friday nights. "Darlin'," I pictured her saying, the twang at full blast, "you go down there and you find yourself some treasure. 'Cause it's the only way you can justify wearing that baggy-ass wetsuit."

I turned the knob at the top of my tank, and my air hoses tensed like a bodybuilder flexing his muscles. "So much at stake," I said. I took a pull off the regulator and breathed out. "And now it's in the hands of a fifteen-year-old girl."

Alvarez nodded. "There's a reason Plan B isn't called Plan A."

"Is time." Wayo cut the engine.

We were in position. I breathed again from the regulator and sprayed a burst of air from the octopus to check the pressure. I pushed a button on my BC, and a hiss confirmed that the vest was inflating.

Wayo motioned for Alvarez to take over at the steering wheel, and then he came over and slid his BC onto a tank and tightened the strap.

"What's the profile?" I said.

"Straight down to one hundred, then a little swim to the coral. La Garganta will take us at a diagonal down to the exit at a hundred and thirty feet—"

"The fissure will be at around a hundred twenty," Alvarez said over his shoulder.

Wayo continued, "We go down, maybe ten minutes bottom time, then start to surface again, with five-minute safety stops at forty and fifteen feet, and then back to the boat."

I checked my gauge. Greater compression at greater depth meant that I'd use more air the deeper I went, but the 3,000 psi of air in my tank was more than enough for me to complete the dive and the safety stops required to avoid the bends.

"Is that a light?" Josh said. "Over there?"

Alvarez turned toward where Josh was pointing. A small light bobbed gently, coming not from the route we took but from the opposite direction, as though it had rounded toward Punta Sur from the other side of the island.

"Did you tell anyone else?" Wayo said, the first traces of worry creeping into his voice.

Alvarez shook his head. "It's probably nobody."

"We go down now. Just in case."

"What does that mean, 'just in case'?" Josh said.

Nobody answered as a nervous energy engulfed the boat. Alvarez stood at the helm, one hand on the wheel. Wayo bounced around, grabbing pieces of his equipment from one side of the boat and the other. Weight belt here, fins there. A mask from a bucket near the motor. Even though we were suddenly in a hurry, the man moved as deliberately as if he were on a Sunday stroll.

I wrapped a six-pound weight belt around my waist and reached for my BC, but Josh sprang from his seat and beat me to it. "I know, I know. Nobody touches your gear but you."

"I'll make an exception."

He put one hand under the tank and the other on the

valve and hefted, and I stuck my arms underneath the shoulder straps.

"See, I learned something before you tried to kill me."

"Come on, guys, let's go," Alvarez said. "Whoever it is, they're getting closer."

I scooted onto the edge of the boat, with the tank hanging out over the water, and Josh helped me put on my fins. I did one last quick check of my equipment—the mask was secure, the headlamp on, my secondary light hung from a D-ring on one shoulder strap, and an emergency whistle dangled from the other. My dive knife was strapped around my left calf. I said, "Ready," stuck my regulator in my mouth, and took a deep breath of compressed air.

Alvarez left the wheel and put his hand on my shoulder. "Don't think I don't know how dangerous this is," he said quietly. "So be careful."

Wayo grabbed his mask and headlamp and strapped on his fins. Then he tossed his tank and BC into the water behind the boat.

"I guess he's ready," Katy said.

Josh leaned in, and I could see the anxiety on his face. "You can do this."

Alvarez was back at the helm. He turned and nodded to me. "We'll see you in about a half hour."

With the heel of my right hand against the regulator and my fingers over my mask, I leaned back and let gravity take over.

First there was a resistance from the water, a splash out and away, and then the ocean came back around to hug me. I was always struck by how awkward it felt to be geared up on land, but in the water everything worked perfectly. There was a grace to the equipment under the surface.

I bobbed up and got myself vertical and touched the top of my head—the universal signal for *diver okay in the water*. Josh, Nate, and Katy were all staring at me, but Alvarez had his attention fixed on the other boat. The light was getting closer. I exhaled, slowly purging the air from my lungs, and began to sink into the darkness.

THIRTEEN

The water was warmer even than I'd been expecting, and for that I was grateful. I kept an eye on my backlit equipment gauge—black numbers over a deep green light—and I equalized the pressure in my ears every few feet. The salty taste of the ocean seeped in through the corner of my mouth.

The descent was when I liked to get my head right, to remind myself that I'd trained more than anybody I knew, and that as long as I kept calm, I could handle almost any situation. My body was like a vampire in a coffin: legs together, fingers laced in front of me with the gauge in my hands. Our depth increased, foot by foot. Wayo shined his headlamp on his hand, giving me the okay sign. I nodded and did the same.

The beam of my lamp was useless in the open water, smothered by the ocean's black. Except for the dim radiance of the glow stick he'd stashed earlier, we were swallowed in absolute darkness. I could feel the current taking us gently north, I guessed at about three knots.

The ocean floor finally rose to meet me: mostly sandy, with the occasional mound of coral appearing from the dark like a shadow. Wayo pointed and gave a signal for me to follow. Tiny puffs of phosphorescence—bioluminescent plankton—sprayed out from behind his fins as he kicked, each one a little swirling galaxy of lime green.

Only inches from the bottom, we kicked gently with the current, past the glow stick, until the coral became more plentiful and created a kind of ravine, first a few feet high and then growing to a canyon that towered above us.

There was no reason to freak out; this was just diving. Yes, it was at night, but I could handle it. I angled my head forward, and my headlamp caught a massive clawless Caribbean lobster scurrying backward into the safety of a reef cavern.

Wayo veered to the left and stopped, and suddenly there it was: the entrance to the Devil's Throat. The opening couldn't have been more than six feet across. Fan coral lined the sides and roof, waving innocently in the current. He turned to me, and I gave him one last okay.

And then we were inside.

Sediment had built up along the bottom, and if we stirred it with our fins, clouds of silt would put our visibility at zero, our flashlights reflecting off the blizzard of tiny white flakes. The slope was gentle for three or four kick cycles before Wayo disappeared over a lip. I slowed and poked my head over the edge; the shaft went straight down for at least ten feet.

This was it.

My depth gauge read 115 feet. Air 2,400 psi. We had seven minutes more bottom time before we had to turn for the surface. I angled my body and kicked straight down with only my ankles, careful not to catch my hoses on any of the sponge coral that groped at me from the walls. Wayo's expended air bubbles played across my face as I swam through them.

He hovered at a spot where the shaft became wider, and pointed his lamp at a small fissure in the coral. I thought he was joking; the crack couldn't have been more than ten inches at the widest.

He covered his headlamp with his hand so I could see his face. The plastic of his mask magnified the urgency in his eyes. He pointed again, and I nodded. I took a slow breath, and the Golden Jaguar roared at the insides of my eyelids.

Nothing like the possibility of long-lost treasure to get the blood flowing.

There was no way I was getting through the crack with my BC on, though, so I kept the regulator in my mouth and unclasped the BC's belt, pulling the vest and tank slowly around in front of me. I gathered all the hoses against the canvas of the shoulder straps and pushed the vest, tank-first, through the opening with one hand. I winced as the aluminum scratched against the coral, but the reef would have to forgive me. Then I kicked and squeezed myself through sideways.

My leg instantly flared in pain. I panicked, wondering

if Cortés might have booby-trapped the room, and I cursed myself for not wondering that *before* I'd wedged myself inside. But there was no Spanish arrow piercing my heart, no spikes shooting from the coral, no falling boulder. I was going to be okay. My shorty wetsuit had left my calves exposed, and I'd rubbed against a patch of fire coral. I bit down on the regulator's rubber mouthpiece until the first wave of pain passed, and with one last effort, I was inside.

I quickly put my arms back through the straps of the BC and took stock of the small cave. It was no bigger than my dad's Ford Taurus. In contrast to the main shaft, where decades of careless divers had bounced into the walls, the coral here was pristine—untouched for nearly five hundred years. I was apparently the only one stupid enough to take my gear off at 120 feet in the middle of an elevator shaft.

A jolt of excitement shot straight to my stomach. I floated, weightless, my buoyancy neutral, as I passed my headlamp over every inch of the coral walls. A small octopus flashed in front of me, stopping for a moment in my beam, its chameleon body changing colors to match a deep-blue sea sponge, and then he was gone. This was no leisure dive, I reminded myself. Time to get to work.

In this compartment the key was concealed, the journal said, *its location revealed by the Southern Cross.*

I saw brain coral, sponges, fans, wire coral, but nothing that could be interpreted as a cross. I looked up. My air bubbles pooled at the top and formed an odd mirrorlike shape, constantly changing as the air searched for a way out. But there was still no cross. What if somebody had beaten us to it? What if there'd never been a cross at all? What if Wayo had left me? What if I couldn't squeeze back into the main passage and ran out of air down here and died? My breathing came faster and faster. This was nitrogen narcosis working on me, I forced myself to remember, otherwise known as "rapture of the deep." Most people get euphoric when they narc, but the main symptom for me was paranoia.

I had to slow down, relax. It was okay, I knew. Even if there was no treasure, at least I wasn't going to die. I'd made it through the first time; there was no reason I couldn't fit through on the way out. I checked my air (2,100 psi), my depth (123 feet). I smiled against the regulator when I saw the claw of a massive crab reach out like Popeye's forearm from—

There it was.

FOURTEEN

'd drifted backward in my forced relaxation, and now my headlamp played across a wider section of the wall in front of me, and there was clearly—so clearly I wondered how I hadn't seen it right away—the shape of an enormous wooden cross emerging from the coral as if it had been embossed. The crab's goofy-looking claw reached out from a small hole in the center, where the two arms of the cross came together.

I squealed, and bubbles escaped out the side of my mouth and bounced up past my ears.

I unsheathed my dive knife and tapped the tip of the six-inch blade against the claw, and the crab disappeared even farther into the hole. A short breath out, and I sank so that my head was level with the hole. Coral had grown in what might once have been a compartment, and I could only pray that I'd be able to get at whatever was hidden inside.

I brought the dive knife against the cross. Hundreds

of years' worth of coral growth had formed a shell, but it was softer underneath once I chipped through, and when I pried down on the knife's handle, a large splinter of wood snapped off and floated out to the side.

The claw shot out at me. I flinched, nearly dropping the knife, and a cloud of bubbles blinded me. This was ridiculous, and I didn't have time for it, so I ignored for a moment the fact that I love all ocean creatures, and stabbed the claw with the knife. I didn't hear the crunch, but I felt it, and the crab freaked out as I pulled back, its legs flailing a protest, its other claw snapping at the blade. It came free of the hole—the body was at least the size of a dinner plate—and I jiggled my arm until it slid off my knife and fell away.

"Sorry!" I yelled through the regulator.

With the guardian crab out of the way, I set to work probing the opening. I stabbed every inch or so, the knife making a muffled thud as it struck the cross. *Thud, thud, thud,* and then I felt the vibrations in my hand, a jolt of pain as the knife hit something hard. *Breathe*, I reminded myself. *Just breathe.* But I couldn't help it: I hacked at the area like the killer in a horror movie.

A rectangular shape became visible as I chipped away at the edges—begging Mother Nature for forgiveness as shards of coral snapped off, dull and gray underneath my headlamp—until finally, unbelievably and unmistakably, I was looking at a box the size of a ham sandwich. I wedged the knife underneath and lifted up, and the box broke free of its centuries-old resting place. It was heavy and rusted and covered with chunks of coral, and it was mine! Only 1,300 psi left in my tank. I'd been down too long, but I had to know what was inside.

The ancient padlock was no match for the knife's tempered steel. It snapped off and tumbled into the darkness. I jiggled the knife under the lid and pried, bracing myself for the possibility that there could be nothing inside. The hinges protested, and the cover opened so slowly that I imagined a creaking noise. I cradled the box with my left forearm and pointed the headlamp inside.

A single disk about the size of my palm was situated underneath a thin film of dust. I nudged it with the tip of my knife, and the disk flipped over and settled back down in slow motion, little tufts of sediment shooting out into the water like puffs of smoke. A flash caught the headlamp and danced against the lens of my mask.

Gold. The disk was gold.

With my knife resheathed, I picked it up and held it closer to the light. Even underwater I could tell how heavy it was. Some sort of design was etched into the gold—a rock formation, it looked like. The other side had another etching but a different design. Heads and tails, but what did they mean?

I ran my thumb over the ridges and I couldn't help but think of every other Pinedale student on spring break. They were sunbathing in Tahiti or skiing in Aspen, sure. They had everything in the world—the money, the famous parents, the designer whatever. But I was the one in this tiny little cavern over a hundred feet below the surface. I was the one holding the disk. Anyone who'd ever made fun of me could just go ahead and eat it.

A high-pitched clanging sound brought me back— Wayo's dive knife against his tank, no doubt. A signal for me to get my crazy little *gringa* ass in gear. I went to put the disk back inside the box, but somehow the lid had fallen closed and become stuck. Because I had neither the hands nor the time to pry it back open with my knife, I slid the disk into the side pocket of my BC and zipped it closed.

One last glance at the cross, which had served its purpose better than de la Torre could possibly have imagined, and I repeated the maneuver I'd used when squeezing in. BC off, hoses in one hand, tank pushed through, and me behind it. I held the box tight with my other hand, so it was a little more difficult this time, but I managed.

Wayo pointed to his wrist, and I nodded. I handed him the empty box and put my equipment back on. It was time to get shallow.

The mandatory safety stops were going to be the longest of my life. All I wanted was to kick triumphantly to the surface, but that would have been disastrous. If we didn't take our safety stops, all the nitrogen that had built up in our blood at this depth would expand like carbonation in an open soda can, and we'd be left with the joys of severe joint pain, paralysis, or even death.

We exited the Devil's Throat, passing across the edge of a wall that dropped into sheer emptiness. I noticed a flash—something—up near the surface. Lights, more than one. There were other divers in the water! I turned to motion to Wayo, but he was no longer next to me, and then my next breath came with difficulty, as though I'd sucked the tank dry. That was impossible. I looked down at the gauge for clarification—

Suddenly something scratched down against my mask. A claw? A shark tail? Water flooded into my eyes. The mask knocked against my regulator. I still had no air. I whirled around to protect myself from whatever had attacked me, to ward off another blow, but none came. What was going on? I opened my eyes to the stinging blackness, in time to see my headlamp tumbling down into the dark void. Wayo's light disappeared up, in the opposite direction. Where was he going? Had he been hit, too?

I managed to put the mask back over my eyes, but it was still flooded, and my lungs were about to burst and my arms started tingling and I didn't have the air to clear the mask. I reached for the manual inflation tube on my BC and took a breath. There wasn't much in there. I tilted my head back and blew out through my nose, and the air pushed the water from my mask, so at least I could see again.

I looked around for Wayo's light, but I only saw the two lights from the divers above. No, there were three. There were *three*?

They were *together*?

Wayo was with them. That's why my hoses were limp.

My dive buddy had turned off my air. *My dive buddy turned off my air!* Worst dive buddy ever!

Oh, hell no. There was no way I was going to die down here, not after seeing what I'd just seen, and not while holding a possible clue to the location of the Golden Jaguar. No way.

I took what little breath was left from the BC, but I could feel myself sinking now that I'd breathed the air that was supposed to keep me buoyant. I unclipped my weight belt and let it fall. It was only a matter of time before I would black out.

I removed the BC vest and pulled the straps around, and my hands felt their way up the tank to the valve, and when I turned it, my hoses flexed up again. I breathed deeply, once, then twice, then a third time, sucking air like a noob diver. I clutched the BC in front of me with both hands. *Relax!* I screamed at myself. Now that I actually had something to be paranoid about, the nitrogen narcosis was working overtime.

My BC strapped back on, I checked my depth: 153 feet. Worse news: only 600 psi of air left in the tank. I cupped my hand over the backlit gauges to shield the light from Wayo and the other two divers, and kicked up gently, keeping an eye on my depth to make sure I didn't rise too quickly. I was caught in no-man's-land—there was no room for error. I needed to decompress or I'd get the bends, but I also had to reach the surface before I ran out of air.

The water was so dark that the mask was almost useless. But for the occasional glance at the three divers above me, I saw nothing. My spare flashlight dangled from its D-ring, but I knew there was no way I could use it, not without attracting their attention. Besides, if there was anything else in the water with me at that point, I didn't want to see it.

The depth gauge held my focus for a while, and when I looked up again, the three lights were getting larger and brighter, no more than twenty feet above me. Of course! We were all riding the same current north, and they were at their safety stop, and I was about to rise right in among them!

I pointed my head into the current and kicked, burning precious energy and oxygen in a desperate effort to increase the space between us. I gave up after thirty seconds, praying that it would be enough.

With just over 200 psi left, I leveled out at fifteen feet. Sure enough, Wayo and his two buddies were at the same depth, probably laughing and telling one another stories in sign language about how awesome it was going to be to find the treasure now that they'd killed the *gringa*. I was only about twenty-five yards from them, motionless and alone in the dark. I wanted to turn on my secondary light and give them the universal signal of "You didn't kill me a hundred feet underwater after all, you losers! Hope that empty box works out for you!" but I decided against it.

They ascended, and I waited.

I heard the muffled whine of a boat through the water, and then it stopped. The three lights left the water one by one. The sound again, this time growing more and more distant. They were gone.

Every minute I could hold out at that depth let the nitrogen escape from my blood and decreased my chances of getting bent, so I ignored the air pressure gauge and concentrated on staying level. Breathing slowly had the double benefit of conserving air and getting my heart rate under control—it was forced meditation.

The air took on a slightly oily taste, and I knew it was time; the tank was almost empty. One last deep breath, and I kicked up, slowly, exhaling a constant but very light stream through my mouth. I could hold my breath like this for over three minutes on a good day, but today was not one of those.

It was so dark that I didn't see the surface until I broke through. I spit out the regulator's mouthpiece and breathed the humid midnight air, and it was only then that I started to cry. I manually inflated the BC between sobs so I could float, and then laid back and let the tears pool at the bottom of my mask. The stars blurred as I reached for the emergency whistle and puffed, gently at first, and then more and more ferociously until I had to stop and breathe again.

I unclipped my secondary flashlight from the D-ring and turned it on and waved it in circles as I screamed. There was nobody out there. I was alone. My death would be nothing more than a footnote on a gossip-blog post about Josh's spring break, if it made the news at all. I slapped the water with both hands and screamed for help, the terror of what had happened to me finally beginning to sink in. What if Alvarez and the others had been killed by whoever was on the other dive boat?

The waves rocked me, gentle and almost soothing, and I started to think that maybe I should just rest for a while.

I caught the vague outline of the island, impossibly far away, and I knew I didn't want surrender to be the last decision I made. My chest surged with adrenaline, and I kicked and kicked toward the shore, but the current was too strong, and soon I had nothing left. I was exhausted.

"Annie!"

I opened my eyes and listened, but there was nothing more. Then a calm breeze played across the waves. Did I really hear it? Was my mind playing tricks on me?

"Annie!" It was Josh's voice—I was sure of it.

I screamed, "Help!" I flailed and splashed and waved my flashlight.

"There, over there!" And then the roar of an outboard motor.

The outline of a small boat approached from the blackness, small lights swinging my way, and tears came once more and I threw my head back and laughed through them. Amazing that the fire coral would start hurting again, now that I was going to be safe. It was as though my body could only take so much, and the pain was waiting to take over as soon as I could handle it.

Eventually, I had to assume, Wayo and whoever he was

working with would open the box. They'd find out I'd survived, and when they did, they would have to decide whether to come after me. I couldn't think about that now, though; all that mattered was that I was still alive.

This wasn't theoretical anymore, wasn't a pipe dream. None of it was—not the treasure, and not the danger. My hand crept down to the pocket of my BC, the trembling fingertips pressing through the canvas. The disk was mine.

FIFTEEN

I told nobody. Not Josh, not the Sugars, and definitely not Mr. Alvarez. The moment they pulled me into the boat would have been the perfect time to shout, "Wayo cut off my air and took Cortés's box!" but I couldn't say anything.

Instead, I cried. I didn't care who saw me, if Katy thought I was a wimp, or if Mr. Alvarez was disappointed in me. I cried as the boat skipped along the water back to town, and by the time my feet hit land, I'd gotten myself as under control as I could.

And when we returned to Tango Divers only to find the door padlocked from the outside, I realized that I couldn't tell the truth. I had no idea *how* to tell the truth, because there was so much I didn't know.

Why, for example, didn't Wayo cut my hoses with a knife? Why did he only turn off my air? The only explanation was that he didn't want to call too much attention in case my body was ever found. I wasn't sure if that meant Alvarez had put him up to it or if Wayo had betrayed him as well.

I didn't know Josh at all, no matter how much I wanted to pretend otherwise, and the Sugars were the Sugars. I couldn't trust anybody. So, when Mr. Alvarez asked what had happened, I lied.

I said that Wayo and I had lost contact midway through the Devil's Throat. Maybe I took a wrong turn, maybe there was too much silt, but whatever the reason, I found myself alone at 130 feet in the middle of the night. I told them I'd wanted to look for him, but it was dark and I was worried about expending too much air. I told them nitrogen narcosis had gotten to me and I'd freaked out.

"It's not your fault. Wayo must have ditched you on purpose," Alvarez said, shaking his head, oblivious to how certain I was that Wayo had indeed ditched me on purpose. "But why? And why would he lock the door and disappear? It doesn't make any sense."

I was too scared to leave the hotel room for the rest of the trip. A headache was my excuse, from going so deep and almost running out of air.

I'd always had little nightmares about losing air at depth—somewhere in the back of every diver's mind is the *what if* scenario—but having it actually happen to me was worse than I'd ever imagined. It's not like you get shot and then you only have a few seconds before your life flashes before your eyes and then you die. Being out of air is like getting a letter in the mail that you're going

116

to die soon. You have time to contemplate how drowning is going to feel.

I had contemplated it. And I had felt it, and despite the fact that I'd ended up surviving, that sensation still haunted me. Like trying to breathe through a swizzle straw.

Every time someone knocked on the door, I thought Wayo was coming back to finish the job. But the hours passed, and Wayo's friend the hotel owner swore he had no idea where Wayo had gone or how to contact him. One of the guys in another dive shop said they saw him getting on the ferry to the mainland.

Alvarez withdrew, muttering to himself with a blank expression that hadn't left his face since he saw the padlock on Tango Divers. He seemed to have no interest in chaperoning, so he finished painting the school himself while the others basically had the run of the island. With every meal he brought me, every visit to check up on me, came another attempt to make sense of Wayo's actions.

I was tempted to tell him the whole story, if for no other reason than to make him stop asking me about it, but I figured it was in my best interests, as a person who wanted to stay alive, to keep my mouth shut. So, whenever Alvarez tried to talk to me about the dive, I kept consistent.

We got separated. I don't know how. I don't know where he went. I freaked out.

"He must have found something and gone off on his own," Alvarez said. "But why?"

I finally asked him the question he'd refused to answer that night. "What was Plan A?"

"We had the dive all set up. Wayo and another diver were supposed to go down, but the night of the dive, after the fishing tournament, the other diver canceled."

"Or maybe he didn't," I said.

"I should never have asked you to do that," he said. The pleas for forgiveness had grown stronger with each day. "I knew it at the time, but I didn't listen to myself. I was so close, I couldn't imagine giving up. But that's no excuse."

At first, the concern he showed me was reassuring. But as the days passed, and as he kept asking me the same questions, I wondered even more if he had something to do with it. What if he and Wayo were still working together? What if Alvarez knew the box was empty? Was that why he kept coming back to "make sense" of what had happened? Did he want to see what I knew? If the box was really empty when I found it?

"I thought you were supposed to be some superdiver," Katy said at one point as she dropped off a lunch of chicken tamales.

How easy it would have been to wave the disk in her face. *I am a superdiver! Here's the proof!*

I wanted to tell Josh, but I didn't know how to bring it up. And I was surprised that my main emotion—overriding even the pride about what I'd done, the relief at having survived, and my fear of what was going to happen next—was shame. I was ashamed to have been used like that, whether it was by Wayo alone or by Alvarez, too.

There was no logical explanation for it, but there it was. So I didn't tell Josh, and I didn't call Gracia; I kept it all to myself.

SIXTEEN

The United States customs declaration form sets a limit of ten thousand dollars on what can be brought back across the border. I was pretty sure that the disk currently pressed between two cheap copper ashtrays and wrapped in a plastic Tienda del Sol souvenir bag—my dastardly plan for getting it past the X-rays in Cozumel—was worth significantly more than that. So I'd checked the box next to "Nothing to declare," which was a lie because of more than just what was in my pack. I had plenty of things to declare, starting with *Someone tried to kill me!*

I clutched the handle of my rolling duffel with one hand and the strap of my backpack with the other. My bag's wheels squeaked when I took a step forward. Third in line. I tried to smile, but my heart was in my throat, and somehow that got in the way. The corner of my eye started to twitch, so I looked down and shrugged into my backpack's shoulder strap.

My palms felt as though I'd soaped them up but forgotten to rinse. I wiped them on the nicest pair of shorts I owned. Black ones, short but not sluttily so. No baggy travel outfit for me. I wore a red tank top, and my hair was pulled back with a diamond-studded banana clip I'd begged Katy to let me use. It was my version of dressing up. I wanted to look put together for the trip home. As unsuspicious as possible.

"Don't worry," Josh said, leaning in from behind me. "Your parents won't ever find out what happened."

I swallowed. "Why would you think—"

"I'm just saying. Besides, it's not your fault."

Katy looked at me from the next line the way a mother might glare at a misbehaving child. She'd made no secret of the fact that she disagreed with Josh's take. To her, it was definitely my fault. My fault we hadn't found the treasure. I closed my eyes, struggling to get my heart under control.

Second in line. A forced smile.

Mr. Alvarez shuffled forward as well, two people behind Katy, by now a shell of his former gregarious faculty hotness. The night before, he'd made us promise to keep everything that had happened—and the real reason for the trip—a secret. There was still the matter of the cheating, after all. Nate called it blackmail, but Alvarez stuck with "mutually assured destruction."

"I'm a big girl, Josh," I said.

And then I was standing in front of the customs officer, extending the declaration form with a clammy hand, the weight of the golden disk in my backpack almost pulling me backward.

"Nothing to declare?" the guy said.

I stole a priceless gold relic! The Mexican government would arrest me if they knew! I think I see a portly diver named Wayo everywhere I look!

"Nope," I said, and then because I didn't trust myself, "Just a school trip."

I thought he was going to wave me along, but right when he lifted up his arm, he stopped. He furrowed his bushy eyebrows. He saw right through me—I knew it. Next stop, interrogation room. Tears. Accusations of smuggling. Loss of treasure. I clutched the strap of my backpack.

"You don't have any alcohol in your suitcase, do you?" he said.

"Huh? W-what?" I stammered. "Alcohol?"

"You're telling me that if I checked that piece of luggage there," he said, pointing to my duffel, "I wouldn't find, say, a bottle of tequila? With a worm?"

I couldn't help looking at Katy, now second from the customs people in her line, who had packed her own liquid souvenir. She stared straight ahead as though we'd never met.

I rolled the duffel in front of me, grateful for the stereotype of the spring-breaking high schooler. "Go ahead and take a look."

He squinted some more, then reached over my shoulder for Josh's declaration form and nodded me along. I stepped through the sliding glass doors, and relief eased into my pores like a lotion. I'd made it. The Los Angeles air was refreshingly dry and empty, with the slight taste of exhaust; I breathed it in deep.

"Hey," Josh said when we'd both reached the other side. "I'm really sorry about what happened—"

"It's okay."

"We could talk about it if you wanted."

The drawback to lying about my misadventure with Wayo was that now Josh saw me as someone who needed his help. Someone who couldn't take care of herself. I was a little girl who'd lost control, and he was the big brother there to protect me.

"No matter what," he said, "I think it was brave of you to—"

"I get it!" I said. Having Josh see me that way made me start to see myself that way. I noticed my dad waiting on a bench underneath the American Airlines sign. "I have to go."

Josh seemed hurt. "At least remember the story, right? We did valuable community service that totally had a positive impact on our worldview."

I nodded once but Josh followed me. My dad reached for my duffel, but then Mr. Alvarez appeared from behind me, inserting himself between us and extending his hand like a politician scrounging for votes.

"She did great, Bill," Alvarez said. "A real leader. You'd have been proud of her." It was eerie, as though he were channeling the predive version of himself. Positive, extroverted, eager to experience what the world had to offer. Josh and I stared at him. Then he leaned in to me, and the concern came crashing back to his face. "Get some rest, okay?"

The ease with which he'd just changed attitudes made me wonder yet again if he was in on Wayo's plan. He was definitely *acting* like someone who'd been betrayed, but if he could so easily flip the switch with my dad, who's to say the whole abandoned-puppy-dejected thing wasn't an act as well?

A woman in her mid-twenties jogged up and tapped Josh on the shoulder. "You ready?" she said, twirling her keys impatiently.

Bluetooth earpiece firmly implanted, blond hair held back with designer chopsticks, she wore tight blue yoga pants and an even tighter white top that showcased both her tan and her sculpted back muscles. Great. On top of everything else, now I had to deal with an unanticipated pang of jealousy.

Josh must have caught me staring at her, because he stepped back and made the introduction. "Violet, Annie. Annie, Violet. My mom's assistant."

"Hi," Violet said quickly and with that flat, eyeless, Los Angeles smile. She nodded to Josh and twirled her keys again. "Come on. I'm in a no-parking zone."

I said nothing as I followed my dad into the garage, but once I was finally buckled safely in the front seat, I stuck to Alvarez's script. The trip was a success. We helped people in need, but that paled in comparison to what we got out of it. The Borders Unlimited representative was impressed with the work that we'd done.

"And the Gold Doubloons?" Dad said.

"You probably know more than Alvarez does about 'Mysteries of the Deep,'" I said, cradling my backpack against my chest like a mama bear protecting her cub. "You could be a guest lecturer."

"I'm sure he'd love that."

I could almost feel the disk inside; it might as well have been pulsating. It was taunting me. *Show me to your dad,* it whispered. *You know he'd love it.*

I was stuck. On the one hand, if I told him about the disk, he'd be beyond thrilled to hold it, to trace his fingers across the formations on either side. I could almost see the wonder in his eyes; I could almost hear our conversations— animated speculation about what the designs might mean and why Cortés might have left it where he did.

On the other hand, although he had once been an armchair treasure hunter, now he was a teacher. And he was still my dad on top of that. I couldn't tell him because I knew exactly what would happen if I did. And I wasn't ready for that. The disk was mine. I was the one who'd braved the Devil's Throat in the darkness. I was the one who'd squeezed into that tiny cavern. I'd earned it.

I caught a glimpse of something in the side-view mirror, and my stomach fell off a cliff. The driver of the car behind us—there was something too familiar. The dark skin. The tuft of thinning hair on top of his head. The car moved into the next lane and accelerated, and I yelped.

My dad flinched, and the wheel jerked to the side before he got it back under control. "What's wrong?"

"Nothing," I said. And there was nothing. The other car pulled up next to us, and I realized that the driver was too thin, and Asian, and he wore glasses.

He looked nothing like Wayo.

SEVENTEEN

"Pair up, everybody," Alvarez said to the class on Monday. "You'll be doing presentations on a topic of your choice. Due the final week of school. Rubric coming soon. Start thinking about what you want to cover. You've got five minutes before the bell rings."

I faced the front of the room while the juniors scrambled for partners all around me. Alvarez dropped into his chair and opened his laptop. He seemed about twenty years older. The light was gone from his eyes, the bounce missing from his step. What struck me the most was his hair: shaggy and unkempt like my dad's. It was as though he hadn't bathed or looked at himself in the mirror in days.

"He's taking it pretty hard," Josh said. He was standing next to my desk pretending not to look at Alvarez.

"Appears to be."

I still couldn't tell if it meant Alvarez was embarrassed that Wayo had used him, or if he felt guilty for sending me down there like that. Was he angry with me for not coming back up with the box? Was he disappointed that his search had reached this dead end?

I'd decided to believe that it wasn't all an act. If he'd had the talent to be so consistent, he would have been out auditioning for movies, not teaching school. This was another reason not to tell him the truth: if disappointment and betrayal happened to be real, finding out that Wayo tried to kill me would push Alvarez over the edge.

"You have a partner yet?"

I shook my head and looked down at the desk. "You don't have to do that." Even as I said it, I knew I was grateful to him. "I'm fine."

A laugh, followed by the screech of desk legs on the floor as Josh whipped his desk around to face mine. "You think I'm taking pity on you? You know more about treasure than anyone in here. It's a team presentation, Annie. This is pure selfishness on my part."

"She might say she'll do the work," Katy whispered, leaning over my desk on her way to her partner, "until it comes time for the presentation. Then she'll get all nervous, and you'll be on your own."

Josh tilted his head over to her and whispered, "I think she should have let you do the dive instead. To see what would have happened."

"If I'd done the dive, maybe we would have come back with something—"

"You have no idea how you would have reacted down

there." A little vein had appeared at the side of Josh's throat. I put my hand gently on his forearm. I pulled it away when he looked down at it.

Katy said, "Oh, I almost forgot, Josh. Much kudos to your family's PR person, whoever it is. Seriously, congratulations. My only question is, how do you balance it? I mean, you're such a rock, such support for your mom, and yet you still find time to devote yourself to humanitarian missions."

Josh said nothing, and Katy—declaring victory—winked and continued across the room.

"What is she talking about?" I said.

"There's a thing in *People*." Josh shook his head, avoiding eye contact. "Don't worry about it."

"*People*? As in, *magazine*?"

"It's nothing." He tapped the desk twice with his palms. "Violet thought you were nice, by the way."

I almost snorted a laugh. "She did not."

"You're right," he said, nodding, including me in a little secret. "She's kind of a bitch."

I wanted to tell him everything right then and right there.

The bell rang, and Alvarez mumbled something that nobody paid attention to. Josh spun his desk back to its original place and motioned for me to go out the door ahead of him. I caught Gracia out of the corner of my eye, but she disappeared almost instantly, blending in to the throng behind me like a halter-topped chameleon.

Josh and I walked outside together. I guess we were headed to craft service, but neither of us seemed to be leading the other. A cool ocean breeze rustled through the palm trees, and a few fingers of wispy clouds had begun to scratch at the clear sky. And I was walking with him, through the middle of the quad, in full view of the rest of the school. The truth was, it didn't matter where we were going.

"It's funny," he said. "At first I thought it was kind of lame, the dive stuff. No offense—"

"Clearly," I said.

"But then, when we were on the boat, and you were putting all that gear on, and you and Wayo were going over the plan, and I didn't have any idea what you were talking about—"

"You said you read the manual—"

"I wished I could have done what you were doing. That's all."

It took me a second to fully understand what he was saying, but when I did, the sliver of a smile parted my lips. "You were jealous."

"*Envious*, maybe, is a better word."

"Of me."

He stopped me with one hand on my shoulder. "You fell backward into the ocean in the middle of the freaking night. Diving for treasure. How could I not have been?"

I sensed them behind me before I actually saw them. Gracia and Mimi, about thirty feet back, but at least they were pretending to be discreet about it. Every time I glanced around, they were talking to each other, heads turned away from me as though they couldn't possibly be following.

They needed to cut it out before Josh noticed. As soon as he and I turned toward the pavilion, I said a quick good-bye and fumbled with an excuse about my dad needing to talk to me. Then I ducked into the administration building and hustled down the hallway, coming out at the opposite end.

The girls were walking more quickly now, scanning the quad, no doubt wondering where I'd gone. I hurried up behind them unnoticed.

"What," I demanded.

The two of them instantly whirled around, their faces frozen in guilt-ridden surprise until Mimi broke the spell. She removed a folded *People* from her purse. "Have you seen this?"

Jessica Rebstock's face filled half the cover. She was leaning forward on a blue couch pillow, her chin resting in her hand and her fingers curled underneath her cheek. She gave a relaxed, knowing smile, and her skin glowed. The caption read, FAMILY FIRST.

"A strange headline for a single-mother divorcée, don't you think?" I said.

Gracia stepped to me. "What were you guys talking about? I saw him put his arm on your shoulder."

"That doesn't mean anything."

"Or it could mean everything."

"What did you think of the article?" Mimi said. "I think he comes off pretty amazing."

"I haven't read it."

This seemed to throw her for a loop. She opened and closed her mouth, her head leaning forward a tiny bit and then coming back as she reconsidered. "You're kidding."

That's not to say I didn't want to read it. With so many of my classmates having spent time in the tabloids themselves, everyone knew that a *People* puff piece was about as good as it got. But I wasn't planning on reading it because I didn't want to be so obvious about my interest: my version of plausible deniability.

Of course, I could just have read it and pretended I hadn't, but I was self-aware enough to know not to trust myself in that situation. Pretending not to have read it and then being exposed as having read it would have been worse than reading it in the first place.

It was a good thing I hadn't overthought the issue.

"That was at least two minutes of conversation you had with him," Gracia said. "Two minutes is a long time. Think of all the things that can happen in two minutes."

"That's an entire commercial break," Mimi said.

Gracia laughed. "Commercial break?"

"No passing value judgment on a person's frame of reference."

"Since when?" Gracia said. "We rip on Scuba Girl over here all the time."

"Scuba Girl?" I said.

Gracia shrugged. "Has a nice ring to it, don't you think?"

"Don't change the subject," Mimi said. "When are you going out?"

"It's not like that," I said, looking away.

Mimi seemed more frustrated than confused. "I can't understand you, Annie. You go on a trip to Mexico with the guy of your dreams. You spend two whole minutes talking to him at school the next day. And you look like you'd rather be pulling detention."

"It's hard to explain."

"If it was me—"

"It's not you, Mimi," Gracia said.

"I know that. But from where we're standing, you're blowing it." And with that, Mimi whirled around and disappeared into the pavilion.

"Vicarious living," Gracia said. "Ain't nothing like it. You sure you're okay?"

"Are you busy this afternoon?"

Katy interrupted us, appearing out of nowhere. How did she always do that? "Looks like your little plan worked," she said, shaking her head dismissively.

"Hi, Katy," I said. Gracia just stared at her.

"I guess I underestimated you." She turned to Gracia as if sharing a juicy little secret. "Never thought I'd hear *those* words come out of my mouth."

"Don't you have to go throw up somewhere?" Gracia said.

Katy half rolled her eyes and went on her merry way.

"I take it your shared experience down in old Mexico didn't result in female bonding?" Gracia whistled when I said nothing. "That bad, huh?"

Katy sauntered down the pathway—slowly, I'm sure, because she knew I'd be watching her leave. When she finally disappeared, I shook my head and turned to Gracia. "Since when am I the kind of person who has a nemesis?"

EIGHTEEN

It wasn't quite like being in the water, but there was something about the dive shop that took the edge off of my day. I felt different there, with the constant traffic on Pico Boulevard, the sun reflecting off the windshields, scattering bursts of light along the walls. Maybe it was the smell of the neoprene—all that rubber, the hoses, the BCs, the wetsuits, the fins. It smelled like comfort.

I was alone behind the counter, my feet propped up on the glass case. I should have been working on Bio, or reading whatever book had been assigned in English, but instead I was staring at my phone, scrolling through the pictures I'd taken of Cortés's golden disk.

One side was a series of different-sized rock formations, like a family of shark fins emerging from the water. The detail was exquisite: individual boulders on the rocks, tiny sea foam on the waves. The other side was more of an archway, although there was no indication whether it was above or below the water's surface. It could have been coral in Thailand or a sandstone in Moab for all I knew.

The door buzzer sounded, and the noise of the traffic got louder, and before I had the chance to look up, a *People* magazine was slapped on the glass counter, and Gracia said, "So it didn't go well. That's okay. To use a metaphor you might be able to relate to, there are other fish in the sea."

"It's not that." I put the phone away as quickly and, I hoped, nonchalantly as possible. "Josh was fine."

She flipped to a page and spun the magazine around. "Josh *is* fine."

The picture spanned the entire spread. His mom perched on a red director's chair, the shiny brunette curtain cascading over her left shoulder as she gazed at her son. Josh stood with his hands on her shoulders, wearing a sky-blue T-shirt and that easy smile of his. He looked confident. He looked like Josh.

I sat forward and scanned the article quickly, feeling the heat rise to my cheeks whenever my eyes passed over his name. The gist was that even an Academy Award winner couldn't do it alone, and that the teenage son of now-divorced Jessica Rebstock provided both the support and inspiration that she needed to survive the cutthroat world of Hollywood. The fact that he'd recently spent his spring break on a humanitarian mission to aid hurricane victims in Mexico only underscored how grounded the Rebstock family had managed to remain in the face of all the hype.

I spun the magazine back around and shrugged. "It's a good picture of him."

"Oh, lord—"

"What do you want me to say? My relationship with Josh is fine. Borderline agreeable, even. We're partners for the final project in Alvarez's class."

The door buzzed, and I looked up to see the guy who'd been the cause of my hybrid fin argument with my mom. Mr. Pockmarks again. He waved.

"Are you following me?" I said, laughing.

"I like a family-owned dive shop. What can I say?"

"How'd the fins work out?" I said, putting on the retail charm.

"Pretty good," he said, but that was all. I let him wander around the shop by himself.

"There's something you're not telling me," Gracia said when the guy was closer to the back, "and I know it has nothing to do with Josh. I can see it in your eyes. They dart."

"My eyes dart?"

"Like minnows."

"What is it with you and the marine-life similes today?"

"Secretive little silver minnows," Gracia said. "I can be patient. See? Here I am, standing right in front of you, being patient."

I put my feet back up on the counter and pretended to answer the dive shop telephone. "Fleet Diving?"

Gracia stuck out her thumb and pinkie as if talking on

a phone. "Yes, I'm calling about a girl named Annie? You may have seen her around: freckles, terrible swimsuit, always used to tell her best friend the truth?"

"Hold, please." I paused for a moment before returning to the fake call. "Yeah, she wants to know if the topic of a certain clandestine romance with Baldwin Forneau would be included in any exchange of information."

We stared at each other for at least ten seconds, frozen with our phones pressed to our ears—Gracia's imaginary; mine real but with nobody on the other line. She raised her left eyebrow a fraction of an inch, sensing weakness in me. I hung up. "Okay, fine."

I started narrow, focusing only on Josh and Katy: the cute little nudges on the seawall, the pole-climbing lesson, the way her hands lingered on his waist, and the way he didn't try to make them not linger. I told her about the night at Club Starzz, how the two of them grinded the night away.

"You're worried about Katy?" she said.

"If you had seen what I saw, you'd understand."

Gracia shook her head and hummed as though I were an item on sale and she couldn't decide whether to buy me. "If that's all—that *is* all, right?"

Of course that wasn't all—there was the matter of me smuggling into the country a golden artifact that may or may not have been the key to a priceless treasure, and the nefarious treasure hunters who may or may not have still wanted to kill me, one of whom may or may not have been my history teacher—but when I thought of it all like that, it just seemed ridiculous. I reached for the shop phone again.

"Okay, fine. Just no more fake phone," Gracia said. "Like I said, if that's all it is, then you have nothing to worry about."

"I could have sworn you and I just had a conversation," I said. "You were standing right there, wearing those exact same clothes. Josh, Katy, the freaky freaky."

"You just have to make him jealous," she said. "I'll take care of it."

"That is exactly *not* what I wanted to hear. Pretty much on the button."

Mr. Pockmarks came to the front with a save-a-dive kit—basically a bunch of seals and O-rings and replacement straps for just in case. "These are the best," I said. "But I hope you never have to use them."

"And I hope your college résumé is now more robust." He smiled and handed me a credit card, and we completed the transaction with the standard pleasantries. I leaned back in my chair.

"Aren't you the friendly saleslady?" Gracia said when he'd left. She knocked my feet to the side, and the chair's spring-loaded back shot me forward. "By the way, now that you're playing in the big leagues, I see a makeover in your future. And not to ruin the surprise, but we may have to start by getting you a pedicure."

Now my *feet* were the problem? I happened to like my feet, even though the nails weren't necessarily polished, per se. "My feet are—"

"Your feet are a window to your soul, Annie. Treat them like dirt, you're broadcasting to the world that you've given up."

The door buzzer rang again. Sounds of the street filled the shop. I glanced up, and the laugh died in my throat.

I snatched Gracia's hand across the counter and gave it a squeeze. "Please," I whispered through a smile, "don't be you."

"Your eyes just did the minnow thing again," she said. "What—"

"Hello, ladies," Josh said as the door swung closed. The street traffic became muffled once again. Or it could have been the sudden thrashing of my heart blocking any sound from my ears. At school there were so many potential distractions that seeing Josh wasn't such a huge deal, but this wasn't school. This was *my* place. The last time he was here, he'd almost died in my arms. And now the only distraction was my anxiety about the sparkle in Gracia's eyes and whatever that meant.

She turned his way with an easy smile of her own and leaned an elbow on the counter. She rested her other hand on her hip and gave her hair a little twirl. "Of all the dive shops in all the towns in all the world, you walk into Annie's."

I reached for the *People*, but Gracia was too quick for me. And where my instinct would have been to hide it— or chuck it into the trash can, or *something*—hers was the exact opposite. She held the magazine up with both hands, out in front of her, so that the cover picture of Josh's mom was almost at his eye level. "We were just finishing the crossword puzzle."

I was surprised my cheeks didn't blister right off my face.

"It's a tough one this week," Josh said.

"What are you doing here?" I managed.

Josh wandered around the front of the shop. His hair looked professionally unkempt, as always, and he wore a cream-colored polo shirt over plaid board shorts. "Unfinished business."

Her face still properly hidden by the magazine, Gracia raised her eyebrows at me and bit her bottom lip. She even squealed so that—I hope—I was the only one who heard.

Josh was acting differently now than the last time he was here. Back then, he could have been asleep for all the attention he paid to the place. But now he wandered through the store noticing things. He poked through the BC rack. He picked a fin off the wall and flexed it back and forth. He chose a mask and pressed it to his face while he looked in the mirror.

"That's totally you," Gracia said.

"Inhale a bit through your nose," I said to him, trying to keep it professional. "If the mask stays in place, it's a good fit."

"Looks like a good fit to me." Gracia again.

I swatted her on the arm. "Stop it," I whispered through clenched teeth.

Gracia pointed to the ground at my feet and whispered back, "You stay right here. Don't move, not even if the place catches on fire."

She left me behind the counter and meandered closer to Josh the way salespeople do when they try to hover without hovering. "What, exactly, is the nature of your unfinished business?"

"I told Annie today, I need to get certified."

"Really?" I said.

"I even read the manual this time," he said. "Cover to cover. There's no way I'm getting stuck pacing the sidelines again."

"What are you talking about?" Gracia said.

He looked at Gracia, whose face was blank, and then at me. I gave him a quick little "no" with my eyes, and he seemed to get the meaning, because he shrugged and moved away from her and toward the shelf of repair equipment.

"Check it out, Annie," he said. "O-rings."

Gracia hurried back to me and whispered, "I have an idea. Tell him to make an appointment."

"What?"

"Just do it. Tell him—"

"You'll have to make an appointment," I blurted.

Josh turned to me and squinted, as though our conversation had suddenly veered in an unanticipated direction. "For what?"

My mind was blank. Why was my mind blank? I looked at Gracia for help.

"Your lesson," Gracia said to him. "But it can't be for tomorrow. She has a date tomorrow."

I gritted my teeth. "Gra—"

"You know Franklin Deveraux? He's a year older than you, I think. He would be a senior, but Pinedale kicked him out. Drugs and stuff. He's a bad boy, but really cute, and—"

"Gracia," I snapped. She shut her mouth. Finally.

"That doesn't seem like your type." Josh didn't look at me, but he did cock his head to the side a little bit. He could have been thinking about the price of a wetsuit for all I knew.

Gracia checked the polish on the tip of her middle fingernail—her nonchalance a bit too obviously played for my taste—and said, "Annie doesn't have a type."

Josh completed his tour of the shop, ending right back at the counter. He leaned on the glass. "I'd like to make an appointment to get certified in open water diving," he said.

"Tomorrow's bad," I stammered. Apparently I was trying to out-idiot myself every time I opened my mouth.

"So I heard."

I broke free of his little spell and turned to the sanctuary of the big calendar behind the counter. I took a pencil from beside the register and wrote down his name. "The day after?"

"Done." Josh motioned with his chin to the *People* in Gracia's hand and said, "I can sign that for you."

She shook her head. "I wouldn't want to ruin the resale value."

"Remember," he said, patting himself on the chest with an open palm, "behind every successful woman is a strong man."

Gracia turned to me and threw up her arms in mock surprise. "Annie! That's what we've been missing! A strong man! A man of strength and courage! Don't you think we could totally ace Bio if we had one of those?"

Josh rested his hand on the door handle and smiled. "See you guys later."

"It's on the schedule," I said, pointing at it, as if to put the cherry on top of my cake of awkwardness.

When the door was properly closed and the lull had settled back into the shop, I collapsed into the chair and tapped my forehead on the counter and groaned.

Gracia whistled. "Interesting."

"There's a speargun over by the fins back there," I said into the glass. "Just put me out of my misery."

"So tempting."

I grabbed the magazine—ten minutes too late—and threw it in the trash. "Who the hell is Franklin Deveraux?"

"Beats me," Gracia said. "But doesn't he sound hot?"

"You made him up?"

"If you're going to use one boy to make another boy jealous, you have to have complete control of the situation. And the convenient thing about using a not-real person is that you can tailor the nonexistent boy to target the real one's soft spots. You saw the look on Josh's face when I mentioned drugs? He's a good guy, Annie—he cares about you."

"What if he asks around? What if he finds out that Franklin Deveraux never went to Pinedale, much less got kicked out?"

"Then you know he's interested, and that's when you lay all your cards on the table. Tell him you made it all up to see what he'd do, and now that you know he checked up on you, you think it's sweet. He'll be so flummoxed it won't be an issue."

"Flummoxed."

"Let me put it another way: even the best checkers players in the world can be beaten," she said, "if you play chess instead."

"Sometimes I wonder if even *you* believe half the stuff that comes out of your mouth."

"Whatever. The point is, Franklin worked today. Trust me."

The door buzzed again, and I thought for a moment that Josh had come back to torment me, but it was just my mom. She rested her purse on the counter and sighed. "Bankers," she said, more to herself than to us.

"Everything okay?" I said.

"Long day." She nodded. "And thanks for covering. Anyone come in?"

I couldn't help but smile at Gracia. Yes, someone came in.

My mom noticed. "What?"

Gracia cleared her throat and wiped her own smile away. She said, "What about Annie's dad, Mrs. Fleet? Did he play checkers or chess?"

My mom gave me a quizzical look, and all I could do was shrug. For a blissful moment, everything was as it had been before Cozumel. Gracia was being Gracia. We were hanging out at the shop, speaking our own language, driving my mom crazy. Everything was okay. Everything was going to be just fine.

But as I tried to sleep that night, I was reminded that everything wasn't okay. Not even close.

NINETEEN

Wayo's features were distorted grotesquely by the dive mask, his eyes magnified, less than a foot from my face. He gave me the okay signal and pulled out his regulator and smiled. We hovered in place, phosphorescence swirling around us in the dark.

He spoke, and his voice was as clear as if we'd been on the surface. "The disk, Annie. The disk."

I saw the whole thing play out as if I were watching myself on-screen. *Don't turn your back!* I wanted to scream, but my voice wouldn't come. And then I realized that my voice didn't come because there was no breath. No breath to make a sound, and I heard his laugh through the water. And I thrashed and rolled around, my hands desperately clasping at my throat, feeling my feet and legs tingling, then my arms. It was only a matter of time.

I squirmed and lashed out with my feet— *Get away!*

A crash, and I forced myself to open my eyes. It was night. Dark, but a needle of light from the streetlamp outside pierced the curtains. My lamp lay fallen on the bedside table, still rocking from side to side. My bed looked as though it had been ransacked. The T-shirt I slept in was drenched. My hand shot underneath my pillow.

The disk. I'd put it there before I'd fallen asleep. It was still there.

I flinched when a knock came at my door. "Annie? Are you okay?" my dad said. He opened the door a sliver and peeked his head inside.

My heart slowed to a trot. I leaned up on one elbow and pinched the sleep from the bridge of my nose. "Yeah."

"You were screaming. You said you couldn't breathe."

"I'm fine, Dad."

The door creaked open another few inches, but then he hesitated for a moment. He nodded and muttered something about me getting back to sleep. And I was alone again. I listened to his uncertain footsteps disappearing down the hall.

My ceiling glowed, the stars I'd put up there when I was little still forming the constellations of my own creation: a daisy, a rabbit, a boat, a slipper. I reached under the pillow and traced my fingertips over the gold disk as though reading Braille.

It weighed at least a pound, so the gold alone was probably worth twenty thousand dollars or more. Twenty grand could go a long way toward easing whatever was going on with the shop, so why didn't I tell my parents about it?

I knew the answer to that question as soon as it formed in my head.

First off, Dad would demand that Mr. Alvarez be fired, or maybe he'd even sue him. Then he would involve the proper authorities—the police, the Mexican government. And he would insist that we donate the artifact to some place like the Smithsonian. No reward, no finder's fee, no twenty thousand. And then it would all be out of my hands. I'd lose my chance at making history of my own.

But I needed to tell someone; that much was certain. I couldn't keep this a secret much longer.

The golden disk was real. It was mine. And it was trying to reveal something to me. I could almost feel it vibrate against my skin, as if its secret meaning was contained within the metal. I stifled a gasp as the thought struck me for the first time: the last person to touch the disk before me had been dead for almost five hundred years.

TWENTY

Josh and I met up at a coffee shop in Santa Monica called Neutral Grounds. The place was bustling, and the ratio of tattoos and leather wristbands to slacks and blue shirts had migrated closer to fifty-fifty as the afternoon hipster-screenwriter crowd had been infiltrated by business types.

The last couple days of dive instruction had gone well; I had to admit that Josh had put some work into it. He'd read the manual, done his knowledge reviews, even gone through the pool stuff we did—buoyancy control, mask clearing, air-consumption techniques—without acting too much like a jackass. I was impressed. All he had left were the open water checkout dives.

And now we sipped our sugar-free mochas at a small circular table by the window while we argued about the topic of our presentation for Alvarez's class. Josh wanted to use the work I'd done on the Golden Jaguar as a stepping-stone for an even more awesome and detailed one on the same subject.

"I told you I'm not doing everything," I said.

"I'm not saying you should. But we'd be stupid not to play to our—your—strengths. We know so much more now! We could take the Jaguar a step further. To the next level. You saw all the research Alvarez had. Maybe we could go to the same place he found all that stuff."

"You should just ask him for whatever he has left," I said. "In case Wayo didn't take everything."

"That's actually a great idea." Josh thought about it for a while. "But even if he doesn't have the research anymore, it all had to have come from somewhere, right? Because the Golden Jaguar is real."

He must have read something in my face, or else my *hrumf* was a little louder than I'd anticipated, because all of a sudden he narrowed his eyes and lowered his voice. "Is it because you freaked out? Is that why you don't want to do the Jaguar?"

What was I supposed to say to that? By all rights, I should have been jumping at the chance to do this presentation with Josh. And not telling him that I had the disk was killing me. I'd seen the moment play out in my mind a hundred times. Me, leaning in close, telling him my secret. His surprise turning into amazement. The whisper in my ear: *Annie Fleet, you're so awesome.*

But I didn't want to tell him, because, among other things, I didn't know if he could keep his mouth shut. So once again I was forced to feign weakness.

"Fine," he said. "I get it. You don't want to relive the memories. So, what else do you want to do?"

"There's plenty of stuff. The *Concepción* is a good one; sank in 1638 near the Mariana Islands. Or the *Flor do Amelia*—that would drive Alvarez crazy."

"Why?"

I smiled. "It's like Sasquatch, or the yeti. The Loch Ness monster. Most people say it doesn't even exist. Oh! We could do the Sinan wreck, if we wanted to give it some Asian flavor. That one was filled with copper coins and fourteenth-century porcelain—"

"You're kind of cute when you talk shipwrecks, you know that?" He drank from his coffee and pointed to me at the same time. "Your eyebrows get all bouncy."

And . . . heart, meet throat.

There was really nothing for me to say after that. I thought taking a sip of my mocha would be a good way to occupy a few seconds, but the shakiness of my right hand surprised me. My choices were: continue and risk a spill, use my other hand to steady it and therefore look like an infant drinking a bottle with both hands, or put the cup back down on the table and look like an idiot who couldn't decide whether she was thirsty or not. I risked it one-handed, and I don't think I've ever been as proud of myself for successfully putting a cup to my lips as I was then.

"You never told me how your date went," Josh said.

It's a good thing I'd finished my sip, otherwise I might

have spat it out all over him. "What date?"

"With Franklin?"

If I could have called Gracia right then and there to tell her that she was a genius, I would have. The girl was amazing. So amazing, in fact, that it made me wonder why she was taking so long with Baldwin; there was no way he could stand a chance against her guy-manipulation superpowers. She must have really liked him.

"He was fine," I said, avoiding eye contact. According to Gracia's rulebook, here was where I was supposed to go into detail about my fantastically awesome imaginary date, but I couldn't do it. I didn't like making Josh jealous. It felt wrong. "I don't know. Not my type, I guess."

"I thought you didn't have a type."

"That's right. I forgot."

Silence. A woman sitting in one of the leather chairs by the fake fireplace was reading a *People*, and I noticed her doing a double take. Something seemed to click and she looked up at Josh, then back down at the pages. I felt famous by association, but of course she wasn't looking at me; she didn't have any idea who I was.

"Are you going to call him?"

"Why would I call him?" I said.

"Because it's a nice gesture." Josh frowned. "It's a lot of pressure to be the one to always make the move."

"What about chivalry?"

"These are modern times, m'lady," he said. "Guys like to be called once in a while. You have to be forward."

"Who are you? My tour guide to Dude World?"

"Dude World is a fun and exciting place, there's no question, but yes, it does help to have a map of some sort."

His laugh made me all proud of myself, and the thought occurred to me that maybe he was telling me this stuff so that I would make the move on him. What if these were hints? Maybe Gracia had made him sufficiently jealous, and now he was giving me an opening. My mouth was suddenly dry, but could I successfully re-create my no-spill maneuver? To sip or not to sip.

Josh's phone vibrated on the table, rescuing me. Or so I thought until I saw the name and face of the person calling. It was Katy.

"What's up?" Josh said, holding his finger out to me as if to tell me to wait *just one sec.* Like I was going anywhere.

They talked for a couple of minutes, the conversation meandering from homework assignments to weekend plans to some band that was supposed to have blown his mind. He even apologized for not yet listening to the song she'd sent him. He smiled at me self-consciously.

I wanted to rip the phone from his ear and delete Katy's contact information and that stupid picture of her that came up when she called, and maybe even throw the phone into the street for having been contaminated in such a way, but I doodled patiently instead—the mysterious rock-and-water image from one side of the gold disk—keeping my face as neutral as possible.

"Sorry about that," he said when he'd put the phone back on the table. "She's been a little weird since we got back from Mexico, kind of like we're both survivors of some intense experience and we're supposed to have this camaraderie."

Rather than ask him if they *did* have this camaraderie, I waved him off and kept doodling. He put his elbows on the table and leaned forward a little as he cleared his throat. "So. Let's say—just hypothetically, of course—that this Franklin guy doesn't work out."

Here it comes, I thought. Here's what he's been planning since Gracia mentioned Franklin's name for the first time. He's just going to throw it out there. He would never wish a breakup on anyone, right? But maybe we could grab another coffee together sometime, he and I, without the books. . . .

"Are there any guys in your class you have your eye on? Maybe I could help you lay some groundwork or something."

And . . . heart, meet floor.

In a desperate attempt to change the subject, I nodded to the lady by the fireplace and abandoned my suave plan to pretend I hadn't read the article. "Is it weird for you for that to be out there?"

He shrugged.

"You came off pretty good, I thought. Except for all that stuff about helping the disaster victims."

"Yeah, that was a bit over the top." Josh wiped his hands on his shorts and looked around. "That's PR people for you. What can you do? Besides, it's not like I have much choice but to go along with the plan."

"Why do you say that?"

"Being seen as family oriented is good for Mom's career. Her agent says it makes her more marketable to the studios if she has those values, but . . ." He trailed off, pressing his lips into a flat smile. "I'm not blaming her, right? The business is what it is, but if she were really family oriented, then maybe she and my dad would have been able to work something out."

My reaction was knee-jerk. "Why is it the woman who has to sacrifice—"

"Ease up, Susan B. You're the one who doesn't want to pick up the phone and call a guy."

"Susan B. Nice reference."

"I'm all kinds of smart." He tapped his temple with his thumb. "And I didn't say she had to sacrifice anything for my dad. But the fact is that her career was blowing up, and she was getting the roles she always wanted to play. Things just got a little out of hand, and pretty soon we didn't even recognize our lives. The paparazzi, the magazines, all the stuff that goes along with the job—that's not what my dad signed up for."

Josh nodded toward the woman and her *People* by the fireplace. "It sucks being known for someone you're related to. And when you can't go to dinner with your family without it being on the Internet, when everyone around you is fake—not that my mom is fake or anything. She's not. She's real. But the agents and the publicists and the producers—"

"Josh?" I said gently.

He looked at me as though suddenly realizing where he was. He blinked a couple of times. "Sorry," he said.

"There's nothing to be sorry for—"

He cleared his throat and finished his coffee, and then he spread his arms just above the table. "I thought you've never been to Hawaii."

"What are you talking about?"

"When we were in Mexico, at that club. You rattled off a long list of places you've never been to—a little self-pitying, if you ask me—and Hawaii was one of them."

"You were drunk," I said, more than a little defensive. "How would you have known what self-pitying sounded like?"

"So if you've never been to Hawaii . . ." He picked up my paper and studied it. Then he put it back on the table and turned it around and tapped his finger right in the center of the doodle. "Why are you drawing the coast of Molokai?"

TWENTY-ONE

We were at my house in fifteen minutes. I made Josh park his car at the curb with the engine running while I sprinted inside. Less than sixty seconds later, I was hustling back down the concrete walkway. I hopped into the car and clicked my seat belt. "Let's go."

"This is where you live?" he said, his left forearm resting on top of the steering wheel as he leaned forward to get a better glimpse through the passenger window.

There was so much going on in my head that I didn't have the energy to be self-conscious about the fact that my house would never adorn the pages of *InStyle*. "No, I just thought I'd run into some random guy's house."

"That's not what I meant—"

"Just drive," I said, looking over my shoulder.

"You put on a jacket," he said. "Were you cold?"

"Left here," I said. "Go straight until you get to Los Feliz Boulevard and then take a right."

"Are you going to tell me what's going on?"

My breathing was shallow, and the tingle of adrenaline was threatening to turn my limbs into pudding. I forced myself to inhale slowly, and it occurred to me for the first time that I was riding shotgun in Josh Rebstock's cherry-red Lexus coupe. The car smelled both new and like Josh at the same time, and the leather seats were softer than black-dyed animal hide had any right being. If only the girls could see me now.

"So," I said, pretending to be nonchalant while keeping my eyes on the side-view mirror, "when was the last time you came over to the east side?"

"You're acting like someone's out to get you."

"I just want to make sure we're not being followed, that's all. No big deal."

We turned onto Los Feliz; the branches of the tall pine trees extended out to the road like claws in the half light. "Who's going to follow us?" he said with a laugh. "Katy?"

This got my attention. "Why would Katy follow us? Are you guys going out?"

"No, I'm just saying that it's so unlikely—"

"You said she was acting weird—"

"No, that's not what I— Forget it." He glanced at me before gripping both hands on the wheel and staring at the road ahead. "I was making a joke."

"Turn left here," I said.

He followed my directions without further comment. We turned up Vermont, through Griffith Park, and snaked around until we reached the Griffith Observatory. The parking lot was empty, and we followed the long circular driveway leading up to the observatory. The sun was down, but the streetlamps hadn't yet reached full power.

"Drive to the end of the parking lot," I said.

"This is cool," he said. "Overlooking the city, the lights, the view."

Except he didn't know what to say when I made him turn around and back into a parking spot so we were facing the entrance.

"Okay, so I may have gone overboard with the whole 'make sure we're not being followed' thing."

"No problem," Josh said. "The paparazzi are ruthless. You can never be too careful."

"You think I was looking out for the paparazzi?"

He shrugged. "I mean, it's not like I'm famous like my mom, but with the magazine article out—"

"I'm going to stop you right there," I said. "Not that you thinking this is about you isn't its own special kind of endearing."

"So, why were you—"

I unbuttoned my jacket as I looked around the parking lot. "I can't believe I'm about to do this."

"Annie," he said, suddenly uncomfortable. "Maybe this isn't the right—I mean—I know I told you guys like it when girls are more forward, but—"

"Shut up."

I reached into the inside pocket. My hand closed around the disk, the gold cool to the touch. "I want you to promise me that I can trust you. No goofy movie star bull—"

"Language," he gasped in mock offense.

"This is serious." I looked at the hodgepodge of shock and discomfort and confusion on his face, and I realized that I was never going to be completely comfortable with this decision, so I just had to take a leap of faith. "I told you guys in Mexico that I'd gotten separated from Wayo in the Devil's Throat."

"Yeah, and then you freaked out."

"That wasn't exactly true." I closed my eyes and took a deep breath, and I removed the disk. It rested on my flat palm as I extended it to him.

He swallowed. "What's this—"

"Go ahead, pick it up."

The streetlamp outside had reached full power, and a wide shaft of white light shone in through the driver's-side window. Josh reached gingerly for the disk, first tracing his index fingertip across the embossed image of the shark-fin rocks.

"You were right about Hawaii," I said. "I've never been."

He slid his fingers underneath the gold—the warmth of his hand gradually replacing the coolness of the metal against my skin—until the disk was now sitting in his open palm.

"It's so heavy," he whispered, his voice filled with wonder. "It has to be solid gold."

I nodded, letting him experience his first moments with it in silence. There was something primal and childish about the look on his face.

"The two sides are different," he said to himself. Then he seemed to remember he was in the car with me. "Do you think it's a map?"

"That's the only thing I can think of. The rocks jut out of the water on one side, but not the other. Maybe the other side is underneath, like a coral formation or something."

He nodded. "Makes sense. You find the one above the water first, and that leads you to the one below."

I pointed to the disk. "And you're sure this is Molokai?"

"Of course." Then, perhaps noticing that I'd recoiled a bit, he said, "I didn't mean it like that. We went there for Christmas vacation one year, my family. This is from Ha-na-something Bay, very picturesque. I had a poster on my wall for a couple of years after that."

"Don't worry about it," I said. "I know how spoiled and out of touch you movie star's kids are."

"Touché." And then: "We have to go find it, don't you think?"

I laughed. "It's just that easy, is it?"

Josh seemed puzzled. "Kind of, yeah. I mean, there are some issues we'd have to work around, but I'm sure we could figure out a—"

"Wayo and I didn't just randomly get separated. This came from inside a small box. I gave Wayo the box right before he left me down there."

"So what? The Jaguar has been hidden for five hundred years. We have as much right to go after it as he does."

I looked away. For some reason there were tiny dots of sweat on my forehead, and my throat had begun to constrict. *Breathe*, I ordered myself. I closed my eyes and wiped my forehead with the first two fingers of my right hand.

"What?" he said. "What's wrong? What else aren't you telling me?"

"I didn't freak out because Wayo and I got separated."

Even in the murky lighting, I could see Josh's expression morph from animated to horrified as I told him what happened. When I finished, we sat in the silence together as he struggled to piece everything together.

"He tried to kill you."

"This is what I'm saying."

He contemplated the disk in his hand for a long, long moment before looking up at me. "Annie, that's *amazing*," he said finally, and laughed. "Seriously, that's amazing."

His jovial attitude caught me completely by surprise. "I think you're missing the—"

"No, really. Some dude turned off your air a hundred feet below the freaking surface of the *ocean*, in the middle of the *night*, and you *survived*?" He breathed out through his lips. "Why didn't you say something?"

"Are you kidding? I was terrified," I said. "I didn't know who I could trust."

"Holy crap. I thought you were hard core before this, but we're talking about a whole new level of—"

"Josh—"

"I mean, there's no way Katy would ever have made fun of you if she knew about this."

"You can't tell anybody."

"Why not? This is the coolest thing I've ever—"

"You have to promise me."

"That's why you were all spooked on the way over here. You think someone's following you?"

"I don't know. Maybe. I tend to see Wayo wherever I look. Maybe he's there, or maybe I'm imagining it. But even if there is somebody following me—whether it's Wayo or someone else—I figure I'm safe as long as nobody knows for sure that I have the disk. That there was something in that box."

"What about Alvarez?"

I shook my head. "Didn't tell him. I didn't know if he was in on it or not."

Josh rubbed his thumb across the surface of the disk and smiled. "Then I guess we're going to have to go this one alone."

"You're not listening to me," I said. "It's not as simple as that. These people will *kill* us to get what they—"

A *tap, tap, tap* at my window.

I screamed, flailing my arms up to cover my face. This was it. I knew it. Even Josh must have known it; he yelped like a terrier.

I peeked up to see a uniformed security guard resting the tip of his nightstick against the glass. Josh started the car and rolled down the window, leaning almost out over my lap to see the guard.

"You can't park here after hours," the guard said.

Josh, bless his heart, somehow kept his sense of humor. "This isn't lovers' lookout?"

"Go home, kids." The guard glared at us for an extra second and then stepped back, his hands planted officially on his hips, waiting.

Josh waved at the guard as we drove away, but I felt frozen in place. Except for my heart, which hammered a techno beat in my chest. I'd finally told someone about the disk, and that someone was Josh Rebstock.

And that meant I no longer had control over anything that might happen next.

TWENTY-TWO

To say that I couldn't concentrate on school would be an understatement. Now that I knew the disk referred to an actual place, I was useless. The first time I Googled it, I nearly fell out of my chair. Type in search term: *Molokai*. Press Enter, and there it was. I held the disk up to the screen for comparison: a perfect match. And the craftsmanship was exquisite. It was as if they'd etched it while at anchor.

Josh and I fed off each other's enthusiasm, and we shared that nourishment with nobody. Not Nate or Katy, not Mr. Alvarez. We were an island unto ourselves. We spent almost a week researching anything even remotely connected to Cortés or the Jaguar. When I'd exhausted every avenue I could find on the Internet, my dad took me to the library, pleased as punch that I seemed to have recognized the importance of primary-source examination.

And it was refreshing to have told Josh; I was no longer in sole possession of some terrible secret. Neither of us had any idea what it would lead to, but our excitement was enough to keep us talking for hours every night, recapping what we'd learned that day or posing hypothetical questions about Cortés and his motivations. We talked about the thrill of the hunt and imagined what it would feel like to see the Jaguar roar again.

As it had been for the last week, craft service on Wednesday was more of a chore than a culinary event. I sat with the girls at our normal table, but nobody said anything. Mimi seemed to have run out of ways to tiptoe around asking me about Josh and his mom. Then there was Gracia.

At one point, Baldwin walked by our table, a plain white T-shirt draped over his pipe-cleaner shoulders like it was still on the hanger. He glanced at Gracia just long enough to shoot her a smile, which she returned just as skillfully. Mimi didn't seem to notice him at all, much less the way he looked at our friend.

I wanted Gracia to spill the beans about him, but she knew I was keeping something from her, and I was sure she'd demand full honesty on my part in return. So I didn't even bother asking; maintaining the exclusivity of my secret with Josh was more important.

Our silent lunch was about halfway done when Mimi slapped her hand on the table and leaned forward. "Okay. Just spill it. You, Josh, Cozumel, this presentation of yours. Have you hung out with his mom? Are they as down-to-earth as the article said?"

"We're partners," I said.

Mimi said, "Now we're getting somewhere."

I smiled in spite of myself. "Not *life* partners."

"Who chose who?"

"*Whom*," I said, deflecting.

"Excuse me, Grammar Police." Mimi rolled her eyes and scoffed. She took a section of her silky hair and twirled the end of it against the tip of her nose. The vibe was bordering on uncomfortable, and it was only a matter of time before I had to start pretending that Josh and I *were* an item, if only to get them off my back.

"It was kind of by default. Everyone else paired up with each other."

"This insecurity of yours is mind-numbing."

Gracia shot Mimi a look. My bodyguard.

"I'm just saying that she can be as hot as she lets herself think she is. By the way," Mimi said, turning to me, "next time you talk to him, could you do me a favor?"

"This should be fun."

"It's not a big deal or anything," she said. "But maybe you could just ask him if his mom's happy with her agency. Don't actually *ask* him that, but if you think you can work it into the conversation somehow—"

I had to laugh. Mimi's mom was a superagent who *Variety* had dubbed "The Most Powerful Hispanic in Hollywood" three years running. The last thing she needed was my help to land a client.

"Work it into the conversation?" I said. "Hey, Josh. Let's do some research for our presentation. What's your favorite candy? Wouldn't your mom be better off with the great Karen Soto representing her?"

"Try not to be so naive," Mimi said. "That's how this town works. That's how the *world* works. You have a connection, you exploit it. Or did you think everything happened by chance?"

"What if I don't want to be one of your connections?"

"Well, you are, whether or not you want it. And lucky for you, I'm one of yours."

"Ladies, please," Gracia said.

I knew Josh was behind me before I felt the gentle tap on my shoulder. The platonic familiarity of his touch was excruciating.

"Hey, Josh," Mimi said.

"Hi, Mimi," he said. He nodded to Gracia, looking a little anxious.

"Is your mom happy with her agent?" I said, glancing at Mimi. She rolled her eyes at me, but at least I'd gotten a smile out of her.

"Sure, I guess," he said. "Hey, can I steal Annie for a second?"

I felt them tracking me as I followed him to the front hall of the pavilion. Josh had a little bounce in his step, and then a smile exploded off his face. He leaned down so our noses were only inches away, and I smelled mint gum on his breath, and for an irrational second, I thought he was going to kiss me right there in front of everybody. Then I noticed he was holding a manila folder.

"Okay," he said softly, glancing from side to side before locking in on me. His eyes practically twitched with glee, but he kept the rest of his body entirely still. "There's a sculpture garden. At the bottom of the ocean."

I scrambled to make sense of what he'd said, but I got nowhere. "Is that a euphemism for something?"

"Sorry. Let me back up. James Cook was supposed to have been the first European visitor to Hawaii in 1778, right? But that was almost two hundred and fifty years *after* de la Torre's journals aboard the *Vida Preciosa*."

"And?"

"The design on the disk is some kind of map, right?"

"Maybe, but we don't know—"

"We already know one side, the side above water, is Molokai. What if I told you I found something else, something at the bottom of the ocean. Maybe a clue to the other side of the disk."

"The sculpture garden," I said.

Josh opened his folder and showed me a grainy picture of a dozen or so pillars rising from a sandy floor. Some were at angles, some rose straight up. I noticed a couple lying horizontally. If they were arranged in a pattern, I couldn't recognize it.

"This place was discovered in the late seventies," he said, pointing to the pillars. "A group of archaeologists restored the statues a couple years later, taking off all the coral and crap. They're Hawaiian. Like, old-school Hawaiian—the archaeologists date them to the mid-1500s—but nobody has ever been able to figure out what they mean or why they're even there. It's like Stonehenge. It makes no sense. I mean, we're talking about the absolute *least* populated of the Hawaiian Islands."

"What does this have to do with Cortés?"

Josh looked around again before leaning in even closer. He spoke almost without moving his lips. "What if . . . and this is a big what if . . . but what if. You know how when the conquistadors first arrived in Mexico and the Aztecs thought they were gods?"

"Montezuma thought Cortés was Quetzalcoatl."

"Right. What if the same thing happened here? But there was no conflict, so there was no record of it?"

"You're talking about a secret discovery of Hawaii. Why would Cortés keep something like that to himself?"

My dad stepped tentatively up to us. Oh, goody! Faculty parents are the *best*! "Annie."

Josh quickly put his hands down, looking like he'd been busted for possession of something worse than a photocopy of an ancient sculpture garden. "Hi, Mr. Fleet."

"Dad," I said, trying to be polite. "You know Josh—"

"How could I forget?" my dad said, nodding, but looking oddly distracted. "Mr. Rebstock."

I caught a glimpse of Gracia spying on me from the lunch table. I shook my head at her, and she smiled all innocent, like "What?"

My dad should have continued on by now. He wasn't supposed to worm his way into my conversations at school! How many times did we have to go over this? He stepped across the hallway and motioned for me to go with him. "Annie? Can I talk to you for a minute?"

I gave him a quick nod and held a finger up like I'd be right there. "You guys know each other?" I said to Josh through an embarrassed smile.

Josh's energy seemed momentarily subdued by his encounter with my dad. He whispered, "Last year. I wasn't able to summon the proper motivation required to succeed at a high level in his course. His words, not mine."

Great. Josh and my dad had a history together . . . Hey-oh!

"Josh," my dad said, clearing his throat as he stepped forward again, "I need to spe—"

"Dad, we're kind of in the middle—"

He put his hand on my shoulder and pulled me aside. This conversation was apparently not optional. I started to protest again, but the look in his eyes shut me up. Sadness. Distress. A little bit of fear. The look you give someone when you're about to deliver news they don't want to hear.

"I just spoke with the police," he said.

I braced myself for his next sentence. A car accident. A heart attack. My mom. My grandfather.

Josh stood across the hall with his arms cradled around his research. Even he could tell something was wrong.

"They're with your mother. No, not that," my dad said quickly, reading the terror on my face.

"Then what—"

"Everything's okay," he said. "I promise. I didn't mean to scare—"

"Dad!"

"Our house was broken into this morning."

Every single molecule of air left my lungs at once. I staggered back, and my dad snaked a hand out to steady me. Fear blinded me, and I tried to blink through it. And then I felt nothing.

"It's okay, Annie," my dad was saying, though I barely understood him. "It's okay. It's just a break-in. I didn't mean to upset you. As far as your mom can tell, they didn't even take anything."

But I knew how wrong he was.

TWENTY-THREE

A police car stood vigil against the curb outside. As I walked up the path, I noticed a uniformed cop inspecting a broken window at the side of the house and another in the living room through the open front door. My mom was waiting for me on the front steps.

"Annie," she said, enveloping me in a reassuring embrace. "Please don't worry. It's okay."

There was no way I could muster the patience to hug her back. I kept pushing forward until she had no choice but to let me go. I'd expected for the place to be torn up, like in the movies, with tufts of cushion bleeding out of knife holes in the sofa, the bookshelves crashed onto the floor, broken lamps. But aside from the broken window, the living room looked like it had hardly been touched.

"They didn't take anything," my mom was saying, following me from the living room to the hallway. "The alarm probably scared them off."

I covered the last ten steps to my room at a dead sprint and slammed the door behind me. Bile was rising in my throat as I scanned the room, grasping for proof that whoever had broken into our house had left my room alone.

"Annie?" my mom said through the door. "Annie, can I come in?"

The mattress, was it off center, or had I left it that way? Were my pillows supposed to be on the floor? I was searching for something, anything, to convince myself that the truth wasn't really the truth.

My mom pleaded, "Annie, I know how violating this feels. But these things happen. We're lucky we weren't home when it did."

"They didn't even take my silver piece of eight, if you can believe it," my dad said.

My dresser. I knew before I opened it. The toe of a sock protruded from the top drawer, blinding white against the dark brown wood. There was no ignoring the truth anymore.

"What do you mean, gone?" Josh said, back at Neutral Grounds because I'd wanted to get out of the house but needed to be surrounded by people. Lots of people.

I'd lied to the police and to my parents—nothing of mine was taken, of course not!—but what choice did I really have? Was I supposed to tell them that I'd put my entire family at risk? That I'd smuggled a priceless artifact over international borders and stashed it with my unmentionables? My parents had spent the rest of the afternoon convincing me that everything was going to be okay, and finally I'd had enough. I told them they were right and thanked them for their reassurance, and I said that I had work to do.

"*Gone* is like *dead*," I said. "Or *pregnant*. There is only one meaning."

A middle-aged woman at the table next to us couldn't help from tilting her head in our direction. Two teenagers, a nervous conversation, and the word *pregnant*.

I leaned my elbows on the table and put my head in my hands. "I'm sorry," I said, staring at a dent in the wood.

"What do you have to be sorry about? Last I checked, it's not the break-in-ee that's responsible—"

"My sock drawer! What kind of an idiot puts something like that in her sock drawer?"

Josh patted the table and leaned back. He shook his head. "We were so close, too. I was sure of it."

"It can't be over."

"They have the disk, Annie. The map. And we don't." He motioned to the backpack at his feet. "We have a folder. Printouts. Photocopies."

I didn't want to admit it, but he was right. Josh and I were just a guy and a girl with a library card and Internet access. Wayo had money, a team, and now he had the disk. My phone rang. I set it on the table and Gracia's face smiled up at me. My phone. My phone!

"I'm a genius!" I yelped, energized as though I'd been

struck by lightning. I spun the phone around and showed Josh, scrolling through the pictures I'd taken. One of each side of the disk. Then close-ups on different parts of each image. Then a self-portrait of me grinning like an idiot and holding the disk next to my face, and another one of me pretending to bite the disk as if it were an Olympic medal.

"Wow," he said.

"Don't pay attention to those ones," I said, scrolling back.

"This is good," Josh said suddenly. "This is great!"

His chair scraped against the floor when he jumped to his feet. Before I knew what was happening, he'd leaned across the table and wrapped his arms around me. But with the table between us, it was not the smoothest of maneuvers. I was so stunned that I didn't meet him halfway, so he could only really get his forearms to me. He sat back down, seeming to realize the clumsiness of his gesture.

The woman next to us could hardly contain herself. She'd turned almost entirely toward us, her eyes wide open, her mouth slightly agape.

"It was negative," I said, giving her a thumbs-up. "Yay!"

She looked away, and Josh said, "What was negative?"

"Forget it." I pointed to the backpack. "Today at school you were going to tell me why Cortés would have kept his discovery of Hawaii a secret?"

"Right!" Josh leaned over and pulled out the familiar manila folder. "Unless it wasn't Cortés who did it. Unless it was one of his men. Or, unless the goal wasn't to discover something but to cover something up."

"Too much *unless*."

"That's what I thought. But then I found this."

He glanced around the coffee shop before sliding a close-up of one of the sculptures across the table. A block, with some sort of embossed design carved into it that looked like a two-headed bird.

"And this."

Another sculpture. This carving hadn't survived the elements as clearly, but it looked like a pyramid of three of the same thing: crescent-shaped images, like bananas with the ends pointing up, and also with a point coming from the center. "Are those ships?"

Josh was biting his bottom lip. He could barely contain himself. "Crowns," he said.

"Crowns? How do you know that?"

He handed me the photocopy of a drawing I did recognize: the *Vida Preciosa* as shown departing for Spain from the New World in 1540. Josh put his finger on the flag, drawn to be rippling slightly in the breeze.

I held up the two pictures next to each other, but I had to squint because the flag was too small to see clearly. "I don't really—"

Josh gave me yet another picture, a close-up of the flag from a different source. Taking up the whole flag was a shield, split into quadrants, with images in each, including a two-headed bird and a triangle of three crowns.

"That right there," he said, "is the crest bestowed upon Cortés by King Charles the Fifth when Cortés became governor of New Spain in 1519. It flew on every one of Cortés's ships."

The flag. The sculptures. The similarities were unmistakable. I tried to lick some moisture back into my lips, but my mouth was just as dry. It was like rubbing sandpaper on more sandpaper. "No way."

"I know," Josh said. "Crazy, right? I bet if we looked at other pictures of the sculpture garden, we'd see more images from the crest. Do you know what this means?"

I struggled to find the words. "You may have just found something that changes everything we know about the discovery of the New—"

"You really are a teacher's kid, aren't you?" He leaned in, whispering, "I just told you that I may have found the location of the Golden Jaguar, and you go *there*?"

"Sorry." I tried again. "It means that you're nowhere near as stupid as you come off in public?"

"Thanks, Annie. I'm trying to do something here—"

"No, Josh, I'm just kidding." It was surprising how cute he was when insulted. It probably didn't happen very often. "So, now what?"

"We're going to Molokai."

"Say that again?"

"Molokai, baby."

"We don't have the resources to handle something like—"

"Alvarez said it himself. All we have to do is get creative. We can turn our greatest weakness right around. Make it our greatest advantage." He pulled out his wallet and removed a small rectangular piece of paper. "Oh, and before you give me a bunch of crap about how spoiled I am and how I don't live in the real world, take a look at this."

"That's a temporary open-water certification card," I said, trying desperately to make sense of everything. The sculpture garden, Cortés, the crest. And Josh Rebstock had just invited me to Hawaii. To repeat, Josh Rebstock had just invited me to Hawaii.

"You have to take me diving."

"You said you spent all last weekend at the library—"

"Check-out dives," he said with a shrug and a damn twinkle in his eye. "Your mom recommended another dive shop, no offense. I got the sense that she wanted to take some things off your plate. I just hope the water in Hawaii is warmer than out at Catalina. That was miserable."

"You're certified?"

"Try to keep up," he said.

I started to let myself imagine the two of us on a treasure-hunting trip to Hawaii, but it wasn't long before reality came thundering in. "Wayo."

Josh started to blurt something out, but caught himself and leaned forward. "He's only had the disk for a couple of hours," he whispered as he pointed to the folder.

"We have this. We have a head start on him. We have to act fast, though."

"What on earth makes you think my parents are going to let me go to Hawaii with you?"

Josh handed me the folder. He laced his fingers together and pressed his palms outward in a stretch. Then he cracked the knuckles of both hands and said, "You'll see."

TWENTY-FOUR

"This is the worst plan ever," I said.

I was sweating, and the back of the shop smelled like extra chlorine, my mom having just recently given the pool a shock treatment. Josh leaned back in one of the folding chairs while we waited, but I couldn't sit still, so I busied myself by filling empty tanks at the fill panel by the rental BCs at the rear wall. Attach the whip to the tank valve, step back, press the button, fill 200 psi per minute. Fifteen minutes to a full tank. Remove the whip. Repeat.

"It's going to work out," he said, his hands laced obnoxiously behind his head. "I promise."

The hum of the compressor out back made it so that I could hear only the general rumbling of my parents' deliberation, interrupted from time to time by Josh's mom's expansive actress voice.

Josh's folder of research lay open on the workbench. I could only hope it had served its purpose. We'd given our parents everything we had on the mystery of the sculpture garden but kept any mention of Cortés or the Jaguar to ourselves. Now our fate was being decided.

"You know what I hate about you?" I said.

"Hold on, I've got to write this down," he said, not moving an inch. "Let me get a pencil."

"It's not your carefree, let-life-come-to-me attitude, because whatever. I just hate that it *works* for you."

He closed his freaking eyes and nestled his head back into his palms. "This is good stuff. Keep it coming."

"Can't you just respect the fact that things don't come so easily to everyone else? Is that too much to—"

"Annie, I'm telling you." This time at least he sat forward and looked at me. "This is a good plan."

The door swung open, and Josh's mom burst through like a gust of freshly shampooed wind. My parents followed.

I turned off the compressor but left the hose attached to the tank. I couldn't read the expressions on any of them. Had they come to a decision? Were they angry at each other? Were they annoyed with us for even proposing this?

Oscar-winning actress Jessica Rebstock looked like she'd just stepped out of the pages of a high-end active-wear catalog. Her luscious hair was held back with a wide green headband, and she wore black capri tights and a fitted white tank. I love my mom and dad, but let's be honest: there's a reason some people are movie stars while other people teach history and own dive shops.

"I'm due for a reading at Warner Brothers," she said, pressing her palms together as if to beg forgiveness. "Call me as soon as we know what's happening, and I'll have Violet make the necessary plans."

My mom flinched at the mention of Violet's name— as though she'd caught herself about to roll her eyes and managed to abort the maneuver.

"Bill, Eleanor," Josh's mom said, offering her manicured hand to my parents, "it was wonderful to see you."

"Jessica." My dad nodded as he shook her hand, and a little smile tickled his mouth.

She squeezed Josh on the shoulder and twirled around, looking over her shoulder at her son one last time before the door closed behind her. With her energy now gone, there was a void in the room, and I think we all knew that none of us could possibly come close to filling it.

My mom cleared her throat. "Josh," she said. "Would you mind? And if anyone comes in, just tell them I'll be right there."

We were alone for at least a minute of silence. My mom disconnected the pressure hose from the tank and replaced the plastic cover on the tank valve. A dull thud rang out as she placed the full tank by the rear door.

I couldn't take it anymore. "Well?"

"Be honest," my dad said. "Do you really expect us to go along with this?"

"It's an amazing opportuni—"

"You're fifteen years old, Annie. And he's seventeen. He's a boy."

"It's not like that," I said, careful to keep any disappointment out of my voice lest they think I wished it were like that.

"I hope it doesn't sound like we don't trust you," Dad said.

"That's exactly what it sounds like."

He waved a quick finger at me as though dismissing a student's obnoxious remark. "Quite frankly, I'm not sure whether Mrs. Rebstock is an appropriate chaperone for a trip of this—"

"That's why Violet's going to be there the whole time," I said.

When we'd come up with the plan, Josh and I had played devil's advocate with each other, offering rebuttals to every objection we could think of. Josh's mom was easy to convince; she practically fell all over herself saying yes, reminding me how in my debt she was for saving her son's life, et cetera. But my parents were much trickier, and only partly because I was younger and a girl. There was the element of me associating with "those people" that couldn't be ignored.

"How well do you know this assistant?" my mom said.

"She's nice. Graduated from Princeton, near the top of her class. Summa cum laude, I think." I was making this part up. I needed to stop. "Super detail oriented. Good person." *Just stop.* "Likes dogs." *What?*

"This isn't how normal people live. You can't just up and go to Hawaii whenever you need to research a school report—"

"Some people *can*," I said. "That's the point. Why do you even send me to a fancy school like Pinedale if you're not going to let me take advantage of the connections I make?"

"What does Mr. Alvarez think about this?" Dad said.

"How many times have we talked about the importance of primary research, of getting as much information on the subject as possible? And here I have the chance to do exactly that."

Considering that I didn't directly answer his question, I convinced myself that it wasn't actually a lie. Of course we hadn't told Alvarez a thing.

A couple of days before, I'd happened to mention that Josh and I were thinking about doing our final presentation on the use of primary-source documents in shipwreck research. I'd said that I knew that a lot of his Golden Jaguar stuff had been lost when Wayo had taken off, but I was hoping he'd made some copies.

"I threw everything away," he'd said. "What little I didn't take down to the island with me."

I'd waited for more, but he was too busy pretending to fiddle with one of the zippers on his satchel.

"You're giving up?"

That's when he finally looked me in the eyes. "We were friends for over ten years. At least I thought so, but now I can't help but wonder, was he just using me the whole time? Pretending, on the off chance that I'd discover something he could use?"

I didn't know what to say to that, so I'd gone with something vague that could be interpreted as insightful. "It's a lot of money. Who knows what people are capable of?"

Now, talking with my parents, I picked up Josh's folder—maybe a bit melodramatically, I admit. I felt like a defense attorney pulling out all the stops in my closing argument. "Printing pictures from the Internet and photocopying old library books can only take us so far. Look at these sculptures. Why are they there? What do they mean? I know you, Dad. Wouldn't you like to find the answers, too?"

"I'm not questioning the validity of your topic—"

"Alvarez is totally on board," I blurted. It was a risk I had to take. Simply not lying wasn't going to cut it. "He practically begged us to go."

My parents exchanged a series of meaningful parental facial expressions: some eyebrow raises, a squint, the shake of a head, the furrowing of a brow. It was like apes doing sign language.

"There will be ground rules," my dad said sternly.

I almost bounced up and down, but I had to prove to them that I was mature enough to spend a weekend with a boy, so I offered a quick nod instead.

The buzzer rang out front.

Annie Fleet! You've just won . . . a fabulous trip to the beautiful and secluded island paradise of Molokai!

"Annie!" Josh called out.

"So it's a yes?" I said. "I can go?"

It was my mom's turn to act all severe. "Please don't make us regret this."

"I won't," I said, clutching the folder against my chest. *I'm going! I'm going!*

Josh again: "Annie!"

I was going to fly on my first private plane for my first trip to Hawaii. I was going to have my own room at the resort. And yes, I was going with Josh Rebstock. I practically floated into the retail shop.

Josh stood by the front counter, his face a mask of surprise and—was it fear? The man he was looking at wore a faded blue baseball cap and had his back to me. He turned his head slowly, following Josh's gaze, and—

Wayo.

"*Hola, señorita.* Is good to see you."

I was unexpectedly grateful that I'd told Josh the truth about Cozumel. It gave me the freedom to be as scared as I needed to be without having to wonder what he thought of me.

"What . . . what are you doing here?" I stammered.

"I hear so much about your dive shop from el Señor Alvarez."

Josh came around and stood at my side. Very casually, he grabbed the folder from me and held it under his arm.

"You've seen him since our trip?" Josh said.

"A little, yes. I was hoping he has more information on the Jaguar, but he tells me he has given up the chase."

"You were supposed to be his friend," I said.

"What is a friend, really?" Wayo opened his palms.

188

"Someone to pass the time with? Someone to get you from one part of your life to the next?"

My parents came from the back, and Wayo turned on the charm. He removed his cap—freeing that familiar wisp of hair—and his eyes lit up. "Annie's parents?"

"Bill Fleet," my dad said, shaking his hand. "And you are?"

"A friend of her teacher, el Señor Alvarez. Annie was come down to Cozumel to help us with the *huracán*."

He was pleasant, friendly, and completely unrecognizable from the man he'd been only seconds before. His posture was different, all laid-back and welcoming. He was a psychopath, or a sociopath. Whatever kind of *path* that shows no concern for other people and no remorse for mistreating them, that's what he was. I wouldn't have been surprised if he had a collection of kitten heads in his freezer.

My dad smiled. "You're from Cozumel?"

"I own a small dive shop myself," he said, looking around. "Not as nice as this one, of course—"

"I'm sure it's wonderful," my mom said. She was *blushing*. "We'll have to look you up if we ever make it down there. I'm sure Annie would enjoy diving with you."

Josh gripped my elbow so hard I thought my forearm was going to fall off.

"I bet she is a good diver, the daughter of a dive shop owner," Wayo said, looking at me. "I am sure she does never panic underwater. She can deal with almost any emergency. Maybe surprising to some people."

"Well," Mom said, "she has had a lot of training."

Wayo let his eyes linger on me for an excruciating moment, and then he replaced his cap. "I only come to say hello."

A nod to each of my parents, a toothy grin to me and Josh, and he was gone. I flinched when the buzzer sounded.

My dad checked his watch and excused himself, citing a stack of ungraded AP essays. "We'll talk specific ground rules tonight, okay?"

He kissed me on the forehead, but I hardly felt his lips. It was as though my entire body had been shot up with novocaine. Josh thanked my mom, and I mumbled that I wouldn't let them down, and the next thing I knew, we were standing on the sidewalk. The rush of street traffic was muted and distant, as though I was hearing it from underwater.

"He knows I know he took the disk," I said. "He's trying to scare me away."

"We have a problem," Josh said.

This was enough to snap me out of my daze. "You think? You think Wayo showing up *at my mom's shop* might be—"

"Easy. Take it easy."

"You take it easy—"

"I mean, we have a problem on top of that. Another problem." He put his hand between my shoulder blades and steered me toward his car. His other hand still gripped the folder. "The people in charge promise the airport is secure, but I've never flown from there without seeing at least a couple paparazzi. One of the staff must tip them off. There's so much money—"

"Focus. The problem."

"The problem is that Jessica Rebstock and her son are going to Hawaii this weekend. Somebody will find out about it. And that means there will be pictures. And if you're there with me—"

"Wayo's going to know."

"He's only had the disk for a few hours, and maybe he doesn't know about the sculpture garden." Josh nodded to himself. "We can still do this. We could sneak you onto the plane beforehand, then my mom and I could get on."

"Unless he's watching you, too," I said.

"If he *is* watching me, then we need to give everyone the impression that what I'm doing has nothing to do with you."

"Like a diversion." An idea flashed into my head, and I knew instantly that it was the right one. "Crap."

"What's wrong?" Josh looked around, suddenly panicked.

We reached the passenger side of his car, and I leaned my elbows on the roof and contemplated a half-eaten Snickers bar stuck in the gutter. "I know what to do."

TWENTY-FIVE

Here's the thing about living in the entertainment capital of the world: if you're going to run a con, you have to do it right. That means production values, full costumes, down-to-the-second choreography. There's no show business without the show, after all, which is how I found myself in the elegant lavatory of Jessica Rebstock's Gulfstream jet on Friday after school, changing out of a flight attendant's uniform.

The skirt was navy blue and knee-length, with a matching suit jacket. The blouse was white and wide-collared, and the costume lady Gracia knew at Universal had topped off the whole ensemble with a red, white, and blue silk scarf tied around the neck like a cravat. She'd even offered little short-brimmed caps, but I had to draw the line somewhere.

When I emerged from the bathroom, now fully changed into simple shorts and a T-shirt, Gracia was waiting for me in one of the reclining leather chairs facing away from the cockpit, drinking an ice-cold Diet Coke, which the actual flight attendant had provided her.

"If all else fails," Gracia said, still in full uniform herself, "you can always go into air hostessing. Navy's a good color on you."

"You look like you should be filming something out in Van Nuys," I said, motioning to the leather, the varnished mahogany, the gold-plated seat-belt buckles, and Gracia's cleavage spilling out of a uniform that must have been sized for a prepubescent.

"I'll call it *Adventures in the Mile-High Club.*"

The interior of the jet was like a narrow suite. Rich leather seats, two facing each other on either side of the plane, plus a bench-type seat on the right side across from another recliner. Plush carpet, varnished wood panels at the front and back. "There's definitely room for that," I said, "even in the bathroom. It's huge. Obnoxiously huge."

Gracia rolled her eyes at me. "Please tell me you're not worried about the carbon footprint of the most awesome trip either one of us has ever taken."

With all the other things on my mind, I hadn't thought of it, but now that she mentioned—

"Mother Nature is going to forgive you on this one," Gracia said. "No, I take that back. She *wants* you to go. When she invented carbon emissions, this is exactly what she had in mind. She's ordered up clear blue skies, gentle breeze, sunsets that will blow your—"

"I get it. I get it."

"Let's hope so."

"Thanks for doing this," I said.

"I want you to know something," she said. "I under-stand. I understand that you told the boy about the break-in before you told me—"

"Gracia—"

"I would have come straight over. You know that, right?"

I nodded. Of course I knew that. I refolded each piece of the uniform and handed her the bundle, which she stuffed into her massive purse. Then I collapsed into the seat across from her. Our windows looked out to the tar-mac, and beyond it the ever-growing bank of paparazzi across the street.

By the time Gracia's driver had deposited us at the airport an hour earlier, three cars were already parked along the street opposite the tarmac entrance. A guy in jean shorts and a brown hoodie stood on the roof of a red 4Runner, setting up a camera with an enormous tele-photo lens on top of a tripod. He'd spun toward our car, camera at the ready, but he'd lost interest when Gracia and I had emerged from the car in our uniforms. We were only flight attendants, after all; we weren't somebody.

"Not that I don't enjoy a little dress-up from time to time," she said, smoothing the front of her skirt. "But one of these days you're going to tell me why we did it. And don't give me the 'I want to protect my privacy' nonsense. That may have worked with Josh's mom and Mimi, but give me a little credit."

My hand dropped to the top of my backpack on reflex. Everything we knew about the Golden Jaguar was inside, including my pictures of the disk. How easy it would have been to show her. I'd tell her about Cozumel and the Devil's Throat, and all the crap she'd ever given me about being interested in lost treasure would disappear. I wasn't a cute little idiot; I was audacious, independent, my own woman.

But I needed a friend, not a fight, so I had to wait. Even though I knew the longer I waited, the more furious she'd be when I finally told her the truth.

"Besides, I had nothing else to do," she said after a pause. "And Mimi wants to hit the Grove after this."

"Why do I feel so nervous?" I said. "I'm getting claustrophobic in here."

"Because you're playing on the varsity now. You have to get used to it. If you're going to be involved with him—"

"We're not involved—"

"Right. He's taking you to Hawaii because he wants to ace some stupid report."

The pilot ascended the short stairway and introduced himself. He was young and well built, and his hair was cropped extremely close, like he'd just left the military. "We're about ready," he said before closing the cockpit door behind him.

"Rebstock Air," Gracia said with a wink. "Our pilots are hot."

"Best slogan ever."

Gracia reached into her purse and pulled out a small package wrapped in pink tissue paper. "Don't open it until you get there."

"You didn't need to do this."

"Yes, I did," she said. "Trust me."

I tucked the gift into the front pocket of my backpack and zipped it up tight. I looked out the window to see six or seven paparazzi now set up across the street. "One little phone call from his mom's agent, and they all come running."

Gracia nodded. "My dad told me Larry Schuster's a bulldog."

Josh and I realized that we had to go over the top. We had to make it clear that Josh was going with his mother on a trip—and more to the point, if Wayo happened to be paying attention—that there was no indication that Josh and I were involved in anything together. We had to separate the *Josh* from the *me*. That meant making sure the paparazzi knew about the flight. And it also meant persuading Mimi to agree to a cameo role.

That part didn't turn out to be too hard.

The town car pulled onto the tarmac, which led to a frenzy from the paparazzi. Those who weren't standing on their roofs ran across the street with their cameras and stopped right at the edge of the airport property, snapping away.

Violet emerged from the front passenger side first. The rear door opened, and Josh's mom stepped out, then Josh. And finally Mimi.

"Here we go," I said. Gracia's face was only inches from the window, but I peeked just around the side.

Mimi reached for Josh's hand and held it close. She wore a red-and-black floral-print sundress, sleeveless and pleated, with a wide black belt that gave her virtually no torso; her legs seemed to sprout from beneath her chest. Her hair was vintage Mimi: blown straight, parted in the middle. There were even some new highlights, I noticed.

The sun was dipping down into the smog layer, giving everything a slightly golden hue; the pictures would look magical.

"This was your idea?" Gracia said.

I averted my eyes long enough to notice the driver unloading bags from the trunk. Mine was slightly more worn than the others, but still in good-enough shape to handle all my dive gear, plus some things I'd picked up from the shop.

Suddenly Mimi stopped Josh, spun him around, and leaned in. He ran his fingers through the back of her hair, cupped her head in his hands, and pulled her lips to his. To say their kiss was intense was like saying nuclear war would be unfortunate. Her hands massaged his entire back as they basically licked each other's faces off. If they didn't stop soon, I was worried they might asphyxiate each other.

Gracia whistled through her teeth. "Whatever your reason for doing it this way, I hope it was worth having to see that."

"Josh and I are looking for Hernán Cortés's Golden

Jaguar," I blurted in a whisper, still looking out the window at Mimi and Josh. "And we think it's somewhere near an ancient Polynesian sculpture garden off the coast of Molokai, but there's a guy named Wayo who tried to kill me in Cozumel, and we're worried that he might be watching us. So we had to throw him off the scent. That's why we couldn't risk my being seen getting on the plane with Josh. That's why you're wearing a porn star's flight attendant uniform."

Gracia stared at me. Then she cleared her throat. "Forget it. Tell me, don't tell me, I don't care anymore."

Before I could say anything else, Violet climbed the stairs. She walked right past us and tossed her purse onto the bench seat, collapsing next to it.

"Hi, Violet," I said. There was no response. Gracia raised her eyebrows and gave me the *sheesh* face.

Josh's mom was next. She gave me a little hello squeeze, but when she saw Gracia, she did a double take.

"I know, I know," Gracia said. "They got the sizing wrong."

"You look very nice," Jessica said, recovering.

"That's pretty good," Gracia said with a smile. "Your Oscar was well deserved."

Josh climbed the stairs and stopped at the open doorway to wave good-bye to Mimi.

"That's my cue," Gracia said, shouldering the bag that held my uniform as Jessica settled into the recliner across from Violet. "Mrs. Rebstock, it was lovely to see you."

"Hey, Gracia," Josh said.

Gracia snapped her fingers in front of her face. "Eyes up here, chief." She turned to me and said, "Good luck on your report."

Mimi climbed back into the town car, following the plan to perfection, not acknowledging Gracia as she walked past the car and into the terminal. The two of them would meet up a couple of blocks away, well out of the prying eyes of the paparazzi.

And then we were moving. The flight attendant brought me a water and Josh a Coke, no ice. He and I sat in recliners facing each other on the same side of the plane. The grin on his face seemed a little too self-satisfied for my taste.

"You want me to get you some floss?" I said.

"Huh?"

"You might have some pieces of her tongue stuck between your teeth."

For a moment there, I thought I saw a flash of regret or even embarrassment, but Josh quickly replaced it with his patented I'm-awesome-and-everybody-knows-it face. "I'm no expert at acting, but I figured we had to sell it."

Even if that's all it was—which I'm not sure Mimi would agree with—he had to have known that I was watching. And he didn't seem to care what I saw.

I knew in my head that doing it this way was worth seeing him and Mimi suck face, and my head also knew that he was right about having to sell it, but that didn't mean that my heart had to be on the same page.

My heart wanted to punch him in the face.

Take-off was almost unnoticeable, and soon we were at our cruising altitude, chasing the sun west, and whatever Molokai had in store for us was only hours away.

TWENTY-SIX

A fleet of polished black Jeeps awaited us at the airport, which was more a landing strip in the middle of a tropical jungle than an actual complex. We were greeted with fresh leis, live music, the whole deal. After a half-hour trip through the jungle in our luxury Jeeps—who knew there was such a thing—we passed through the gates of the five-star Hanauma Serenity Resort.

There are only around eight thousand people on Molokai, and according to Josh's mom, only one resort on the island is worth visiting. Lucky for us, it is on the northern shore, only a thirty-minute boat ride from the sculpture garden. I couldn't decide which I was more excited about: staying at a five-star tropical resort, having my own room in said resort, hanging out with Josh in said resort, or using said resort as the launching point in our search for the Jaguar.

The lobby was open to the breeze, providing a combination of exquisitely polished marble and billowing linen curtains. I expected that we might check in at the front desk, but there was no front desk. Instead, four bellmen were lined up beside a flower vase the size of a Smart Car. They wore cream-colored sport coats over yellow-and-blue Hawaiian shirts, and the moment we walked through the doorway, each of them approached one of us.

"If you'll follow me, Miss Fleet," one said.

I leaned in to Josh and whispered, "How does he know my name?"

"That's all Violet," Josh said. "She e-mails our pictures to the staff before we go anywhere. It's a nice touch, isn't it?"

Josh's mom put her hand on my shoulder like a politician. "Why don't we all get settled. We can meet back down here for dinner in an hour?"

I nodded, my mind coming to grips with the concept of individual bellmen who knew our names. I noticed our luggage being hustled on a cart behind us and through a set of doors, probably to a service elevator so the process was hidden. My bellman—Kenny—offered to take my backpack for me, but I politely declined.

"She's a little particular about her stuff," Josh said.

I blushed. I felt out of place enough as it was. I didn't need him making me look like a moron in front of everyone.

We each paired up with our designated servants, and while the others went down the hall one way, I followed

Kenny in the opposite direction to an elevator. As we rode the short trip to the second floor, he apologized profusely for not having enough beachfront rooms available on such short notice. I said I was pretty sure I'd be okay.

When he unlocked the door for me and held it open, I realized with some amazement that I didn't have my own room after all.

I had my own suite!

Two steps led to a sunken living room that spilled out onto a wide balcony overlooking the ocean. The entire floor was covered in a carpet so thick it might as well have been a beige cloud. A sitting area with a couch and matching chairs faced the balcony, and a gleaming wooden table took up much of the dining area behind the couch. Tucked around the side was a full kitchen—as if there were a grocery store within miles of this place— with a massive stove and copper pots hanging from a carved wooden rack on the wall.

White French doors opened to a bedroom dominated by a king-size bed. A fifty-inch television took up half the wall opposite the bed, but the notion that anyone would want to watch TV at a place like this seemed preposterous.

Kenny opened the closet door and pointed to a small steel box with a keypad on the door. "That's the safe for your valuables."

"It's a little late for that," I said.

"I'm sorry?"

Then I almost asked him how he knew I was planning on coming back with any valuables, but I was able to stop myself and cover it with a laugh. God, I was the worst at playing it cool in the history of playing it cool. I unzipped my backpack and searched for my wallet. "Do I . . . I mean, what's the . . . ?"

"It's been taken care of, Miss Fleet," Kenny said.

"Please, call me Annie."

"Of course. If you need anything at all during your stay with us—day or night—please don't hesitate to call."

I felt a strange urge to act like this was no big deal, to pretend that I stayed at five-star resorts all the time. But as Kenny in his linen sport coat opened the door, I couldn't take it anymore. I had to tell somebody.

"This place is amazing!" I pointed out the windows to the ocean. And yes, I admit it: I squealed. "Have you ever seen anything as gorgeous in your entire life?"

Kenny smiled.

"Rhetorical question," I said, clearing my throat. "Of course you have."

Kenny backed through the door with another wide smile. "Enjoy your stay, Miss Fleet."

"Thanks, Kenny."

After he left, I locked my turtle pendant and all my research safely inside the private safe, which made me feel all stealthy and important. If only we'd had one of them at home.

I thought about going down to eat with everyone else, but I wasn't quite ready for that. I needed to gawk at the view and gape at the flowers and roll around on the bed and laugh and marvel at the fact that I had just flown on a private jet. And I had to be free to do all of that without reservation.

"You sure?" Josh said when I called him. "We have a big day tomorrow."

"All the more reason to get some sleep."

I was hungry, though. I lifted the phone and pressed the little button with a fork and knife on it. Immediately, a cheerful voice on the other end said, "Good evening, Miss Fleet."

"It's Annie, please," I said. "I can't find a menu."

"That's not a problem. What are you in the mood for?"

"What do you mean? Is there a menu?"

"We'd be happy to prepare whatever you'd like," she said with a chuckle that was remarkably non-patronizing.

"You mean, if I wanted cornflakes and oysters with a side of goat cheese—"

"We would certainly make that happen, yes."

I thought for a moment. "Do you have hamburgers?"

"Yes, ma'am."

"How much are they?"

"It's all been taken care of," said Cheerful Room-Service Voice.

I was a hundred yards from the sea; by all rights I should have wanted a fish of some sort. Or lobster, and maybe caviar, considering that my stay had been taken care of. But I ordered a burger, medium rare, with a side of fruit and homemade sweet-potato chips anyway. The planet would have to forgive me, just this once.

I texted Gracia: *My burger = massive carbon footprint*

:-(btw whats the most thread count of any sheets you've ever slept in?

I stepped onto the balcony. It was dark out, with only a sliver of moon rising above the cliffs ahead. The wide beach was spread out in front of me; small waves broke against the sand with a rhythmic gurgle. Massive banana trees swayed in the breeze. The air tasted of salt water and something else, something sweet and tropical.

My phone buzzed with Gracia's response: *u aren't supposed to sleep in those sheets! go get him!*

Before I knew it, Kenny was at the door with my food—a burger of fresh ground Kobe beef grilled over imported mesquite wood coals, as he informed me—which was literally served on a silver platter.

My dad might have thought that real people didn't live this way, but real people didn't dive for lost treasure, either. I took my burger onto the balcony and gazed out at the cove below, steeling myself for the task ahead. If Josh was right about the sculpture garden, our discovery of the Golden Jaguar was possibly—astonishingly—only hours away.

TWENTY-SEVEN

I awoke the next morning to the light spilling in through the translucent curtains. It was early, but exhilaration tightened my chest; I couldn't sleep any longer, no matter how high the thread count of my sheets.

I was about to go down for breakfast when I remembered Gracia's present, and I laughed out loud when I opened it: a bikini. The fabric was both soft and tightly elastic, a shimmering light blue like the shadows of sunlight on rippling water. Boy-short bottoms—for my active lifestyle, of course—with a wide-strapped, triangle halter top.

I put it on and checked myself out in the bathroom's full-length mirror. This was only a billion times better than the lesson suit; it might as well have been stitched out of magic. I thought about sending Gracia a picture, but I didn't need myself to go viral, so I decided on a simple thank-you text instead.

I plastered on sunscreen like a good girl and threw on

my shorts and a top and went downstairs.

The restaurant was as ridiculous as the suite. Three levels cascading toward an open wall overlooking the ocean and the jagged black cliffs, impossibly green and lush at the top. The breeze came just enough to carry the scent of seawater without rustling any of the enormous tropical floral arrangements—birds-of-paradise that were larger than my head.

Violet sat alone on the bottom level, reading a book. I went down and put my hand on the chair across the table from her. "Mind if I join you?"

She looked up, nodded, but didn't say anything and went back to her book. I sat. A waiter appeared tableside before I'd pulled in my chair, and coffee was served. I stirred milk and pink fake sugar into it while I thought of something to say.

Violet seemed to sense the deliberateness with which I swizzled, because she finally broke the silence. "I shouldn't even be here right now."

I looked out onto the crescent-shaped beach, the sand white as flour, the gently rolling turquoise waves. "Yeah, this is awful."

"You seem like a nice person, Annie, so I'm going to give you some advice. The glitz and the glamour feels great, I'm sure. The private plane, the king-size bed. This." She gestured to the ocean with her paperback. "But remember one thing: the whole business is built on illusion. And if you're not the one creating the illusion, then you're always going to be at its whim."

"What's wrong?"

"I was supposed to go to Catalina this weekend with my boyfriend—" She stopped and looked up as though seeing me for the first time. "Did you just ask me what was wrong?"

"Yeah, why?"

She nodded, and then her features softened, and she took a sip of fresh-squeezed, five-star orange juice. She smiled at me and said, "Look, I don't need to babysit you guys. Jessica had me book her spa treatments all day, so you're on your own. Just don't die, and everyone will be okay."

"Thanks."

"She's not that bad. A little overwhelming."

"So I've seen."

"Dinner is at seven tonight. Whatever you and Josh do, wherever you go, just don't be late."

"I promise we won't die."

"Fair enough. Now, if you don't mind, I'm going to take the world's longest bath while I pretend to keep tabs on you."

She took her juice with her, leaving me alone with a basket of fresh-baked breakfast rolls to contemplate what lay ahead. According to what Josh and I had been able to come up with, the sculpture garden was in about fifty feet of water off the coast of Ha'upu Bay. We planned on two dives: the first to get a general sense of the area, and the second to explore any areas of interest in greater detail.

I was unexpectedly anxious about diving with Josh for

the first time. I knew that whatever he felt about diving would have nothing to do with me as a person, but I couldn't shake the feeling that his not enjoying his dives would make me look bad. I'd wanted us to be able to share Cozumel as an experience, and that didn't work out at all. It was stupid, I knew, especially since we weren't exactly going on a pleasure dive, but even so—

"You ready?" he said, sliding into the seat across from me. I couldn't tell if he'd showered or not; his hair looked the same either way. "We missed you at dinner last night. Lobster and mahimahi."

My orange juice arrived; I downed half of it in one luscious gulp. "I suppose I'm glad that you talked me into this."

"Right. I twisted your arm." Josh asked the waiter for a peeled mango on a stick and said to me, "They have the freshest fruit here."

"Imagine that."

A boat pulled up to the dock outside. In addition to giving the concierge a picture of Wayo from our spring-break trip and asking him to keep an eye out—thankfully, the trip so far had been Wayo-free—Josh had asked him to arrange for a private dive trip. No dive master, just a boat and a captain. There was reluctance when the concierge found out where we wanted to go, but Josh could be very persuasive, as I knew, and before long we had our very own boat and a captain to go along with it.

"That's us," he said. "Now we just have to figure out how to get rid of Violet."

"Already done," I said. "We have until seven p.m."

Josh reached across the table and speared my last wedge of cantaloupe. "Look at you, pulling your weight."

"The only thing is, we can't die."

"Or she'll kill us."

"Something like that."

I carried my gear down to the dock after breakfast, but Josh's new stuff was already on the boat. And wow, had he gone all out. Poseidon regulator, Zeagle BC, three-hundred-dollar fins. Apparently, when you've got the means to take a private jet to a dive location, you're not going to blink about spending a few grand on your equipment.

"Check this out," he said, gesturing with his half-eaten mango.

At the stern of the boat were two torpedo-shaped diver propulsion vehicles—DPVs—battery-powered underwater scooters with handles on either side of an encased propeller.

"Are those for us?"

"Yep. Bought them last night. Had 'em charged up and everything. I saw this movie with Navy SEALs in it when I was a kid—"

"We're not exactly planning an underwater assault."

"Not literally, maybe. Anyway, I've always wanted to try one."

I was torn between a witty—but admittedly snarky—comment about how annoying he was, and a compliment for buying gear that would allow us to search a wider area. "I'm not the only one pulling my weight," I said, going for non-snarky.

"You know how to use them, right?"

"Please," I said, pointing to my chest. "That hurts me to the core."

The boat was no bigger—though considerably nicer—than Wayo's runabout. The brilliant yellow canopy was new, and the reflection of a fresh coat of paint sparkled in the water. Our captain was a local named Goofy. He was short and sinewy, with a single deep crease across his forehead whenever he raised his eyebrows, which was all the time.

Captain Goofy took my gear, helped me onto the boat, and pushed off. "We'd best get there early." Just saying the words seemed to make him uncomfortable.

The sun sparkled already, and the air was thick and tropical, so I kicked off my shorts and pulled my T-shirt over my head. I felt Josh's eyes on me, but I did my best not to look his way, focusing instead on rolling the shirt, then the shorts, and stuffing them in my dry bag. Finally, I tucked the dry bag away and looked back at the resort as it disappeared behind a cliff.

"Nice suit," Josh said, taking me in. He stood, absorbing the motion of the boat with bent knees, holding on to the canopy bar with one arm. Before I could thank him, he said, "You could use a tan, though."

"I hate you," I said.

Josh slurped on the mango, the thick yellow juice dripping from his grin. "No, you don't."

Damn if he wasn't right about that.

"How much do you know of the island's history?" Captain Goofy said.

I shared a knowing look with Josh. "A little," I said. "Not too much."

"Molokai is so much more than a leper colony," the captain said, shaking his head.

Josh nearly choked on his mango. "I'm sorry?"

"It was, almost a hundred and fifty years ago, but still, when people think of Molokai, they think of Father Damien. Yes, he was made into a saint. It's a great story. But a saint who cared for lepers doesn't drive tourism, if you know what I mean."

We didn't have to know what he meant to agree with him.

The boat sliced through the water. For all of Josh's bluster, I could tell that he was getting nervous. Was it about the dive? About the treasure? Theoretically, it was my job as the more experienced diver to get him to calm down, but how was I supposed to do that if I was just as nervous as he was?

"They call me 'Goofy' because of how I surf, okay?" the captain said, as if sensing, and misinterpreting, our unease. "It's no big deal."

We rounded a promontory into Ha'upu Bay, and my legs went completely boneless. There it was. The exact image on the disk. Jagged rocks piercing the water like a family of sharks, massive cliffs in the background. The surf broke against the rocks in short clouds of white water; one of them looked like a vanilla ice-cream cone smashed down onto a bright blue plate.

Josh pinched me. I wasn't dreaming, but I was so giddy that I couldn't do anything but pinch him back.

"The sculpture garden is one of our great mysteries. How did they get the stone for the sculptures? How did they position them fifty feet below the ocean? Fascinating, like the Moai on Easter Island."

The captain slowed the engine. We approached the cove at about half speed, the shark-fin towers now looming above us like skyscrapers.

"There's no diving allowed here," he said. "It's a cultural preservation site, so please hurry. I don't want to lose my license."

"It's going to be fine," Josh said. But no matter how much Josh had paid him, the captain didn't seem any more receptive to the movie-star-kid nonchalance than I was.

We nestled the boat between the rocks jutting out of the surface, about a hundred feet offshore. The captain pointed to a thin strip of water cascading down the face of a cliff that must have been at least three hundred feet tall. "You'll find the garden about thirty feet to the right of the waterfall. I'm staying here; I don't want to get any closer to those rocks than I have to."

"No problem," I said.

"Are you sure you can navigate your way back?" The captain squinted at me as though he didn't trust the rating on my certification card. "A surface swim is not advisable, even in these conditions."

Before I had the chance to scoff at him, a low, whining siren pierced the morning air. We heard the sound before we saw the boat it came from: STATE POLICE in bright red letters across the hull.

A distant and crackly—yet decidedly agitated—voice traveled across the water. "To the small vessel. Please cut your engine *immediately*."

"You guys might want to go book a massage," the captain said. He flipped a switch, and the engine went silent.

TWENTY-EIGHT

"We're doing a research report for school," Josh said. He splashed *innocence* all over his face and held up an underwater camera I'd never seen before—you couldn't say that he hadn't outfitted himself. "It's no big deal."

The police boat was almost twice as big as ours, with a two-tiered observation deck above the wheelhouse. The hull's deep blue paint reflected off the lighter blue water, as if it were casting a shadow in plain sunlight. A uniformed policeman—short-sleeved white shirt, knee-length blue shorts, baseball cap, sunglasses, radio, gun—stood at the bow, perching one leg atop a locked trunk like a pirate captain. His partner stood at the helm behind the wheelhouse glass.

To be so close! Just sixty feet below us was the sculpture garden, and with it . . . who knew?

"This area is off limits. Unless you happen to have permission from the governor himself, you are not allowed here." He shot our captain a devilish glare that made the captain clear his throat and turn away. "I'm going to give you—"

"The concierge at Hanauma said we could dive here, no problem," Josh said, lying. When he'd told the concierge what we wanted, it had taken five of the who-knows-how-many crisp hundred-dollar bills Josh carried in his wallet for him just to call Captain Goofy.

"This area is under the jurisdiction of the Hawaii state police. Not local PD. And certainly not the concierge of a resort."

Something clicked in my head, a little piece of the puzzle falling into place, and I jumped into action as if hit with a cattle prod.

"Hold on, just a second." I scrambled through my dry bag, finally finding my cell phone. The signal was low, but it was there. Eight a.m. in Hawaii meant eleven in LA, so there was a good chance she was awake, even though it was Saturday. While the policeman continued to berate our poor captain, I wandered away from them and toward the stern of Goofy's boat.

"Mimi?" I said when she answered. "I need a favor. Fast."

"Another one? You should see the pictures from yesterday. They're already all over the Internet."

"I'm sure that's killing you."

"That's not the point. How's Josh?" she said. "Did you guys, you know—"

"Mimi—"

"If I'm going to get plastered all over the tabloids so you can get a little Honolulu nookie, the least you can do is tell me what—"

"Can you stop? I don't have time to argue with you about this right now."

Mimi's annoyance was unmistakable. "What?"

I gave the policeman an apologetic smile and held my thumb and index finger about half an inch apart. The look in Josh's eyes as he argued unsuccessfully with the policeman was one of disbelief, as if he'd never even considered the possibility that his devastating charm would find its kryptonite.

I said to Mimi, "A while ago you said your parents were throwing a party for the governor of Hawaii. Do they actually know him?"

"I thought you didn't want to use your connections," she said.

"Can you call me a hypocrite when we get back, please?"

When she finally let me explain what I needed, she agreed to make the call, on one condition. "Yes," I said. "I'll spill it. Everything you want to know."

I asked the cops to give us five minutes, and with nothing to do but wait and hope, Josh and I prepped our gear. This seemed to make the police even angrier. Not only were these punk kids not immediately leaving the scene, but they had the nerve to act like they'd be allowed to dive anyway!

I pretended not to hear their grumbling, and focused

only on my equipment. BC onto the tank, regulator properly attached to the valves. I was glad to have my own gear for this: computer, compass, small knife, dive light. I clipped Josh's camera to a D-ring on my other shoulder strap. I couldn't help but be impressed by Josh. He was so much more comfortable around the equipment; he bore no relation to the guy who'd nearly killed himself in the pool.

I checked the battery level of the DPVs, trying to make it look like I knew what I was doing, but no matter the impression I'd given Josh, everything I knew about the scooters came from watching the certification videos and tooling around on our rental unit in the shop pool. I could have taken it out into the Pacific, I guess, but I was saving my first experience for clearer waters, where I could see. Warmer waters, where I didn't have to swim with a bulky wetsuit.

Now that I was here, the question was, would I get to use it?

The policeman hung two large inflated rings from the edge of his boat and lashed the two boats together. Captain Goofy still wasn't allowed to touch the throttle, so at least this way the police boat could keep us all from drifting against the rocks.

My phone rang, a number I didn't recognize, from an 808 area code. I handed it to the officer. "I think this is going to be for you."

He glared at me as he answered. "Yes, sir . . . Yes, I understand. . . . Of course . . . Thank you, sir." By the time he gave me back my phone, he was a hundred times angrier than when he'd first arrived.

"I don't know who you are, but you've got an hour. If you break the surface one second late, I *will* arrest you for trespassing. Are we clear?"

We were clear.

I set the timer on my dive computer to go off after thirty minutes, established a compass bearing toward a spot thirty feet to the right of the cliffside waterfall, and with no time to waste, Josh and I dropped backward into the water. When we bobbed to the surface, Captain Goofy handed us each a DPV, and we descended.

The visibility was spectacular. With the ocean floor at only sixty feet, and white sand at that, it was as though the area were being lit both from above and below. Down here, we could see that the shark-fin rocks were like icebergs below the surface: gnarled pillars of rock and coral that became gradually wider before finally disappearing into the sandy bottom. Small tropical fish surrounded them like little airplanes buzzing around King Kong.

When we reached the floor, Josh added air to his BC without my having to tell him to; he hovered fairly well, neutrally buoyant, and I gave him the okay sign. He gave it back, but from the look in his eyes, he was better than okay.

I was, too. I belonged here—not in the halls of the school, not with my friends around egging me on, but here. And we were alone. And I was responsible for the look in his eyes. There are always kids who want to be the ones to introduce you to booze, or weed, or more. They seem to get some sort of thrill out of taking you past your boundaries. That was me now.

I gave him one last okay, then checked my compass bearing and motioned for him to come alongside me with his DPV. I engaged the trigger, and a high-pitched whine suddenly interrupted the hushed silence. The DPV pulled me forward with a slight jolt, and in seconds I was parallel to the ocean floor. I heard Josh engage his scooter, and we were off.

If current diving made me feel like I was gliding, then holding on to the scooter was more like spaceflight; I could actually feel the scooter pulling at my arms. I was probably going at about three knots, much faster than I could have kicked. The water tugged slightly at my regulator as it pushed past my face.

Josh screamed.

I turned to him, expecting to see a shark or a bad guy with a speargun, but he just gave me the okay sign. His was a scream of joy. I squealed back at him.

I found out quickly that if I leaned in one direction, I could make gradual banking turns, almost as if I were on a roller coaster, and so I serpentined just above the bottom, careful to keep the propeller wash from stirring up the silt. Two minutes into the dive, a series of massive stone columns appeared in the distance as if from a lifting fog. The sculpture garden.

The pictures Josh had found did no justice to the size of the pillars. Each one was at least fifteen feet tall and as wide around as a large tree. Some lay on their sides, some protruded from the floor at a slight angle, and one was perfectly vertical. No wonder the place was protected by the government. If everyone were allowed to dive here, it would take a bunch of yahoos—like Josh, I had to say, given the hooting and hollering he was doing as he weaved in and out of the garden—hardly a week to destroy it.

It had been nearly three decades since the archaeologists had restored them, so the sea was well on its way to reclaiming the pillars as artificial reefs. Even so, I could still make out—underneath the coral that had begun to encrust one of them—the faint image of the three crowns from Cortés's family shield.

Partly to keep up our cover story, but mostly because the pillars were amazing, I unclipped the camera and snapped some pictures while I held on to the scooter with one hand. After a couple of shots, though, I didn't bother looking at the viewfinder. Instead, I kept my eyes out for something—anything—that didn't seem to belong.

Near the cliff wall, I spied a wooden stake, slightly mangled at the end as though it had been hammered into the sand. When I moved closer to investigate, I noticed a pear-shaped opening in the stone wall, wide at the bottom and then tapering closed as it rose, like a curtain being peeked through. In contrast to the rest of the ocean floor, it looked like the sand around the stake had been disturbed, and recently.

I disengaged the scooter and set it aside. I fell gently until my knees touched the seafloor. The stake felt like wood when I pulled it out—there was hardly any algae growth at all. It couldn't have been there for more than a few days. My air started to taste of adrenaline.

Josh cut off his scooter, but he didn't exactly nestle down. By the time he figured out to empty the air from his BC, there was a fine mist of silt floating up to our waists. I removed a slate from one of my BC pockets and wrote: *Did u see anything around sculptures?*

He shook his head.

I pointed to the opening and wrote: *U ok to go in here?*

His eyes went wide behind the mask.

I confirmed the time on my computer. Forty-six minutes before we were due back. I checked my air gauge and then his. The scooters had made it so we hardly had to do any work, so there was plenty of air left for both of us. The only problem, and it was a big one, was that Josh didn't have a dive light. I took his scooter from him and placed it on the ground.

I wrote: *Trust me. OK?*

The eyes didn't get any less wide, but he gave me the okay sign anyway. I put away the slate and removed a safety reel with bright yellow twine. There was nothing else I could find to attach the twine, so I clipped it securely to Josh's scooter handle and wedged the DPV against a small outcropping on the cliff wall.

I don't know what happened next.

One second I was motioning for him to hold my ankles, and then I was hyperventilating, my vision blurry and my heart racing. No matter how hard I breathed, it wasn't enough. I needed more air. I was choking.

TWENTY-NINE

flailed my arms behind my neck, reaching for my tank valve, but I couldn't reach it, and my fingers weren't working enough to unclip the front of my BC.

I needed more air.

A cloud of silt surrounded me. I wanted no part of that little sliver in the rock. That opening. I couldn't go in. Who knew what waited in the darkness? What if Wayo was in there?

I felt hands on my shoulders and screamed. The explosion of bubbles from my regulator blinded me.

But it was Josh. He shook me once, gently, and motioned for me to calm down. The silt around us began to settle, and I could see more clearly. Josh brought his hands up to his chest and pushed down. Repeated the movement slowly. *Breathe in. Breathe out.*

He reached for my dive slate and wrote: *I am here.*

I nodded. The terror had subsided, only to be replaced by the inevitable shame that Josh had seen me that way.

Are u ok?

I nodded. One more deep breath, and I knew we had to get moving. I clipped the reel onto my D-ring and motioned for Josh to come around behind me. I pointed to my ankles and made a motion with my hands, like "grab on hard." He did, and I engaged the scooter and pointed it toward the opening. As soon as we went inside, darkness overcame us, and I fought another wave of panic. I held the scooter handle with one hand and the flashlight with the other. Josh was a presence behind me, his hands gripping my ankles with more force than I'd planned for.

I decided to be grateful that it was dark; had Josh been able to see me from this position, Gracia's bikini gift would not have left much to the imagination. As it was, I knew he couldn't see anything, and given the strength of his grip, he was probably too nervous to fantasize about anything other than making it out of this cavern alive. Probably.

With the scooter pulling the two of us, we went more slowly, which gave me the chance to shine my light across the cavern walls. It must have been a lava tube; the walls were jagged with pockets like craters from popped bubbles. The width of the tube varied wildly. At times it was no wider than a hallway, but occasionally it opened up into rooms so big I could hardly see the sides. We turned so many times I lost count, but I could tell that the bottom followed a gentle slope upward. We were ascending.

I shined my light quickly down onto the reel—the

twine was halfway gone. We were about a hundred feet from the opening.

When I pointed the light forward again, directly in front of me was a solid white wall. I couldn't see through it. Flashes of silver. I yelped, instinctively releasing the scooter's trigger. Robbed of our forward momentum, we began to sink. Josh squeezed so hard I thought my feet were going to fall off.

I passed my light back and forth in front of me, and what had been a solid wall became a living thing. Expanding and contracting, as if breathing. Pulsating back and forth. Darting.

A wall of tiny fish.

I hit the trigger again, and the scooter nearly leaped out of my hand, and we jolted forward, the fish parting at the last second, my flashlight like high beams through a snowstorm.

A heart-stopping ten seconds later, the cloud parted, and the tube became wider. The walls were slightly visible even where I wasn't shining my flashlight, and up ahead, in the distance, there was literally a light at the end of the tunnel.

I kept my finger securely on the DPV's throttle, and soon the bottom of the cavern floor pitched up at a steeper incline. The light was above us now, shimmering on the other side of the water's surface.

I bent my legs and reached behind me for Josh's hand. He came around the front, and we kicked up together.

We broke the surface, and I motioned for him to keep the regulator in his mouth, but when I saw a shaft of light from a cleft in the ceiling about twenty feet overhead, I figured that the air was okay to breathe.

"Congratulations," I said. "You've just satisfied the requirements for your totally insane, scooter-propelled, cave dive certification."

Josh spat his regulator out. "I don't think I can feel my fingers."

"And thanks," I said, looking away. It didn't seem right to ignore the part about me freaking out, no matter how much I wanted to. "For the—"

"Stop," he said, waving me away. "I'm just glad I faked it well enough for you to trust me."

I hefted the DPV out of the water and laid it gently on the flat expanse of coarse rock that passed for a shore. We climbed out and removed our gear. The light from above made it almost like dusk inside the room, so my flashlight was helpful but not essential. The trickle of running water came from somewhere.

I laid my BC and tank gently on the ground but left the reel connected; there was less than a half-inch of twine left. "We're about a hundred and fifty feet from the entrance."

The floor was rough and sharp in places—all the tiny holes reminded me of a dried sponge—but it was slick, too, so while our booties protected our feet from the sharp rock, the rubber soles made it more slippery. We had to take short, gentle steps.

"When do you think was the last time someone was in here?" Josh said.

"I bet the locals know all about this place. The question is, when was the last time someone was in here with the same goal as us?"

"That wooden stake at the entrance?"

"It could have been an anchor for a line like—"

And that's when we saw it. On the floor toward the rear of the cavern, away from the water, was a pickax.

"No way," I said.

A metal spike and a small sledgehammer lay next to a pile of jagged stone. I shined my light in the corner, hoping that the shadow on the wall was just a shadow, but I knew better.

The cavern wall was gouged, with a pile of rock on the floor beneath. The damage to the wall was extensive; I could have wedged myself inside. I bent down and sifted through the pile of stones below; some were brittle, flat, and thin, like shards of broken glass. I noticed carvings on one side. I found a big-enough piece, and the design was unmistakable: a two-headed bird from the neck up. The crest of Cortés.

I grabbed the pickax and swung it as hard as I could against the ground. My hands went instantly numb as the vibrations rattled up the handle, and I screamed, as much from frustration as from pain. In a room of solid rock, the sound built upon itself, growing exponentially.

My chest heaved as the sound lingered before silence

came to the cavern once more. I wobbled, unsteady on my feet.

"Did you think it was going to be easy?" Josh said gently. "That we'd just hop a private jet down to Hawaii over the weekend and be back with a hundred million dollars' worth of treasure by Monday?"

Of course not. Okay, yes. Maybe.

It was stupid, I know, but everything came so easy to him that maybe I hoped it would rub off on me somehow. Even being in Hawaii with him in the first place—the jet, the resort, the diving—seemed more like fantasy than reality. What was a little treasure on top of all that?

I grabbed one of my fins and laid it on the rough lava right next to the water and sat down on it, sticking my feet in the water up to my calves.

"I don't know what I thought," I said.

Josh came over and sat on the jagged ground next to me. "Do you see anything in here that looks like the other side of the disk?"

I looked back at the rock pile. The space that had been hacked out was large, about the size of a refrigerator, but nowhere deep enough to have hidden a twice-life-sized statue of any animal bigger than a ferret.

"So it wasn't the Jaguar," I said. "Another clue maybe, but not the Jaguar."

Josh gave me a crooked smile and put his fists on top of each other and swung once, imitating my pickax maneuver. "I love it when you get all feisty."

My heart was thrashing—the excitement of the dive, the disappointment, the Josh.

"Besides, at least we know something was here." He gave me a wink and said, "Not to mention we pretty much disproved the whole James-Cook-discovered-Hawaii nonsense."

I wasn't exactly feeling what you'd call sexy, not after coming up short yet again. But in the dim light of the cave, my lack of tan wasn't as noticeable as it was outside. Josh reached a tentative hand out and patted my thigh— Did he leave it there a fraction longer than gentle and reassuring?

My fingertips trembled. I made fists.

"Sorry if I held on too hard," he said.

My god. It was going to happen. Here. It was my new swimsuit; Gracia was a miracle worker. It suddenly felt way too stuffy in the cavern, and I glanced up behind me to make sure that nothing was blocking the opening above.

"I'd never swum through a minnow cloud before," I said.

"That was pretty awesome."

Did he just scoot toward me, or was he in pain and shifting his weight because he'd made the mistake of not sitting on a fin?

I became more nervous than my body knew what to do with. This was a guy who had dated princesses. This was a guy who'd walked the red carpet, who had profiles written about him in magazines. What if really rich people went to kissing school or had hook-up tutors? How far behind the curve was I going to be?

Shut up, self. Stop it. We are alone. Nobody is peeking through the keyhole.

He leaned to me. Stopped. Smiled. I smiled back.

It happened. His lips on mine. Tentatively at first, so gently that I thought I might have been imagining it. Then again, and my nervousness vanished. The slight taste of the ocean. I kissed him right back.

Forget that talk about how things never happen in real life the way they happen in the movies; this was as Hollywood a moment as I was ever going to have.

A high-pitched beep filled the space. Shattering the silence.

Was it my alarm clock? Waking me up from a dream? Was I even here?

"What the hell is that?" Josh said, pulling back. He was startled, almost uncomfortable, as though he'd just been caught cheating on a test.

I faced forward and rested my elbows on my knees, letting my head fall into my open palms. I thought briefly about ignoring the beep, about sacrificing the future for the present. But even if I'd been willing to do that, it wouldn't have been any use. The moment was ruined.

"That's my dive computer." I stood on the jagged rock and walked gingerly to my gear. "Come on."

"You okay?"

Sure. No problem. Just the double disappointment of being beaten to a treasure site and having to cut short our first make-out session. "We have thirty minutes to get back to the boat before we're arrested."

THIRTY

I leaned on my balcony, observing the dinner setup as the sun cast ribbons of golden light across the bay. An open space just off the beach had been converted to the outdoor dining area. Men in Hawaiian shirts set up instruments on an elevated stage across the polished dance floor from a thatched-roof tiki bar. An animal of some sort was being roasted on a huge spit over an open flame. Waiters arranged circular tables around the dance floor, white tablecloths billowing down.

This phenomenal dinner was only an hour away, and a sense of dread was building inside me with every creeping minute.

After we'd returned to the boat, sliding under the cops' curfew by no more than five minutes, Josh and I had hardly said a word to each other. I couldn't tell whether it was disappointment at not finding what we'd come for or regret at having kissed me, but Josh spent the return trip to the hotel sitting near the bow, staring off into the distance. We were tired, and sunbaked, and we'd agreed to see each other at dinner.

Once I'd made sure our research was still in the safe—it was—I'd napped, soaked myself to a raisin in the Jacuzzi-sized bathtub, flipped through the channels on the television I swore I'd never watch, and napped again, but I couldn't get rid of the knot in the center of my stomach. Did I feel it because of what we hadn't found? Or because of what we had done?

So there I was, resting my elbows on the balcony railing, contemplating the answers to those questions and watching beautiful women in hula skirts and bikini tops rehearsing with muscular, shirtless men what I could only assume was a traditional Polynesian dance, when I heard a knock at my door.

"Miss Fleet," Kenny said, sporting his patented smile. He held a cloth garment bag in one hand and a cream-colored envelope in the other. "I have a delivery for you."

"Why, Mr. Kenny. You shouldn't have." I ushered him inside.

"Technically, I didn't," he said. "Where would you like me to put it?"

My grin was bordering on cartoonish. "Where do people usually choose?"

He started toward the bedroom, but quickly—though subtly—veered away when he noticed the unmade bed. He draped the garment bag across the back of the couch in the living area, then turned to me and handed me the envelope. "I hope you enjoy the show tonight. Our fire dance is quite something." He gave me a little bow. "I'll leave you to it."

I thanked him, and the door latch echoed through the silent room. My eyes bounced from the envelope in my hand to the garment bag on the couch and back again. I decided to attack the envelope first.

I tore it open to find a handwritten note on Hanauma Serenity Resort stationery:

> Dear Annie,
> Thanks for not dying today. See you at dinner.
>   XOXO,
>   Violet

I crept toward the garment bag and opened it slowly. Something shiny and aquamarine was inside. A dress. What was Violet doing sending me a dress?

I carried it into the bathroom with two hands—cradled it, really, as though it were a sleeping baby. I unfurled the dress and stepped into it instead of putting it over my head, so it wouldn't bunch and wrinkle, and when I looked up, the only thing I could do was laugh. One quick "Ha!" before I covered my mouth in disbelief.

The dress was something of a phenomenon. Fancy without being obnoxious, it fit me better than anything in my closet. It was sleeveless, with just the right amount of width at the straps so that my shoulders looked broad but not like a linebacker's, and it tapered in at the waist and fell just above the knees.

And the fabric. It was light and flowing, pure silk. The color changed depending on which direction I turned; sometimes it was deep blue with hints of silver, other times it took on more of a dark emerald color. The design itself was vaguely ocean-inspired, with the four or five inches above the hem resembling the roiling foam of a wave crashing against the shore and the foam gradually giving way to the solid colors as it moved up toward the waist.

The person standing in the mirror was like the Annie Fleet from an alternate universe.

I'd always liked to think that I'd be the same if my family had money, that I would love the ocean and diving and be friends with the same people. That I would still be me, basically, but with better dive gear. I didn't *need* all those fancy clothes. I didn't *need* to go on exotic vacations where the bellmen knew my name before I even got there. But now, seeing myself like this, I had to admit I felt different. Not better, definitely not worse, but different.

I retrieved my pendant from the safe. The scoop of the dress was just low enough that the turtle hung against my skin an inch from the fabric. The only problem was that this outfit screamed for thin-strapped sandals, but all I had in the sandal department were my old black flip-flops.

There was something I definitely needed to do before dinner. I'd been reluctant to send Gracia pictures of my new swimsuit, but this was a whole different story.

I texted a few quick pictures; she called no more than ten seconds later.

"Shut up," she said.

"I know!"

"Is that Prada?"

"I didn't see a tag. Maybe? How would I know?"

"Seriously, what the hell?"

I felt drunk, like I had nitrogen narcosis on the surface. I tried to tell Gracia, but it took me a few tries before I was able to stop myself from giggling. The island, the resort, the upcoming dinner with tiki torches and hula band. When I got to the kiss with Josh—leaving out the real purpose of our cavern dive, of course—it was like I was trying to walk through a pounding surf. Every time I got a few steps forward, silly laughter would crash over me, and I'd have to stop, take a deep breath, and start again.

"Annie Fleet," Gracia said when I'd finally gotten it all out, "you are going to have yourself a magical time tonight. There's no way around it."

Contemplating my reflection, it occurred to me that my new dress had the potential to swallow me up. "What do I do about my hair, though? Makeup?"

Gracia *tsk*ed me through the phone. "A dress like that's going to do all the work for you. Your job is to let it happen. No makeup. Just a little gloss. You have gloss, right?"

"Yes, Gracia. I have gloss."

"What do I know? Maybe no gloss is part of your eco-chick persona."

"I don't have a persona."

"Everyone has a persona," she said. "But, whatever. The hair is simple, too. You have amazing natural highlights, Annie. It's going to be perfect."

"Dirty-blond qualifies as highlights?"

"Would you stop? You're active, you're on the go. Accentuate what you already have. Go with the tousled beachy look."

"Okay," I said. "That's good."

"You're not going to go all glamour on us, are you?"

"Nah." I couldn't stop checking myself out in the mirror. "But it's nice to know I have it in me."

"What do you think we've been trying to tell you?"

"There's a dance floor down there. With tiki torches and a hula band. What do I do?"

"He'll ask you to dance. But be careful. He's going to stick his butt out in order to hide his excitement, if you know what I mean."

"Gross, Gracia."

"I'm just saying. Be prepared to pretend not to notice. You don't want to make him more self-conscious than he'll already be."

"Any word from Baldwin?" I said, eager to change the subject. Gracia said nothing, but there was something in the nothing that felt like something. "Is he there? Laugh once if he's there right now."

"Ha!" she said. "That's a good one."

"You little tramp. I bet he's showing you his hard drive as we speak, isn't he?"

"Okay, now. Bye-bye."

"I hope you're using a surge protector."

"I said good-bye, Annie."

We hung up, laughing.

THIRTY-ONE

There's an important element in the story of Cinderella that always gets left out. We hear all about her magical evening with the prince, but we never get what she must really be thinking. She has to know she doesn't belong there, no matter what she looks like. She has to feel like an impostor, knowing that her dress isn't really a gown and her coach is really a pumpkin and that if not for the presence of a fairy godmother, none of the people at the ball would even look at her.

I walked slowly through the open lobby to the top of the wide stairway leading down to the beach. I stopped for just a moment to take it all in. There was a dance floor. There was a bonfire. There was a band. There were at least forty or fifty people scattered around a dozen tables—far more than I'd seen at the resort up to this point, and some of them appeared to be close to my age— high school or early college. It was nearing dusk; the sun hung just above the rocky horizon, but the air was still tropically warm.

My close personal friend Kenny stood at attention near the top of the steps in front of a marble vase filled with six-foot birds-of-paradise. Like all the bellmen, he had changed into black shorts and a brilliant yellow-and-orange Hawaiian shirt. "You look lovely, Miss Fleet."

"Thanks, Mr. Kenny," I said, giving in to the formality. "I like your shirt, too. Very festive."

"We like to mix it up a little bit at the Hanauma."

I nodded to the mass of new guests milling about at the tables and on the dance floor. "Where have you been hiding all these people?"

"Saturday night is open to all," he said. "Not a ton of nightlife on Molokai."

I had a momentary, reflexive worry that "open to all" might include Wayo, but then it struck me that sticking around the island after finding whatever was in the cavern was the last thing he'd do. In fact, for the first time since Cozumel, I didn't need to worry about Wayo at all.

Kenny pointed to my feet. "It's okay to go barefoot, if you'd like. I'll take care of those."

I smiled as I kicked off my flip-flops. Who needed a fairy godmother when I had a Kenny? "Can I take you back to school with me?"

He gave me a quizzical look as he pressed my flip-flops together and held them behind his back. He nodded to the festivities. "Now, go have fun."

Relieved of my inappropriate footwear, I bounced down

the stone steps, the day's residual warmth against my feet. I made a conscious decision to embrace the night, to live in the present moment no matter how out of place I might feel; to revel in the dress, the drums, the stars. Who could say when I was ever going to get another crack at something like this? For all I knew, that's exactly what Cinderella was thinking, too.

There was a tap on my shoulder, and I spun around, and there was Josh in a floral print shirt and rolled-up khakis, barefoot just like me. "You look amazing."

I tucked a few tousled beachy strands of hair behind my ear. "It's different, I know."

"Not different," he said. "Just amazing. Here's where I would normally make the obligatory 'you clean up real good' joke, but I don't want to give you the impression that I thought you needed cleaning up in the first place."

"I'm glad you didn't overthink that one."

I'd made him laugh.

He led me to the tiki bar, where a pair of virgin strawberry daiquiris appeared in no time, and then somehow we started walking away from the party and toward the beach. The drummers began to hammer out a tribal beat, but it was just background noise now. Everything was background noise.

"What did Franklin have to say about you coming down here with me?"

"Who?" I said. The name sounded familiar, but I was distracted by the present moment, and I couldn't think clearly.

"Franklin Deveraux?"

"Oh, of course." My fake boyfriend. How could I ever have forgotten? "He's fine with it. Or, I should say that he doesn't know."

"Hmmm," was all Josh said.

The sand was cool against my feet. The sun sank behind a promontory at the other end of the bay, and gentle waves tickled the shore. We made small talk. I closed my eyes and tried to sear an image of the moment into my brain. Remember this. Remember what it feels like. Remember everything about it.

If only we could have re-created the atmosphere in the cavern. That's the only way the moment could have been better.

"About what happened today," Josh said, as if reading my mind. My bosom, as they say, threatened to heave, but then I noticed a hint of resignation in his voice, and it terrified me. "I just want you to know—"

"It's okay," I said before the other shoe could drop. I knew what he was going to say, but I couldn't hear it. Not tonight, with the tiki torches and the beverages. Not after I'd decided to revel. "You don't have to explain. The emotion of everything and the adrenaline. We can just pretend it didn't happen."

"Why would I want to do that?" He was legitimately surprised. Almost offended.

"Do what?"

"Pretend it didn't happen."

"You don't want to pretend it didn't happen?" I said.

Had I misread him that much? Was my bosom about to be given permission to heave again?

"Of course not." He put his arm on my shoulder. "That was amazing."

Finally!

"I want you to know that I'm not discouraged," he said. "Not at all. I'm totally committed."

Uh-oh. I tried the old take-a-drink-to-stall tactic, but the daiquiri was suddenly too cold and didn't taste like anything. "Totally committed?"

"To the Jaguar. I know you're disappointed we got beat to the punch today, but I'm not giving up." He leaned back as if to get a better view of me. "Why? What did you think I was talking about?"

"Oh. That," I said, turning back to the ocean so he couldn't read the truth. I shrugged as if uninterested. "What did you think I thought you were talking about?"

"I'm confused."

A blinding flash lit up the dusk. The drums stopped. Smoke machines covered the stage in a thick fog, and a shirtless linebacker stomped onstage holding a flaming torch. He wore a green-and-orange kilt-type thing, and his calves were covered by what looked like small grass skirts.

He began to whip the torch around, creating a comet-like tail of yellow flame at least three feet long. The drums returned, and he stomped with the beat.

"We should tell Alvarez," I said, using the interruption as an excuse to shift gears.

"Are you crazy? I bet he sold us out. Your dad must have talked to him about our trip."

"You can't blame this on the faculty lounge," I said. "Wayo had the disk for long enough. And even if my dad did tell him we were coming here—"

"Which he probably did—"

"I'm pretty sure Alvarez wouldn't knowingly have gone along with what Wayo did to me in Cozumel. It just doesn't make sense."

The fire dancer knelt and leaned his head back so that he was looking straight up. Then he opened his mouth and pulled the flame end of the torch across his face. He was licking the flame. There were *oohs*. Applause.

Josh said, "I still don't trust him."

"I don't see what choice we have. What if we told him the truth about the sculpture garden? He's lived and breathed the Golden Jaguar for years. If there's a connection, maybe he's the one to find it. Otherwise, we're stuck. Dead end."

"We got this far on our own," Josh said. "We can start over at the beginning. Get back to the primary sources."

Now the dancer grabbed a handful of fire and brought it down to the other end of the torch, sending flames burning from both ends. He spun it around like a drill teamer from hell, at one point tossing it thirty feet into the air, where it hung for a moment, the deep yellow outline of a sun. The drums grew both louder and faster, and the audience started to clap to the beat.

"The guys who beat us down there were pros," I said. "They brought tools."

"Telling Alvarez is too risky."

"We bribed a captain and pissed off some cops. I'd say we did just about the best we could have done."

"Maybe there's another way," he said.

"Would you rather put something on the Internet? 'Treasure hunters wanted! Knowledge of Cortés a must. Lack of desire to kill fifteen-year-old girls underwater preferred.'"

The drums reached a fever pitch as another dancer appeared onstage with a flaming baton of his own. They swung their fire at each other, flung the batons back and forth through the air. It was like the ancient Polynesian version of glow sticks and house music, and it was breathtaking. We watched in silence, inching closer to the stage.

"You know something," Josh said. "I bet you could get any guy out here to dance with you."

I laughed, but Josh just kept looking at me out of the corner of his eye like he was sizing me up. "Are you serious?" I said.

"As hell. That's how good you look. Any guy."

I tried to convince myself that he hadn't said what he'd just said. "There are about five even remotely close to my age."

"Then one of the staff, whatever. My point is, you look good enough to get anyone you want."

"What do you mean?"

"Choose someone, anyone. I'll bet you a hundred dollars that I can get him to come over and ask you to dance. All you have to do is stand there looking hot."

The drums stopped, and the dancers howled, and a wild applause came from the audience.

Don't cry, I commanded myself. *Don't let him think it's a big deal.*

"You're not mad that I said you were hot, are you?" he said, picking at least something up through his monumental obtuseness.

My smile was as plastic as the girls he was used to dating. "Of course not, Josh. I think it's sweet that you want to pimp me out to the staff."

"What?" He whipped his head around to look at me directly. "What? Pimp you out—"

Josh's mom ran up to us, flailing her hands as though they'd caught fire. "Come on, you two! Dance lessons."

Stars: They're Just Like Us! They embarrass the hell out of their kids!

Josh reached after me. "Annie, wait—"

"Dance lessons," I said with a shrug as I let his mom pull me away from him.

I ditched my now-flavorless daiquiri and joined everyone on the packed dance floor, all of us facing the stage for our authentic fire dance lessons. There was a lot of clapping and some stomping. From the looks of it, everyone was having a wonderful time. Even Josh. I did my best to play along, but I was in too much of a daze to do much more than stumble through the steps.

By the time the lesson was over, I had composed myself just enough so that when Josh turned to me for the inevitable "that's not what I meant," I was able to wave him off and laugh. He said he would meet me with more drinks, and gestured to where Violet and his mom were sitting. I took a moment, dabbed at the corners of my eyes with the tip of my pinkie, and joined them.

Mrs. Rebstock wore a flowing translucent top over an ankle-length floral-print skirt. "You look stunning, Annie," she said. "Really, that dress is phenomenal."

"Oh, this old thing?" I said. Then I turned to Violet and mouthed, "Thank you."

Violet raised her glass and gave me an almost imperceptible cheers.

Josh's mom leaned over the table and tapped her fingers on the back of my hand. "Before we get anywhere, I know you didn't spend the day with Violet."

I struggled for the appropriate response. She didn't look angry or disappointed. More like she was sharing a juicy little secret. Never mind the fact that she was this famous person. Or that she was the mother of my crazy crush. She was magnetic, and she gave me—and everyone?—the impression that we should be best friends.

"Truth be told, I didn't expect you to." She flashed a Cheshire cat grin and said, "I won't tell your parents if you don't."

"No, I . . . I think that's fine—"

"Because, really, I got the sense that they didn't trust me very much."

The idea that she would care what my mom thought of her made me laugh out loud.

"What's so funny?" Josh said, pulling up to the table with a fruity drink in each hand. "You're not talking about me, are you?"

"How was it today?" his mom said when we were all seated. A waiter offered folded napkins from a stack with a pair of silver tongs. "I want to hear everything."

Josh laid his napkin daintily across his lap as if stalling for time and said, "Violet came with us on the boat. She watched while we dove, and then we came back together."

I would have stopped him, spared him the embarrassment, but I hadn't quite gotten over the fact that he saw me as bait in a hundred-dollar bet.

Finally Violet interrupted him. "She knows."

Josh cleared his throat and smiled at his mom. She shrugged. He licked his lips. "Violet didn't come with us."

His mom acted shocked. "You don't say."

"We did go diving, though," he said. He mentioned the sculpture garden only briefly and left out any details about the police boat or the underwater scooter trip up the lava tunnel. "It was amazing. It really was. It's like you're flying. You don't belong down there, but you're there anyway. It was like magic."

Hearing Josh talk about diving that way should have been my dream come true. It should have been a sign that we were perfect for each other. That he valued what was most important to me, that we'd spend the rest of our days together, diving and treasure hunting and just being the happiest people on the planet. Instead, his words grated on my ears.

"I could never do it," Violet said. "I get too claustrophobic."

"You need to have Annie teach you. She's the best." Josh elbowed my arm. "That is, when she's not trying to kill you."

"You mean saving your life," I said reflexively, defensively. A bit too harshly, judging by the rise of Violet's eyebrows.

Josh continued as if he hadn't noticed. "People freak out because they don't trust themselves to handle whatever situation comes up, so the anticipation of trouble causes anxiety, and then it multiplies, and then when something tiny happens, they overreact and panic instead of dealing with it."

Was he still talking about diving? Or was he reading my face?

"It's all about preparation," he said. "Mental state. See, Annie, I told you I was listening."

I looked down at the dress. If I could have run right then, I would have. Fairy godmother be damned. I would have sprinted back to my little cottage before the dress turned to rags. Coach into a pumpkin, white stallions into mice. It was midnight somewhere.

THIRTY-TWO

The pictures had hit the Internet with a vengeance. Everybody knew; everybody had seen them. TMZ ran the headline DADDY'S LITTLE GIRL MEETS HER MAMA'S BOY over a picture of Mimi and Josh in mid-kiss, Mimi with her heel kicked jauntily up behind her. Wherever I went, like the background soundtrack in a horror movie: *Did you hear? Did you hear? Did you hear?* Yes, I heard.

In Alvarez's class, Katy—of all people—leaned over and said, "That show she was in was just stupid. Where's the comedy in growing up in a bar? And what was up with the laugh track? What are we, in the eighties?"

"It's not what you think," I said, feeling at the same time defensive about a friend who had only done what I'd asked her to do, appreciative of Katy's gesture of solidarity, and suspicious of the motivation behind that very gesture. It was too much.

"The pictures speak for themselves," Katy said. "A thousand words, you know?"

"Ladies," Alvarez said, "do you have something to say before we begin?"

I shook my head. Katy grunted. Alvarez flipped off the lights and showed us a presentation from his computer.

He was different now, better, as though he'd turned a corner. He wasn't the same old Alvarez, but he no longer looked like he wanted to shoot himself in the face. And he'd moved the class focus from Spanish and Portuguese galleons to what he called the underappreciated riches of sunken Chinese junk ships.

"I know porcelain and copper coins don't seem as flashy as gold bullion and silver pieces of eight," he said, directing his laser pointer to a slide of a replica of a Chinese junk, its three square-sailed masts all at different angles. He touched the keyboard, and a picture of stacked blue-and-white bowls filled the screen. "But take the Vung Tau wreck off the coast of Vietnam. Millions of dollars' worth of dishes and vases, coins dating back to the time of Emperor Kangxi in the late sixteen hundreds."

He went on and on about how fascinating it all was, even going so far as to try to engage me in some reciprocal eye contact, which made me wonder whether this new-found disdain for all things gold was just him protesting too much.

Craft service was the worst of all. Without the busy-work of a class to distract me from the rumors, I had to sit and take it. I was trapped in a fishbowl, but I wasn't even the fish. I just had to share the bowl with her.

When Mimi sat down, I told her I didn't want to talk about my weekend until Gracia got there, which was good for me because I knew Gracia wasn't coming.

"There's something weird going on with her," Mimi said.

Too many secrets, I thought.

I had my own stuff, Gracia was off somewhere with Baldwin and she hadn't told Mimi about it, and Mimi couldn't—or wouldn't dare—tell anyone that she and Josh weren't actually an item. After she drizzled vinaigrette on her salad and gave it an aggressively self-satisfied mix, I couldn't take it anymore.

"You didn't have to kiss him," I said.

Mimi said, "He kissed me too."

When Josh appeared at our table, it was as though all conversation in the cafeteria stopped. There they were, the new power couple, and the rest of the school now had the chance to see it in person. Mimi let it get to her, batting her eyes, twirling her hair, even pursing her lips.

"Mimi," I said.

She got herself under control. Josh nodded at her and smiled at me, and I knew what he wanted. I grabbed my backpack and excused myself from the table, leaving poor Mimi in a puddle of disappointment.

All eyes were on us, but neither of us said anything until we were outside the pavilion doors. "I hope you haven't given up," Josh said as I followed him to a bench near a replica of *The Thinker.* "We can still find the Jaguar; I know we can."

"You know the kid with his face pressed up against the window of the candy store? With tears in his eyes as he watches the kids on the other side of the glass take down Milk Duds and Skittles and Tootsie Rolls the size of his arm? That kid is close, too. But he knows he's not getting the candy."

"There's something I need to show you. I was going through my research—"

"You're not listening," I said. "We could stay at it for the rest of our lives and never get to the other side of the glass, because the fundamental difference between us and them remains the same. They have whatever they found, and they have the resources to go after whatever else is out there."

"I want you to close your eyes," Josh said.

"What? I'm not closing my—"

"It's cool. My therapist does this all the time. It's called visualization."

"And I'm visualizing with my eyes closed?"

"If you have your eyes open, you're visualizing me instead of visualizing what matters."

Oh, the irony. Barf, barf, barf. I closed my eyes.

"Okay, so I want you to imagine the Golden Jaguar. Everything you know about it. See it like it's a movie and you're zoomed in close. Imagine the places you've been searching for it, and think about the men who must have put it there. I want you to imagine yourself standing next

255

to it. How tall would it be? Now touch it. What does it feel like?"

"Why are you doing this?" I said.

"What does it feel like?"

"It feels smooth," I said. "And warm, as though it's absorbed heat from the sun. It feels alive. Can I open my eyes yet?"

"Now this. Imagine a pile of cash the same size as the Jaguar. A hundred million dollars, at least—"

I opened my eyes. "It's not about the money."

"Sure, sure. It's about the thrill of the hunt, about being a part of history, et cetera. But it can be about the money, too. Eyes closed."

"Okay," I said, doing as I was told. "Lots of cash."

Of course I'd daydreamed about this before, but there was something different about it after going through Josh's visualization. First the Jaguar, then the money. It felt more real than ever before, so all the things I could use it for felt more real, too. The Marine Park Conservancy Fund, the shop, ridiculously awesome dive gear. I could even pay my own Pinedale tuition so my dad wouldn't have to teach if he didn't want to. I couldn't help but laugh.

I put my hand on top of my backpack and scooted it closer up against my leg. It was a reflex more than anything, but Josh seemed to notice.

"You have the folder in there, don't you?" I said nothing. His jaw dropped when he figured it out. "You're going to tell Alvarez. I can't believe you."

"We can't do this on our—"

"Why are you the one who gets to tell him?" Josh said. "Why are you the one who gets to decide what we do?"

His sudden irritation took me by surprise. "Why am *I* the one? I found it."

"And I got us to Molokai. So, were you just using me? How am I supposed to feel about that?"

"How is this about you?" I said.

"How is this about *you*?" he said.

"Are you serious?"

We were silent for far too long. I didn't know what to say, and I didn't want to hear what he had to say, either. I stood up and shouldered my backpack and told him I'd see him later.

"What just happened?" I overheard him ask himself as I walked away.

THIRTY-THREE

After school let out, I planted myself in the middle of the Wozniak Family Computing Center's second-floor hallway. "Gracia!" I yelled. "I know you're in here. Don't make me knock on all these doors." I waited a moment and yelled her name again.

Five seconds later, the third door on the left creaked open a sliver. I went to it.

Gracia was at a computer, and Baldwin was sitting in a chair next to her. "Hey, Baldwin," I said.

He blushed. "Hi, Annie."

Though a bit gaunt for my taste, he was cute; I had to give Gracia that much. He wore his patented white T-shirt and black shorts.

His blush gave way to a worried expression. "Gracia promised you wouldn't tell anyone about us."

"We have reputations to protect," Gracia said. "Both of us do."

"Both of you?"

Baldwin shrugged. "My friends would think I'm a sellout."

"They wouldn't be happy for you?" I said. "I mean, look at her."

"Nah, it would shake their world to its core. Intelligence and social success are supposed to be on opposite ends of the same spectrum. The more you have of one, the less you get of the other. We complain about not going out on many dates, but at the end of the day, it's a trade-off we're all willing to make." He whistled and shook his head as if dreading some catastrophic future event. "But for me to be smarter than everyone *and* get the girl? That's not supposed to happen."

"Out of respect to your friends' worldview," I said, "my lips are sealed."

Baldwin looked relieved. Gracia winked at me.

"What are you guys doing?"

"It's not what you think," Baldwin said.

"He was just teaching me how to program in Objective-C."

"I'm sure that's supposed to mean something to me."

Baldwin puffed out his slender chest like a proud sparrow. "She said she wanted to make some mobile apps," he said. Gracia clenched her teeth as her eyes widened just a fraction. I got the message: *Drop it.*

"Okay," I said. "Can I steal her for a second?"

Gracia kissed Baldwin on the cheek and followed me

down the hall into an empty room. We closed the door behind us. I said, "Mobile apps? Don't you already know how to do that?"

She shrugged. "He gets to think he's showing me new stuff, and we get to hang out. It's a win-win. The hard part is not correcting him when he makes mistakes."

"You're duplicitous."

"And it was working, too. We were just about to make out before you barged in. Oh, and by the way: *I'm* duplicitous? Does that mean you already blocked Mimi's return to tabloid heaven out of your mind?"

"I have to tell you something. No, that's not true— I have to tell you *everything*." I motioned for her to sit down. The look on her face went from confused to surprised to skeptical until it finally settled on something I couldn't quite read.

"It's okay if you're mad," I said when I finished. "I should have told you the second we got back from Mexico."

"You should have. Can I see it?"

I turned the lock on the doorknob and unzipped my backpack. Gracia took the folder and sifted through the full-page color printouts I'd made of the disk. She leaned down and squinted at them in her lap; she held them up one by one, as if seeing the pictures from a different angle made any difference.

"How do I know this is real?" she said, so I took out my phone and showed her the picture of me taking a nibble of gold.

She yelped a laugh and looked up. "You're not really

going to let some boy get in the way of you and the treasure, are you?"

"I don't know what to do."

"Well, then, I guess there's just one thing you need to ask yourself." She took a meaningful, overly dramatic pause and said, "Are you Dorka the Explorer, or aren't you?"

"Gracia—"

"Seriously. You've been going on and on about buried treasure, sunken treasure, hidden treasure, lost treasure ever since I met you. Treasure treasure treasure." She held a picture in my face as if giving me a red card. "And now you actually touch some and you want to let a *boy* stop you? Where's your self-respect?"

"Says the girl in the midst of a secret computer-center love affair."

"You either suck it up and get Josh on board, or you suck it up and make the decision to go on without him. Either way, this is happening." She grabbed my hand and placed it on the picture as though it were the Bible. "Say it with me!"

"Say what?"

"I. Am. Scuba Girl!" She laughed when I did not say it with her. "Okay, fine. We'll work on that. Now let's go tell Alvarez."

"Wait, what?"

"You said it yourself; that's the next step. I'll go with you. If Josh is out of the picture, you need a new sidekick." She laid on the twang. "And I do believe I fit the bill?"

"What about Baldwin?"

She bit her lip. "Mo-niques before geeks?"

"That doesn't even make any sense."

"You know what I mean. Anyway, he won't mind if I leave him in there." She pointed her thumbs at her chest and said, "He's got two good reasons to get over it."

The quad had completely emptied out by the time we left the computing center, but Alvarez usually stayed a couple of hours after school, so I figured we could still catch him.

"Will you please let me do the talking?" I said.

"What could I possibly have to add to this?"

"Something. You'll add something, and we both know it."

I shifted the strap of my backpack. The closer we got to Alvarez's classroom, the heavier it felt on my shoulder. I realized that I was looking forward to telling him, just as it had been a relief to tell Gracia. With the *should I or shouldn't I* resolved, we'd be able to focus on the next step. I reached for the front door, but it swung out to me just before I could grab the handle.

It was Wayo.

"*Señorita* Annie," he said.

I stumbled backward, bumping into Gracia as he took a step outside. I even threw up a little bit in my mouth when I recognized the man who came out the door behind him.

Mr. Pockmarks.

I tried to act normal, but my brain was about to explode.

So many thoughts buzzed in my head—realizations that hit me one after the other—there was no way my skull could hold them all.

First off, Pockmarks and Wayo knew each other. That meant Pockmarks was keeping tabs on me every time he'd come into the store and that he was probably part of Wayo's original betrayal back in Cozumel.

Second, the two of them were still talking to Alvarez, which must have meant they were all still involved together.

And third, there was the little matter of all my research shouting at me, "Tell-Tale Heart"–style, from my backpack.

"You must be Wino," Gracia said, steadying me with a hand on my shoulder. "Or Wayo, or whatever."

"I have a reputation?"

"I hope you're proud of yourself," Gracia said, her voice cracking and rising as though at the brink of a full-on breakdown. "You took the one thing Annie loves. She hasn't even been in the water since Cozumel."

"I am very much doubt that," Wayo said.

Gracia looked at me like a trainer checking his boxer for signs of life, but I had nothing for her. I wanted to get out of there.

"And *you*," Gracia said, pointing to Pockmarks as she stepped ever so subtly between me and them. "I've seen you before. You were at her store. You were *stalking* her. Ewww. You're a pervert! I bet you're not even allowed to be within two hundred yards of a school, are you."

Her voice became louder and louder with every word, until the smug bad-guy look on Pockmarks's face was replaced with one of discomfort. He shook his head and brushed past us.

Gracia wasn't done, not by a long shot. She called out after them, "I bet if we checked the registered-sex-offender database, we'd find your picture!"

By the time she got to that part, they were both out of sight.

I staggered over to a pine tree and collapsed against the trunk, hugging the backpack tight against my chest. "Thanks for that."

"The pizza-face guy was totally casing the joint, wasn't he. Checking you out." I nodded, and Gracia sat next to me, tucking her heels to the side. "I guess that means we're not telling Alvarez, huh?"

THIRTY-FOUR

As soon as we were alone in the back of my mom's shop, Gracia peppered me with follow-up questions about everything: my out-of-air experience, my cunning use of Mimi both as a diversion at the airport and as a liaison to the governor of Hawaii, Violet's magical dress. But Gracia saved most of her curiosity for Cortés and the Golden Jaguar.

"So now you're interested?" I finally said.

"Come on. You know how it goes: if you're poor, you're crazy, but if you're rich, you're eccentric? Now that all this treasure nonsense is actually true, I see you in a whole new light!"

The buzzer interrupted us, followed by my mom calling, "Annie, someone's here to see you!"

"Your face just went all white," Gracia said. "I'll check if it's Wayo."

Before she could even get up, Josh appeared in the doorway looking surprisingly un-Josh-like. He shifted back and forth, put his hands in his pockets, took them out. His tongue darted out along his bottom lip, and he cleared his throat.

"There's something you should know about Cortés," he said finally. "But I want to make sure I tell you something else first. Can we talk?"

Gracia crossed her arms and wiggled her shoulders, giving him the finest reality-show sass she could muster. "Whatever you want to say to her you can say in front of me."

"She's right," I said. "She knows everything."

Josh nodded. He stepped toward an empty tank and lifted it up. It hit the ground with a soft thud. "About Hawaii. I was trying to give you a compliment. I'm sorry."

"It takes a big man to admit that," Gracia said. "What else you got?"

"What else is there? I shouldn't have said what I said, even though I didn't mean it the way it came out." I could see a trace of irritation on his face; he didn't like having to explain himself to her, but he was stuck. If he was going to get what he wanted, he'd have to play the game. "Are we looking for the Jaguar or not?"

Gracia bent a stick of gum onto her tongue and started an exaggerated chew. "She'll think about it."

It wasn't even that I was mad at him. Of all people, I understood that we shouldn't be held accountable for things coming out wrong. I was more frustrated with myself, given that I couldn't seem to keep from falling back into his charming little trap. If I could trust myself to think of him as a friend, only a friend, and nothing but a friend so help me God, we were definitely looking for the Jaguar. But how was I supposed to trust myself to do that?

"What did you find?" I said finally, and the tension seemed to vanish from the room.

Josh wandered to the side door and poked his head into the alley as if checking the place for surveillance. He opened up a folding chair and sat across from Gracia and me, then scooted in closer and leaned forward, resting his elbows on his knees.

"Okay, so Montezuma dies and Cortés takes over Tenochtitlán, dismantles the Aztec Empire, and renames it Mexico City. He basically rules there for five years, but then he starts to feel all underappreciated. People accuse him of holding back on gold that was due to the Spanish Crown, so he has to go to Spain in 1528 and prove to Charles the Fifth that he hasn't been stealing from him."

"We know all that already," I said.

Josh nodded to Gracia. "I thought she might appreciate a recap."

"This is a considerate young man, Annie," Gracia said. "Don't stifle him. Go on?"

"So the king buys whatever Cortés is selling, but when Hernán gets back to Mexico, the place is a mess. There's another guy, Antonio de Mendoza, who has most of the governing power, but Cortés still has control of the military, and the freedom to explore stuff. Then he gets accused of murdering his first wife, and the government refuses to exonerate him, even though he's never convicted. So in 1536, he figures, 'This sucks. I gotta get out of here,' and he goes off to the Pacific and discovers Baja California."

"That's where we get the Sea of Cortés," I said to Gracia. "Now called the Gulf of California."

"You're kidding. The *very same* Cortés?"

I smiled at her sarcasm and turned back to Josh. "So what's the big revelation?"

He scooted forward on his folding chair even more, unable to contain his excitement. "In 1539, Cortés paid a captain named Francisco de Ulloa to go back to Baja California. According to most of the information I found, the route he took was only to verify the existence of the Baja Peninsula. But there is evidence that he might have gone farther north than originally thought."

"That seems like a pretty big deal," Gracia said. "I mean, wouldn't historians be all over that?"

"Taken by itself, not really. Reports of expeditions like these were super unreliable. But when you take into account what we know about the Golden Jaguar . . . that's when the questions start popping up. Where, exactly, did Cortés go for the three years between 1536 and 1539? And more importantly, why did he send Francisco de Ulloa back to Baja, at roughly the same time the archaeologists on Molokai say the sculpture garden was created, and only a year before Juan de la Torre's journal entry puts the disk Annie found in the Devil's Throat? What was Ulloa doing there?"

"Did you find out anything about him?"

"He died in 1540, and that's where it gets even weirder. Some reports say he was stabbed to death by a sailor when he got back from his expedition, but other reports—equally trustworthy, by the way—say he never even made it back, that his ship disappeared at sea."

"Oh, boy," Gracia said, rubbing her hands together. "Now we're cooking."

"How far north did Cortés get?" I said.

"North of what's now San Diego, at least," Josh said. "Remember that Alvarez said Cortés's life was in chaos before the *Vida Preciosa* headed back to Spain? I think he needed the Jaguar as an insurance policy, but he couldn't leave it anywhere near Mexico City. He had to protect it, so he took the risk of losing it all, just in case he had to get it back someday. So he commanded the one man he could trust, Francisco de Ulloa, to take it to a spot that only Cortés had discovered before: Alta California."

I continued for Josh, reaching a crescendo as the pieces all started to fall into place. "Ulloa sent a ship west, with the key to the Jaguar's location, which they deposited on Molokai. And that was reason enough to keep their knowledge of the island's existence a secret from recorded history."

"And he returned to Cortés with the golden disk to

show where the Jaguar was hidden, only to die in a knife fight soon thereafter." Josh slapped his hands on his thighs and leaned back in his chair as if to say, *Eureka!*

"I have to admit, this treasure hunting thing is pretty exciting," Gracia said. "But whatever that key is, you don't have it, right? The other guys, Wayo and his dermatologically challenged buddy—can we call them the 'bad guys?'—got to Hawaii first."

Josh nodded. "True, but we still have the pictures of the disk. And we already know one side leads to Molokai. I bet whatever was in that cave leads to the other side of the disk."

"So you'd need both items to make the map work," I said.

"Right. And the rock formation on the other side might be where the Jaguar is hidden. Besides, no matter what the bad guys—"

"Thank you," Gracia said.

"—took from that cave on Molokai, we still know that Cortez spent time in Alta California, and that he sent Ulloa back there—at his own personal expense, no less—almost immediately after his return to Mexico City."

The look on Josh's face was exactly the reason I should have avoided getting involved in treasure hunting with him. Could anyone have been cuter talking about Spanish conquistadors and buried treasure? Impossible.

Gracia said, "What's the connection between Cortés and California? Right? That's what we have to find out."

"Primary sources!" I said, nearly knocking the air tanks over as I jumped to my feet. It was as if the conversation up to that point had built the pressure bit by bit, and my little exclamation caused it all to blow.

"Annie?" Josh said.

I yelled to my mom that we'd be right back, and led a confused Josh and Gracia out the side door just in case prying eyes were watching out front.

"Come on," I said. "Alvarez told me Cortés had a wife here."

THIRTY-FIVE

The Iglesia de la Virgen Madre was a historic building across the street from the train station in downtown San Juan Capistrano, with enormous red bougainvilleas shrouding the exposed stone walls of the bell tower. We followed an uneven path to a set of thick wooden front doors. Fortunately for us, the father was in.

We stood on the brick floor and waited, each of us in our own zone. At the beginning of the nearly two-hour trip, Josh's car was abuzz with theories and conjectures, wild pledges about what we would do with the money when we found the treasure. But gradually all that had dissipated. We'd focused only on the cars around us, making sure we weren't being followed.

Father Rubén Gonzales was a freakishly tall man. He stepped through the door at the end of the passageway and covered the twenty feet in three or four extraordinarily long steps. For some reason, I'd been expecting to see him in robes, but instead he wore slacks and a white button-down shirt with a brown name tag clipped above the breast pocket.

"How can I help—"

"We're doing a report on Cortés?" Josh said quickly, waving our folder of research as proof and speaking in one long uninterrupted sentence, with his patented charm absolutely nowhere to be found. "Hernán Cortés, the conquistador? The explorer?"

"I've heard of him," Father Gonzales said with a smile.

"What my classmate means," Gracia said, stepping ever so elegantly between Josh and the father, "is that we are in need of some primary sources for our report. Our teacher mentioned that you are the archivist."

Father Gonzales checked his watch. "Normally it would take some time to organize everything for you, but you're in luck. Lots of interest in Cortés recently."

"Yeah," I said, catching a worried glance from Josh. "He's pretty hot right now."

We followed the father down the chipped brick pathway through a side door, and suddenly we were walking on clean white tile.

"What happened back there?" I whispered to Josh. "I thought you said you could handle it."

He shook his head, blushing as he hustled forward. "I don't want to talk about it."

"I'm a big Cortés fan myself," Father Gonzales said,

leading us down a wooden staircase into the basement. "I find him the most interesting of all the conquistadors. Almost a tragic figure, really."

"Why tragic?" I said.

"I believe he should have been exonerated in the death of his first wife." Father Gonzales opened a thick steel door marked ARCHIVES. "But politics were politics, I suppose, even then."

A slight chill greeted us when we entered the room, and my jaw just about fell to the floor. "Wow."

"You were expecting a dusty old room? With bricks falling from the ceiling? You'd have to read the crackling scrolls with a lantern?"

"Something like that," I said.

The room was bright and clean, with three long aisles and a series of tables, lit from underneath, in the center of the room. Lamps were clipped to each of the tables. The father handed us each a pair of white cotton gloves.

"We are in the process of digitizing the archives, but this will have to do until then." He picked up a huge thick folder at least three feet across and laid it gently on the table closest to us. "This is everything we have on Cortés and Francisco de Ulloa, who, as you may not know, was sent by Cortés to Baja California in 1539."

I winked at Josh, who looked particularly proud of himself.

"Please leave everything in the order and condition you found it," the father said. "No eating, no touching without the gloves, no flash photography. The lamps use special lightbulbs so as not to damage the documents." He checked his watch again. "Now if you'll excuse me, I trust you'll take utmost care. And remember, God is watching."

He laughed and pointed at a blinking red light in a corner of the room.

"You wouldn't happen to have the names of the other people who were looking at the Cortés stuff, would you?" Gracia said. "I was thinking that maybe we could talk to them for our project?"

Father Gonzales shook his head. "We don't keep a visitor's log."

As soon as the father left, Josh set our research on the adjoining table and helped us spread out the contents of the large archival folder. The papers seemed to be journal entries and maps, most of which had been encased in protective plastic sleeves. It was all in Spanish, and in cursive, which made progress slow, but finally Gracia shouted, "Yahtzee!"

Josh and I hustled to either side of her.

"Alvarez was right," she continued, pointing to the flowery calligraphy of what looked like a short obituary. "Cortés *did* have a wife here. She died in 1559."

"That's twenty years after Ulloa came back," I said.

Gracia swung a lamp down closer to the table's surface and squinted. "It says here her name was Salento Torres García del Nacimiento."

Josh's head shot up, and he bit the inside of his cheek. "I've heard that name before." He went to our folder and searched through the pages, scanning each one quickly before slapping it down on the table and moving on to the next.

The name sounded familiar to me as well, so I leaned down over a primitive-looking map of the California coast and tried to decipher the handwritten markers. And then, at exactly the same time—

"Found it!" I said.

"Here it is!" Josh said.

I looked at him, a wide smile planted on my face. "You first."

"No, you."

There was a connection here—I knew it. The same connection that had led us to that fleeting kiss in the Hawaiian cavern. The same connection that I'd sworn— only hours before—I wouldn't become distracted by. But there you have it.

"Enough!" Gracia said. "No foreplay around the archives!"

I ignored her. Josh held up a color photocopy of an article. Circled at the top was a picture: a stone statue of a woman overlooking the ocean, staring directly out into the water, holding her hands beneath her chin as if in prayer.

"This statue dates to the mid–fifteen hundreds and has been restored to close to original condition. Carved at the bottom is one simple word: *Salento*."

Gracia gasped. "And do you know where it is?"

"Dana Point," I said triumphantly. "Only three miles down the road from where we are right now."

This time, Gracia shook her head. "How can you be sure?"

"Because Dana Point was originally called . . ." I spread my white-gloved palms across the surface of the map and pointed to a knob of a peninsula, like a big pointed zit on the Southern California shoreline. "Punta Salento."

"It's there," Josh said, looking at his picture. "Out there in the ocean. That's the next step. That's where Ulloa hid the Golden Jaguar."

"Not to burst y'all's bubbles," Gracia said, "but we have no idea what Wayo and his evil pizza-faced henchman already know. They could still be way ahead of us."

A memory flashed into my head, and I smiled, then giggled, and then I flat-out laughed, the sound echoing off the concrete floor.

"*Pizza-faced* isn't that funny," Josh said.

"It's not that." I glanced up at the camera's blinking light, and my laughter died down as I started replacing the documents carefully in Father Gonzales's large folder. I whispered, "He used a credit card."

We were back at the dive shop less than eighty minutes later, thanks to the carpool lane and Josh's high-performance machine. It was well past sundown as we hustled through the alley and entered the shop through the back.

"Josh," I said, "I need you to distract my mom. Tell her

about how much you like to dive, or ask her about wet-suits or something. Just get her away from the register."

"Done."

We hit the retail area at a jog.

"I didn't expect to see you back," my mom said, looking up from a display of dive-computer brochures.

"Struck out," I said. "No luck with the research."

Josh waved at her. "Mrs. Fleet, can I talk to you for a second? I was hoping for some feedback on dry suits, but Annie said you were more knowledgeable than she was."

"What are you looking for?" my mom said, clearly pleased. Flattery will get you everywhere.

"All I know is that I don't like the cold."

He walked away from the register as he talked—slowly, though, so as not to seem too obvious—and my mom followed right along. He was good.

I went to the front and waved Gracia around the counter. It took me a couple of seconds to access the register database, and I could tell that Gracia was doing her best not to leap in and help me.

"What are you looking—"

"I remember what he bought," I said. "And shhh."

Gracia whistled in mock reverence. "You're like the idiot savant of treasure myths and retail transactions."

Finally, there it was. "I knew it. Anthony Snow. Paid with a credit card two weeks ago, $15.99 for a save-a-dive kit."

"If he'd only known that his save-a-dive kit would end

up ruining everything for him," Gracia said. "Irony, thy name is scuba-retail-shop receipt."

I printed out the receipt and handed it to her. "Can you do something with this?"

"Who do you think you're talking to?" She pshhhawed me and snatched the paper and stared at it for a few seconds. Then her eyes lit up. "But not here."

THIRTY-SIX

osh stepped delicately through Gracia's basement as if discovering an exciting, unexpected, and ultimately terrifying new world. He spun as he moved, taking it all in. What little light there was came from a string of butterfly-shaped LEDs tucked up against the ceiling on the far wall. He stopped dead in his tracks—I thought he was going to fall to his knees in prayer—when he saw the size of her HD screen.

"What is this place?" he whispered.

"This," Gracia said, flipping the light switch, "is the Lion's Den."

I laughed. "You touch anything, and mama lion gives you a mauling."

Gracia sat on the couch and plugged a cable into the back of her laptop. She tapped out a few keystrokes, and the huge plasma screen came to life. On it was a picture of a kitten in full Princess Leia costume—robe and side buns—pointing a laser gun at the camera.

"That's quite the desktop background," Josh said. "Do you think I could—"

"Don't even think about it." Gracia was hammering away on the keyboard, but her voice was icy cold. "If you mention a single word of this place to anybody at school, I *will* come after you. We're talking blog posts. Photoshopped pictures. Total cyber-destruction. It will get nasty for you and your very public family, and it will get nasty in a hurry."

Josh looked around uncertainly. "I was just going to ask where the bathroom was."

"Oh. Through that door." She gestured with her head while her fingers danced across the keys. An application window opened over Leia kitty, a blue screen with some kind of computer code scrolling down the screen.

When the bathroom door closed behind him, I collapsed next to Gracia and said, "The Lion's Den? Where did that come from?"

"Every superhero's headquarters has an awesome name. Zorro has the Lair of the Fox. Superman has the Fortress of Solitude. Even Batman has the Batcave—"

"We're not superheroes."

"Aim high, Annie."

"That's the Air Force."

"Okay, here goes." An American Express online-account page covered half the screen. Gracia scrolled down from the top. "I'm showing purchases on Molokai, Cozumel—"

"He's been around the whole time," I said. "I bet he's

the mastermind. I wonder what his lair is called."

"Whatever it's called, I don't think he's going to be hanging out there much. Not for a while, at least. Look at these purchases only today: dive shop, salvage shop, gas station, adult video store—"

"Really?"

"Just kidding," she said. "But the other stuff is true. He's spent a whole lot of money in a very short period of time."

My stomach disappeared on me, and I started to get a little light-headed as I realized what it all meant. "He's going after it."

"Oh, new activity. Just now. A charge from Dana Point Marina LLC. Let's see what it's—"

"A boat. He rented a boat."

"Yep," Gracia said. She navigated from the account to the specific receipt and then opened another window showing a picture of the boat in question. "A big one, too. Fifty-nine feet. *Aquatic Diamond*—who names these things?"

"We don't have much time. Whatever they found in the cavern pointed them back here. I bet they're going out there tomorrow."

Gracia pointed to the screen. "Uh-oh."

I followed her gaze. "Uh-oh."

The sound of water rushing through the pipes, and then Josh came out. "Wha-oh?"

"Our guy here isn't a registered sex offender," Gracia said. On-screen was a three-foot mug shot of a scowling Anthony Snow. "But he is a convicted felon. Spent three years in prison for aggravated assault, attempted robbery, wow. You name it, he's been accused of it. Except for the touchy-touchy."

"We have to go up against that guy?" Josh said.

"My dad said treasure hunting was nasty business," I said. "No more sword fights—pirates have guns."

"What did Alvarez get himself into?"

"He's not our problem anymore," Gracia said. "Not getting killed by that dude is our problem."

I went closer to the TV and pointed to the credit-card-account window. "Can you keep that active? We need to know what they're going to do as soon as they decide to do it."

"No problem. I can create a permanent link to the server, using an elegant little worm that—" Gracia looked at me and Josh and rolled her eyes. "Why don't I just do a lot of cool stuff that you won't understand?"

"I thought you'd never ask."

"So, great," Josh said. "We have his credit-card activity. But we can't just sit back and watch them go after the Jaguar."

"I have an idea, but I don't know if you're going to like it." I smiled apologetically at Gracia. "I think it's time we broke in the Lion's Den."

Mimi was first to arrive. "This better be important," she said.

"Thanks for coming," I said, motioning to the couch. "I'll explain everything in just a sec."

"FYI, Josh," Mimi said, "my publicist arranged an interview with *OK! Magazine*. Don't worry, our plan is to 'no comment' anything related to the Rebstocks. We'll make sure to give the impression that there's nothing there."

Josh looked puzzled. "But there *is* nothing there."

"That's what I'm saying. It's all about maintaining an image."

"I do love me some Mimi Soto." Gracia laughed and pointed at her with a wink. "I'm glad you're here."

Mimi shook her head. "As much as I enjoy getting the group together, I enjoy not bombing the English exam tomorrow morning even more."

"It's going to be worth it," Josh said.

I checked my watch. "Should be any minute now."

The doorbell rang, and Gracia went upstairs to answer. Seconds later, Nate and Katy Sugar walked down the stairs as if every step was against their collective will.

Mimi let a snort escape. "What is *she* doing here?"

Ladies and gentlemen, we had ourselves a dismissive-off, and Katy was winning; she rolled her eyes without saying anything, as if Mimi wasn't even worth responding to. She was very, very, good.

"So," Nate said, "now you have us in your basement."

"Don't touch anything or your face will explode." Josh laughed.

Katy's disinterest seemed to be thrown off when her eyes landed on all the electronics on Gracia's desk. "You like computers?"

I motioned for everyone to gather around the coffee table. There were now six of us: Gracia in her recliner, Mimi and Nate on the sofa with Josh sitting on one armrest. Katy stood across the table from Mimi, and I rolled over on Gracia's desk chair.

"You sure you don't want to get Baldwin in on this?" I said.

"I knew it!" Mimi said. "I knew there was something going on with you! Why didn't you tell us?"

"Baldwin doesn't want to ruin his rep," I said.

"Ruin *his* rep?"

I nodded. "It's complicated."

Gracia opened her laptop. "I'm not sure he's ready to see me like this, anyway. Last night I was *this close* to blurting out the solution to a bug he was trying to fix, and I almost had to come clean. I don't think he could handle knowing that I am part of a treasure hunting team, too."

"What do you mean, treasure hunting team?" Mimi said.

"Um," Nate said, shooting a glance at Katy, "I'm not sure that really worked out too well last time."

I cleared my throat and nodded to Gracia. The TV sprang to life. The disk looked gorgeous on the big screen, my pictures tiled across to show all the different shots of both sides.

The Lion's Den was silent for at least a minute until Mimi yelped and covered her mouth in astonishment. "Is that your room, Annie?"

"May I?" Gracia pressed her keyboard without waiting

for my answer, and the other two pictures I'd taken appeared on-screen. My little thumbs-up grin looked even lamer than I'd remembered.

"Gracia," I said.

"Sorry." She typed again, and now Snow's mug shot covered one half of the screen. The other half included pictures of the Golden Jaguar, a map of the coast near Dana Point, a picture of Snow's rental boat, and the credit-card account.

I told them everything, filling in the Cozumel blanks for Nate and Katy, and dumping a ton of new information on Mimi, who was clearly struggling to process it all. I talked about Wayo and Alvarez and their connection to a convicted felon, and I came clean about the real reason we'd needed Mimi as a diversion at the airport. After I'd brought everyone up to speed, I outlined my plan for what to do next.

There was silence when I finished. Snow's gnarled face growled down at us.

"It's okay if you don't want to help," I said. "I wouldn't want him coming after me, either."

More silence.

Mimi finally broke it. "What do you need?"

"That depends on—"

"Don't give me that. You know exactly what you need, and everyone here knows you know. In a perfect world, if you could have it all, what would it be?"

"A perfect world?" I said. "Okay, a perfect world. If

we're going to do it right, we'd need at least two rebreathers, for the silence and lack of bubbles that would give us away. Plus, we get extended bottom time and don't have to worry about tanks. I'd want computer-integrated masks so we keep our hands free. We'd need a way to communicate fast underwater—no writing on dive slates this time—so I'd want full-color wrist-mounted HD touch screens for text messaging. And there's a company that just came out with a wetsuit/dry-suit hybrid with Yamamoto Geoprene. . . ."

I trailed off, and they must have read the concern on my face.

"What?" Gracia said.

I shook my head. "All that stuff's way expensive."

Mimi's hand came down on the table with a slap. She removed it, and there on the table was a black American Express card with her name on it. "My grandfather gave me this. For emergencies only, no questions asked. I think this counts?"

I had to admit that sometimes going to school with spectacularly rich people had its advantages. Like, for example, if you happened to find yourself needing fifty thousand dollars' worth of dive gear and equipment.

"You're going to need to reschedule that English exam tomorrow," Josh said.

Mimi laughed. "Let's call this experiential education."

"We can use our family's boat," Katy said. "It'll be perfect. We'll do the old drunk-kids-on-daddy's-yacht maneuver."

"There's already a name for that?" I said.

"Duh."

Josh nodded to Nate. "Are you sure you'll be able to handle your part?"

Nate's only response was an eye roll, so Josh took two steps toward him. The next thing I knew, Josh was on the floor, gasping for breath. Nate stood above him, one foot on Josh's chest, pulling with both hands on Josh's wrist, which was bent at the strangest and most painful-looking angle. There'd been some punches, I think. And maybe a kick or two, but Nate didn't look like he'd exerted any effort at all.

"Any more questions?" Nate said.

Josh wheezed through clenched teeth. "I'm good."

Nate released him and pulled him to his feet.

"Belt test went well, I take it?" Josh said.

"Okay, then." My limbs were starting to feel all tingly as the anticipation of what we were about to do took hold. "Now the only question is, can we get all the gear we need before it's too late?"

The five of them passed around an annoyingly knowing glance. I was the only one not smiling; yet again, one of these things is not like the others. "What?"

"You're so cute," Mimi said. She picked up the card and tossed it into my lap. It was a tiny bit thicker than a normal credit card, and it didn't bend at all. "That card is made out of titanium, silly. We can have everything here in an hour."

THIRTY-SEVEN

We pushed off from Marina del Rey early the next morning in the Sugars' boat, *Constant Bliss*. The marine-layer clouds were a thin mist in the predawn glow. It was a Tuesday, a school day. I had never ditched a single class before, let alone an entire day of them. Even the simple lie I'd told my dad when Gracia picked me up so early—that she and I were going to a coffee shop to work on an English presentation—was enough to get my heart racing.

At fifty feet long, the *Constant Bliss* was the biggest boat I had ever been on. The forward deck stretched twenty-five feet, and even without the sails up, the rigging formed a complex web of ropes and pulleys. Behind the cockpit was a ten-foot deck and a small dinghy with an outboard motor hanging off the stern. It wasn't quite to the level of the Rebstocks' private jet, but it was definitely nice.

Even so, Nate had acted apologetic when we'd arrived

at the marina with all our gear. "Sorry it's not bigger."

"It's the motion of the ocean," Mimi had responded with a smile. "Not the size of the waves."

"You were way funnier on TV."

"I know," she'd said. "Better writers."

We left the sails in their blue sleeves and headed south under engine power, sitting cross-legged on the forward deck, our coffees offering a barrier against the predawn chill. Nate and Katy wore matching tracksuits over the outfits they'd need when we got there. Josh, Mimi, Gracia, and I would change when the time came.

Whether it was due to the sense of entitlement fostered so heavily by the Pinedale Academy or from some other mystical treasure-hunting source, the six of us felt empowered enough to take matters into our own hands. We knew it was dangerous, but we also knew we were special; we'd been told as much every single school day.

Nevertheless, I felt a burden growing gradually, inexorably, over the two-hour trip to Dana Point. I quietly left the others up top and went down into the main cabin.

Seeing all our new equipment laid out neatly on the floor—the rebreathers, the masks, the dive computers and wetsuits—I couldn't help wondering if I had given myself too much credit. I wasn't a Navy SEAL, wasn't a grizzled veteran of treasure hunts near and far. I was, after all, just a fifteen-year-old girl whose dad had once taught how to use a metal detector.

The HD color screen of my new wrist-mounted computer was the size of a deck of cards. I turned it on and scrolled through the images I'd uploaded earlier that morning: sixteenth-century maps of the Dana Point coastline, a few pictures of the statue of Salento, shots of Cortés's crest, and finally the disk. I paused the screen on a close-up of the non-Molokai side. The formation looked like a tunnel I would have made out of Play-Doh when I was little. Wide at the bottom, narrowing toward the top, like a poorly drawn triangle.

I wanted so desperately to see the real thing that I'd almost convinced myself it was below the surface.

But what if it wasn't? Or what if what we found was just another clue, which led to another clue, and another? Or even worse, what if there was no Golden Jaguar at all? What if it was all a wild-goose chase designed by Cortés to keep his enemies spending money and manpower? What would I tell everyone?

The possibility—inevitability?—of failure was paralyzing, and I hadn't even allowed myself to fully contemplate what might happen if Wayo got the chance to finish the job he'd started in Cozumel.

"You doing okay?" Gracia said. She braced herself in the doorway, clutching a to-go cup in one hand and the railing in the other.

"Sure," I said. "Just a little seasick."

"You"—she came down the short flight of stairs and sat across the small table from me—"are pretty much the worst liar I know."

I swallowed. I turned off the screen and laid the computer next to me on the bench seat.

"Out with it," she said. "We don't have all day. Literally."

"Fine. I'm scared." Now that I'd said the words out loud, I felt tears welling up in my eyes no matter how hard I tried to force them down—and I tried *hard*. I motioned upstairs. "Terrified is more like it, and everyone up there is counting on me. What if we don't find anything? What if I screw up? What if . . . ?" That last one didn't need to be completed.

Gracia leaned forward, her elbows on the table and her coffee in both hands. "Let me tell you something. My dad runs a 'reality' show in a bio-dome where even the thunderstorms are scripted. Mimi spent ten years pretending to be the daughter of a bar owner. Josh's mom gets on the cover of magazines because she's good at make-believe."

"What about the Sugars?"

"Who the hell knows about those freaks?" She laughed and continued. "My point is that we're here because we're sick of make-believe. We're here because day after day, class after class, test after test, everything we do is geared toward positioning ourselves for the future, which means that even the parts of our lives that *aren't* built on fantasy have nothing to do with today—with right now."

She picked up a wetsuit and tossed it onto the table. "This is as close as any of us are ever going to get to something special. Something real. We're here because we believe in you. And we want what you're giving us the chance to experience."

"But—"

She brushed the words away before I could get them out. "And if you fail, you fail. We fail. It's worth it. Conversation over."

I nodded, more to myself than to her, and then I took a deep breath. "You're not going to tell the others, are you?"

"What, that you're mentally weak? That you're about to have a nervous breakdown?"

"That's enough—"

"No way; my lips are sealed on that one."

A distant *BOOM* drifted through the open cabin door, and Gracia and I turned toward the sound. "Was that an explosion?"

A couple of seconds later, we heard the sound again, but this time in a rapid succession of three. We jumped from our seats and were on deck before the noise of the last explosion had dissipated.

It was considerably lighter outside, the morning sun having crested the shoreline horizon, and the marine layer was almost a memory. Nate trained his binoculars toward the distance. The explosions were getting louder now, punctuating the constant low rumble of our engines like timpani drums. He dropped his binoculars and turned to us. "That's cannon fire."

"Cannon fire?" I said. "As in the Spanish Armada?"

"Check for yourself." He handed me the binoculars and pointed to a cliff-walled promontory jutting out over the water. "That's the Dana Point headlands right there. Now look just offshore."

I gasped the moment I put the binoculars to my eyes. Just visible through the fog in the distance was a ship like something straight out of a pirate movie. Two huge masts with four rectangular sails on each, and three triangular sails from a mast pointing straight out from the bow. A plume of smoke shot out from the side, with the accompanying boom coming a full three seconds later.

"It's the Tall Ships Festival," Nate said. "Goes on all week."

"Oh, god," Katy said with an eye roll. "Our dad used to make us come every year. They re-create old naval battles or something."

"It was fun," Nate said, offended. "We got to tour the ships."

"If your idea of fun is shuffling behind hundreds of people through stuffy, BO-filled enclosed spaces, then yes, it was absolute—"

"Guys!" Josh said.

"They stage the battles in pretty tight quarters," Nate said. "So unless Wayo is right in the middle of it all, we shouldn't have to get too close."

Josh grabbed the binoculars and looked for himself.

I said, "This could be good. Everyone's going to be paying attention to the battle, so we'll be able to do what we need to."

There was another burst of cannon fire. Josh pointed to the tip of the headlands. "That's the statue, right there."

"Go," Nate said. "We'll be there in twenty minutes." Katy immediately stepped behind the wheel. Nate grabbed the binoculars from Josh and scrambled through the rigging up toward the bow, and without another word, the rest of us went below.

We made Josh change in the bathroom, which was fair based on the numbers but still unfortunate for him. Every two or three seconds, we'd hear a bump followed immediately by a groan or a shout.

"No, no, no," Gracia said when she saw the suit I was wearing. "Not the sensible one-piece."

Mimi sighed. "I thought we were past this."

"It's my lucky suit," I said, admiring the faded stretch-challenged black material, the tiny hole above my right hip bone.

"This is the last time," Gracia said as she threw a wetsuit at me. "You have to promise."

"Cross my heart."

The wetsuits were unlike anything I had ever worn; no wonder they were so expensive. They were thin and smooth inside, with integrated booties and watertight seals at the neck and wrists. A single waterproof zipper spanned diagonally left to right across the front, so we had to step into the legs and pull the upper bodies over our heads. The design was even an aqua-camouflage pattern: dark blue and dark green interspersed with lighter blue and gray. I squeezed my little silver turtle for good luck before I zipped the suit closed.

"These things are amazing," Gracia said.

"I don't know what Geoprene is," I said, "but it beats the heck out of neoprene. It's supposed to—"

"Do something awesome and technical?" Mimi said. "We heard."

Josh knocked from inside the bathroom. "Are you decent?"

"Better than decent," Gracia said, admiring herself in the mirror. "That means you can come out now."

Josh strode into the room. His wetsuit accentuated his shoulders and biceps and came in tight around the waist; it fit him perfectly. It might as well have been a superhero uniform.

"What?" he said.

Gracia slapped me on the shoulder with the back of her hand, and I realized that I'd been staring. "Do the booties fit?" I managed.

Mimi stifled a giggle.

Now Gracia slapped her on the shoulder.

Mimi and Gracia put their clothes—long-sleeved shirts and sweatpants—back on over their wetsuits for just in case, and they fastened their HD computers to their wrists like oversize watches. I gave them a quick tutorial.

"Do these come with unlimited diver-to-diver?" Mimi said, keeping things light.

I wrapped a dive knife with a six-inch blade to the outside of my right calf and handed one to Josh. "It's for the kelp," I said in response to the concerned look on his face. "I'm not planning on an underwater knife fight."

The rebreathers were essentially BCs with hard-shell backpacks that carried two small tanks—one air and one 100 percent oxygen that would be blended to exactly the right mix depending on our depth. The shells had been custom-painted deep green, thanks to the all-powerful Black Card. Unlike on a traditional regulator, the mouthpiece stuck out from a thick hose that went around my neck like a hands-free harmonica. I'd breathe in from it and out to the constant circulation of computer-blended air.

It was lighter than a conventional BC and tank, but the rebreather was still about thirty-five pounds even before I slid the weights into the integrated side pockets, so I had to hold on to the table for stability as the boat rocked back and forth in the waves.

Josh and I pulled on matching Geoprene hoods and affixed our HD computers on our right wrists. The rebreathers had small monitoring screens we strapped on our left wrists. Then came gloves, and finally we were fully equipped.

"You guys look like cyborgs," Gracia said.

Mimi laughed. "Are they setting off your geek-dar?"

"There it is," Nate called down. "The *Aquatic Diamond*. Katy, kill the engine."

The silence that enveloped the boat was as disconcerting as it was sudden. Nate said, "I see someone at the helm, and two people on the top deck, getting gear together. One of them is Wayo, I think."

"Does the other guy look like a bulldog that got shot

in the face with a shotgun?" Gracia said.

"That's not really— Wait, yeah. He kind of does," Nate said.

It was Snow. He and Wayo were about to get in the water. My stomach clenched. "What about Alvarez?" I said.

"Nope," Nate said. "I don't see him. He must not have made the trip."

"Let us know if anyone else comes up from below."

Josh pulled his mask down and said, "Let's do this."

"You're going to be okay." Gracia squeezed my shoulder. She looked me up and down and said, "And I take back everything I ever said about you and buried treasure. You are officially a badass."

THIRTY-EIGHT

The dinghy had a hard bottom with inflated sides and a fifteen-horsepower outboard motor. We lowered it from the stern, hunching to stay out of Wayo's sight. Gracia was the first to climb down the ladder and into the dinghy. Josh and I followed, and Mimi came last with our fins.

I tied a rope to a D-ring at the front of the dinghy and tossed it to Katy, who secured it to the stern of the *Constant Bliss*, leaving us trailing about ten feet behind.

The ocean breeze was mild, but when Nate reengaged the engine, the dinghy bounced forward, spraying us with a cool mist. Josh and I strapped on our fins and waited.

The sound of the cannons grew louder as we bobbed toward the *Aquatic Diamond* and—finally, we could only hope—the Golden Jaguar. All at once the fog was gone, and a golden hue spread across the water's surface, glittering sparkles into the horizon.

Mimi put her hand on my shoulder and gave me an expression I could only describe as beseeching. "Please don't get killed."

Josh laughed once, a burst of sound as though he'd been kicked in the stomach. I exhaled through a forced smile. "I'll do my best."

"Seriously, it's shark season, you know. It's not uncommon for great whites to come this far dow—"

"Mimi!" Gracia said.

"The Black Card also comes with emergency evacuation services. Just in case. If anything hap—"

"Not helpful, Mimi." Gracia engaged the outboard motor enough to keep us out of view of Wayo's boat.

"What? I'm nervous."

I ignored both of them. I put the regulator in my mouth and breathed as normally as I could, and Josh did the same. I pressed a button on my computer, bringing up the full-color artist's rendering of the Jaguar to remind myself exactly why I was doing this.

Breathe in. Breathe out.

In.

Out.

Katy reappeared at the stern in what seemed like no time at all. "Okay," she said. "We're a hundred feet away. Are you ready for this?"

Josh and I gave each other the okay signal; then we turned and gave it to Katy.

She took off her tracksuit top, revealing a bright orange

bikini. She grabbed an empty wine-cooler bottle and said, "I'm up."

The *Constant Bliss* slowed.

Gracia cut the outboard to nothing more than a crawl. Josh and I pushed ourselves up onto the pontoon sides. Now that we weren't moving forward as quickly, the waves pitched us from side to side even more, so we grabbed the rope handles for support.

Then we heard yelling. It was indecipherable at first, but the closer we got, the more it sounded like actual words. Irate words.

Nate hollered a drunken "Waahoooo!"

"Hey!" said an angry voice. Not Wayo or Snow. Not Alvarez. "Watch out!"

"Here we go," Gracia said under her breath.

No matter how much I had been bracing for the sound, the sudden thump of boat against boat still caught me off guard. The dinghy's momentum would have carried us directly into their line of sight if Gracia hadn't gunned the engine and spun us off to the side.

"Whooopsie!" This was Nate at the helm, his voice high-pitched and giggly like he was wasted.

The angry voice again: "What the hell?"

Nate yelled, "My bad!"

"Damn it!" This was Snow. And he was livid.

"Now," Gracia said.

With that, Josh and I leaned back.

The water came around my hood to slap me in the face,

cold enough to take my breath away, but I was relieved to discover that I had full range of motion without having tiny daggers of cold water pierce the folds of my wetsuit. These new space-age suits were actually *warm*.

We'd removed all the air from our BCs so that when we hit the water, we didn't bob back up to the surface, and it took me a moment to orient myself. The galaxy of bubbles disappeared. I saw the keel of the dinghy above me.

Now that we were in the water, a small LED display came to life in the bottom-right corner of my computer-integrated mask, showing me information on depth, time in the water, and water temperature—a brisk sixty-two degrees. And, my god, the rebreather was astonishing. Not only were there no bubbles to give us away, but there was also no raspy in and out like with traditional regulators; my breathing was completely silent.

Josh hovered across from me as if enveloped in a cloud. The visibility was nowhere near as good as in Cozumel, but not bad for here—about thirty feet. I engaged the computer's touch screen, typed a quick *test*, and pressed the Send-to-Buddy button. I heard a short beep. He looked at his wrist and gave me the okay sign.

I pointed to the hull of Wayo's boat and kicked toward the stern. Josh followed, and we came to the edge of an underwater forest. Thick towers of dark olive kelp undulated in the waves like gigantic moray eels. When Josh and I were in position, we grabbed on to the bottom rung of the ladder.

I typed: *Ready.*

Josh beeped, but the message wasn't for him. We held on to the ladder, rocking back and forth with the waves, having nothing to do but stare into each other's masks while we waited.

He winked at me.

Our wrists beeped with a message from Mimi: *Go! Everyone distracted.*

Yeah, no kidding. I pulled myself up the ladder so that only my head broke the surface. The arguing voices had grown so loud that they almost drowned out the noise of the cannons.

"Iz jus a lil' scratch!" Nate said.

"You're getting in the way of the tall ships," Katy screeched. "The tall ships! We come here every year, and you're *ruining it*!"

"Calm down!" Snow said.

"Eeew, gross! Stop looking at me like that! You're a dirty, dirty man."

Nate said, "Tha's my sister you're starin' at!"

"Gross, gross, gross! I'm calling the cops!" Katy was amazing, I had to admit.

Snow yelled a string of profanities that ran together, and another voice joined the fray.

"Hey, look! It's Wayo!" Nate hollered.

We knew he'd recognize Nate and Katy, so we figured the only way to deal with that was to freely acknowledge the coincidence. Even if it didn't fool him for long, it might add to the confusion. And Josh and I only needed a few minutes.

"Oh my god! Wayo!" Katy squealed. "You like cannons, too! I should have known!"

"Wayo! My amigo! Tell yer cap'n to watch what he's doin' to my daddy's boat!"

I noticed that Mimi had clambered back up onto the deck and was hiding behind the cabin, poking her head up for the occasional glimpse. She pressed some buttons on her computer, and my wrist beeped again: *Go!*

I slipped off my fins and nestled them on the small platform at the stern. Then I hoisted myself up the ladder. Josh followed quickly.

"In and out," I reminded him.

Josh opened the cabin door, revealing a long living room with an open kitchen at the far end. I had only made it three steps into the room when I heard my name. And it wasn't Josh who'd said it.

The voice belonged to Mr. Alvarez.

"Annie?" Alvarez said again. His legs had been roped to a chair, and his hands were tied behind his back. "Annie!"

Of all the things I'd prepared myself for, seeing Alvarez helpless in the corner like that was not one of them. The combination of my surprise and a particularly large wave rocked me off balance, and I staggered into the coffee table by the small couch. It took everything I had not to scream in pain.

"I guess you're not in on it after all," Josh said as he lumbered past Alvarez and toward the lower helm controls. He pried off the control panel with the tip of his knife and stabbed at the wires leading to the fuse box.

"What's going on?" I asked Alvarez as I rubbed a sharp throbbing from my shin.

"You shouldn't be here," he said.

"I could tell you the same thing," I said, finally able to tear my eyes away from him long enough to do my job. I scanned the room for any clues, any information Snow and Wayo might have gathered about the Golden Jaguar.

"Snow said he'd kill me if they didn't find the Jaguar," Alvarez babbled in an exaggerated whisper. "Everything we have points to right here, but if they don't find it, I've got nothing else."

"What *do* you have?" I said.

He nodded toward a table near the kitchen. "Snow was our partner. He's the one who brought Wayo and me in on the job. We kept hitting dead ends. When we ran out of money, he borrowed from some black market dealers. Mexican Mafia, I think. I don't know, something bad."

"And when he couldn't find it on his own," I said, "he came back to you."

The wall above the long table was covered with maps and images of the Jaguar, much of which Josh and I had already seen, but there was some new stuff. The gold disk sat on a pile of full-page color photos, being used as a simple paperweight.

Next to it was a two-foot gold statue I recognized instantly as a replica of Salento's statue on the headlands above us.

Josh noticed it, too, as he stepped away from the helm controls. "Was that inside the cave on Molokai?"

Alvarez said, "How did you—"

"Primary sources," I said. "Remember?"

"That's why—" The sound of Josh unsheathing his knife stopped Alvarez short.

I gasped. "Josh—"

"I'm just cutting him loose."

"The statue was in the cavern, along with Francisco de Ulloa's log," Alvarez said. "But the log was so poorly preserved, it fell to pieces almost instantly."

I sifted through pictures of the fragments—some containing as much as a sentence or two, some with only a word. One picture showed an entire page of the log, meticulously reassembled as if it had been a shattered china plate.

"The log led us back here," Alvarez said. "We were able to figure out the rough location based on descriptions of the headlands and the location of the statue—"

"We know," Josh said. His knife cut through the rope, and Alvarez shook out his hands as Josh freed his feet.

"You don't understand," Alvarez said. "These people will kill you."

Josh scoffed. "Like Wayo tried to kill Annie in the Devil's Throat?"

I glanced briefly over my shoulder, in time to see Alvarez's face pale. "What? No. He didn't."

"Turned off her air and left her to die."

I led Alvarez toward the exit door. "Come on. Gracia's

on the other side of the Sugars' boat. You can swim there."

"I swear, Annie, I didn't know Wayo was going to do that. I recognized Snow down on Cozumel; that's why I knew we had to hurry that night. But it was the first time I'd seen him in months. I had no idea he and Wayo were still working together. I would never have—"

"Does he have anything else on the Jaguar?" I said, pointing to the table.

"The log said 'three hundred paces beneath his true love's gaze,' so the GPS puts it right below us," Alvarez said. "Let me go with you."

Josh shook his head. "No time."

The room rumbled with the loudest burst of cannon fire yet. Alvarez veered to a dry box and opened the latches. Inside was a pneumatic speargun pistol, cocked and ready to go. He wrapped my hand around the holster. "Just in case."

"In case what?" I said.

"Please," Alvarez said. "If you're going to do this, at least take it."

Josh motioned impatiently. "We have to get moving."

I grabbed the speargun and strapped it around my thigh. The tip of the spear extended through the holster, past my knee, but I was able to move freely without it stabbing me.

"Go," I said to Josh. "Get him out of here."

I sent a quick message to Gracia—*Alvarez coming back*—and I was about to follow them when I noticed something else on the table. Underneath a large printout of the ocean-floor topography was a file stand with a series of manila folders inside. I recognized the words written on each of the files: SAN PABLO, MARIA ROSADA, SEÑORA DE BELEN—all names of as-yet-undiscovered shipwrecks.

Then I gasped. I wobbled a little, whether from the unsteady boat beneath my feet or my suddenly unsteady legs, I wasn't sure. One of the files was labeled simply FLOR DO AMELIA. Bigfoot. The mythical Portuguese ship of gold. My hand trembled as I grabbed the file and looked inside. It was thick with documents and photos, a few data CDs, even a flash drive.

Josh stood alone outside, motioning to me frantically through the tinted window, but I couldn't leave, not now. I dumped the contents of a small trash bin onto the floor and tore out the plastic bag. I stuffed the file inside and wrapped the rest of the bag around it.

I unzipped my wetsuit and tucked the bag tightly against my damp skin. The Geoprene wasn't completely watertight, but it was close enough. I zipped the wetsuit up, shrugged under the weight of the rebreather, and went outside just as Alvarez disappeared, swimming around the stern of the *Constant Bliss*. The cannons' explosions were almost on top of us now.

"Care to explain?" Josh said, handing me my fins.

"Later."

Our consoles beeped a message from Mimi: *Holy crap. Nate just went Jackie Chan on Snow. Katy took out captain. Boat is secure but Wayo in the water.*

Another beep, this one from Gracia: *Alvarez safe.*

Josh and I put on our fins and secured our masks. This was it.

"You ready?" I said, my knees bending with the gentle rocking of our now-disabled boat.

Before I knew what was happening, Josh leaned down and put his lips on mine.

Our masks bumped up against each other, and the waves jostled us back and forth. Josh held on to the railing with one hand for support, and at one point he almost pitched backward into the water. The gear made it impossible for us to hug each other, so we wobbled in our fins, kissing like overweight penguins on an ice floe.

It was fantastically awkward.

"What was that for?" I said when Josh pulled away.

He leaned down again and put his forehead to mine. "In case we don't make it. No regrets."

I was overcome by a surge of energy, a sensation unlike anything I'd ever felt before. It wasn't adrenaline, and it wasn't happiness; it was just new. Everything was sharper, more brilliant. It was as if I saw things more clearly, as if I felt things more deeply.

I had a knife on one leg and a speargun on the other. I was wearing twenty-five thousand dollars' worth of equipment. There was treasure in the water below me. And Josh Rebstock just kissed me on the lips.

"No regrets," I said.

He smiled at me, and we put our regulators back in and took long strides forward into the water.

THIRTY-NINE

We passed a school of barracuda at thirty feet, their silver flashing in the cold blue light. At forty feet, I noticed a snail—its brilliant blue-and-yellow shell the size of a dime—stuck to a gently swaying kelp leaf. Without the regulator's intermittent drone, I felt more part of the underwater world than ever. And with the LED readout in my mask, I didn't have to worry about checking any external depth gauges. I forgot about myself, forgot about my equipment, and was able to concentrate on everything around me.

We descended at the border of the kelp forest, directly beneath the boat, our bodies horizontal like skydivers in slow motion. At seventy feet, the ocean floor came into view below us, as did the biggest striped treefish I had ever seen. It left the security of a coral mound and braved the exposed openness long enough to reach a much larger coral formation.

An arching tunnel, wide at the base, narrow at the top, and achingly familiar.

Still descending, I danced my fingers across the computer screen as I scrolled through the images, finally settling on the one I wanted. I held my wrist out in front of me.

There it was. A perfect match.

I screamed victory into my regulator.

Josh screamed, too. I turned to flash him the thumbs-up, but what I saw was so unexpected, I could only process the images as individual pieces of information, not as the parts of a whole.

Josh was still screaming.

He was doubled over, clutching his upper left arm with his right hand.

A silver barb the size of my pinkie stuck out from between the fingers of his right hand, glinting even in the low light of the depths.

A dark cloud seeped from beneath his hand, the maroon liquid dissipating into the water.

A black cable stretched about twenty-five feet behind him and just to the left, where Wayo now hovered. He was holding the body of a speargun. And he was starting to pull Josh toward him.

There was no time to do anything but act. I unsheathed my knife and cut the cable connecting the shaft to Wayo's speargun.

Wayo was charging now, so I grabbed Josh's wrist and

kicked frantically for cover in the kelp forest behind us.

Josh wasn't going to like what I did next, but I couldn't see that we had much of a choice. The shaft extended a good three feet behind Josh, but there was enough of the point sticking out of his biceps for me to wrap my gloved hand around it. I gripped the spear's barb end and pulled it all the way out, and Josh screamed again.

The spear fell swiftly into the depths. We were in the kelp, hidden for the time being. His wetsuit had closed around the wound, but even so, the blood seemed to flow more freely now that the spear was out. That wouldn't necessarily have been too bad—at least not for me— except for the shadowy outline that had just meandered into view behind an unsuspecting Wayo.

Classic. There was a freaking shark in the water with us. What was next? Wayo turning into a merman?

I pulled Josh deeper into the kelp forest. He was moaning, so I put my finger in front of the regulator as a reminder. He glared at me but stopped moaning anyway. We sank down lower, at ninety feet now, running silent and bubble free.

It was only a matter of time.

Sooner—not later—either Wayo or the shark would find us. In spite of that, or maybe because of it, a sense of calm swept through me. I knew that everything depended on the next ten minutes. I knew what we had to do; there was no other option. I held Josh's face in front of mine to make sure that he wasn't about to pass out. I typed: *follow my lead*. He nodded.

And then I did something I could only have imagined the movie version of myself even contemplating.

We were only ten feet above the bottom. Based on where I'd seen the rock formation, I knew we would have to be out in the open for at least a few seconds. I held Josh by his good hand and kicked as hard as I could.

As we bolted from the kelp, I caught a hazy glimpse of Wayo about twenty-five feet above and to the left. He noticed us, and his body tilted down like a dive-bombing falcon.

Josh and I entered the formation no more than three seconds later. It was longer than I'd anticipated—more than a simple arch. From the top of the tunnel to the sea-floor was no taller than twenty feet, and while a pair of SUVs could have driven comfortably through, side by side along the bottom, the walls tapered severely up to about five feet apart at the top.

I noticed an indentation in the tunnel ceiling—as if an ice-cream scoop had been taken from the underside of the rock—and kicked up to it. An uneven hole no wider than a basketball allowed a glimpse through to the ocean above. I quickly pulled an emergency buoy and spool from my BC pocket and filled the buoy with a burst of air from my octopus. Then I knifed the spool into the rock and let the buoy float through the hole and up to the surface.

Josh and I, now parallel with the ocean floor, pressed our backs up against the rock. I eased the speargun from its holster and waited.

The buoy spool was no longer spinning, so I glanced back to make sure that my knife was still in place.

There was something on the rock.

My knife had chopped away a crust of coral, revealing what looked like the corner of an embossed design. I reached the tip of the speargun to scrape away the growth, revealing a wing, then another, then a neck. The familiar double-headed bird of the Cortés crest.

It might as well have said, "Ulloa was here!"

I scanned around me for anything else. Anything out of place. Anything that would indicate the location of the Jaguar itself. Wayo would be appearing at any second, but I couldn't help it. One eye on the opening below, one eye inspecting the formation. It had to be there. Farther down the slope was a line, too horizontal, a shelf carved into the rock.

It was like staring at an anthill, how for a moment it looks like there's nothing there, but once you see the first ant, you notice all the others, and you wonder how it was possible that you hadn't noticed them before. The centuries of growth had covered the Jaguar so completely that it appeared to be nothing more than part of the rock. If I hadn't been looking for it—if the roaring beast hadn't been seared into my retinas—there's no way I would have seen it. But now, knowing everything I knew, with the double-headed bird staring me in the face, the silhouette of the Golden Jaguar's head was unmistakable.

Josh elbowed me, wide-eyed, and pointed angrily down to the mouth of the tunnel.

Wayo. He was too far down to see us, and he wasn't looking up. Not yet, at least. He moved slowly, kicking so as not to disturb the silt on the ocean floor, and his head scanned to the left, then to the right.

A shadow of the shark swam across the entrance behind him but didn't come inside. My throat tightened, and I had to force the air back into it.

I turned the speargun back up into the rock and squeezed the trigger from point-blank range. My wrist recoiled slightly, but the bolt buried itself past the barb, and I unspooled the twenty feet of cable below the barrel of the gun.

Josh grabbed my arm, but there was no time to argue or explain. I shrugged him off and—while keeping my eyes on Wayo—motioned for Josh to stay where he was. I arranged my body vertically upside down, so my legs were in a crouch and my heels were pressed against the tunnel ceiling.

When Wayo came almost directly below me, I pushed off as hard as I could. It took me only two strong kicks, and then I was there.

I grabbed his tank valve and leaned back, pressing my knees on either side of his tank and pulling on the valve as hard as I could. It took him just a moment to realize what was going on, and that moment was enough. He started to flail like a turtle on its back, but it was too late; he was helpless. I had him securely in the panicked diver hold, and there was nothing he could do. It didn't matter how much bigger or stronger he was.

I thought briefly about giving Wayo a little taste of his own medicine, but there was no time to turn off his air. The shark was back. It made another pass across the entrance and turned toward us.

I wrapped the speargun cable around Wayo's valve as many times as I could while avoiding his thrashing limbs, and when I ran out of cable I jammed the spear pistol itself between Wayo's tank and BC and pushed off of him and up toward Josh. The shark was closer now, on the other side of Wayo, whose panicked writhing had caused him to become even more entangled in the cable.

Josh came down to meet me at the opposite end of the tunnel, and I grabbed his hand, and we kicked out through the opening as hard as we could. Our computers beeped frantically, warning us that we were ascending too fast, so I flattened us out to a more diagonal ascent without slowing down the kicking. We swam up and away.

It was only when we reached about sixty feet—and when we hadn't been munched on by the great white—that I had the nerve to turn around to see what was behind us.

Josh and I hovered side by side as we caught our breath. He squeezed my hand, and we watched the coral formation together. It was just at the edge of our visibility, a hazy outline against the deep blue water.

Wayo's bubbles percolated gracefully up through the hole in the tunnel ceiling. I stared at the tunnel exit for any movement, but there was none. The ocean rocked us gently back and forth—movement that became more motherly and protective with each passing second. After five minutes, I began to breathe easier.

There was no shark. And there was no Wayo.

FORTY

'd always thought I wanted to be famous.

Sure, I'd pretended otherwise. Whenever people swarmed Mimi on the street, hounding her for autographs or quick pictures, crowding me off the sidewalk or against the side of a building as though I didn't exist—or worse, asking me to take the picture for them—I would scoff at the whole spectacle.

Deep down, though, surrounded as I was by the idea that fame was the ultimate goal, I envied her—as I envied Josh's mom. I envied all the people at school who never had to introduce themselves to anyone. Fame was the be-all and end-all in part because it seemed so attainable; as the stars of Gracia's dad's reality shows had proved, you didn't even need to accomplish anything in order to get it.

But when I finally had the choice, and when I forced myself to consider the repercussions of that choice, I realized one important fact: there is a difference between a famous person and a real person, and that difference is simple. Famous people do things for recognition. Real people do things for the experience.

The experience, for example, of riding the Golden Jaguar like a horse as an industrial-strength crane lifted it from the ocean floor.

I sat bareback, one hand clutching a rope around the Jaguar's neck, the other holding the winch controller, watching the excavation area disappear below me as I rose at a safe, gradual speed. Above me, Josh waited on the trawler. Poor Josh, who hadn't been cleared to join me below because his arm was still in a sling three weeks later.

When it came down to it, I wanted to be a real person. I wanted to be me.

Tempting though it might have been, I even turned down a fawning pitch from Gracia's dad about what he swore was a "can't miss" new reality show. *The Real Adventures of Scuba Girl*, which would follow me and my new team of high school treasure hunters around the world as we searched for history's most valuable undiscovered shipwrecks. The bulldog agent Larry Schuster, who'd salivated at the chance to represent me, couldn't believe I'd pass on such an opportunity.

Josh was crushed at first, in spite of what the fame machine had done to his family, and he struggled to understand why I wouldn't want the whole world to know what I'd done. Maybe it was because fame was all he was familiar with. Or maybe he wanted the cachet, now that he and I were actually "together" or "a couple" or "dating" or whatever we were calling it. Eventually, though, he came around. *Scuba Girl* would have to stay a nickname.

There would be no media event celebrating my fantastic discovery. No paparazzi waiting eagerly on the shore. Josh knew who'd found the Jaguar. My dad knew who'd found it. I knew. That was enough for me.

The credit for the find—publicly, at least—would be given to the students of the Pinedale Academy, but the full story of the Jaguar was yet to be written. Though the statue had been deposited well within American waters, claims had been put in by cultural agencies within the Mexican and Spanish governments.

I'd requested that Father Gonzales be brought in to oversee the restoration. Eventually, once the ownership claims had been settled and the statue fully restored, the Jaguar would go on tour. Starting in California, it would cross the ocean to Spain before completing the circle. Finally, the Golden Jaguar would return home to its original location in Mexico, the heart of the Aztec Empire.

Besides, who needed the credit when we had the finder's fee? Snow would have gotten his couple hundred million on the black market, but we settled for the customary single-digit percentage. No matter which government it ended up coming from, my share would be enough to take care of the dive shop and set up a college account, with a little extra for the Marine Park Conservancy Fund. Maybe even some more of those magical dresses.

But that would all work itself out. Right now, the Jaguar and I had a few more minutes to ourselves.

At fifteen feet, I pressed the Stop button on the winch controller and typed *safety stop* on my dive computer. Seconds later, my wrist beeped. A message from Josh on the trawler: *You're milking it.*

He was right. Even if only a handful of people ever knew that I'd found the Jaguar, my life was going to be different the moment I broke the surface. It already was, at least to me. Over the past three weeks I'd stopped thinking of myself as plain old Annie Fleet. I had a new full name: Annie Fleet, the Girl Who Found the Golden Jaguar.

And now I was about to ride the Golden Jaguar as it tasted sunshine for the first time in five hundred years.

Snow was tucked safely in jail, charged with all sorts of fun stuff, including the felony kidnapping and aggravated assault of poor Mr. Alvarez on top of some additional parole violations. He wouldn't be bothering anyone soon, and neither would Wayo.

After a furious six-hour search, the Coast Guard found him bobbing, exhausted, among the waves, over a thousand yards offshore. Wayo might have escaped the great white, but the long arm of the law was another matter, and his premeditated speargunning of my boyfriend had gotten him charged with attempted murder.

Things had been such a whirlwind, what with the permits, the salvage planning meetings with underwater archaeologists and college professors and museum curators, that I hadn't even had the time to do half my homework, much less look through the folder I'd swiped from Wayo's boat. All I knew so far was that the fancy Geoprene had done its job. Everything in the folder was readable, even the flash drive.

My wrist beeped again: *You still alive?*

I smiled into the regulator and took another moment to enjoy the tranquility, the gentle swaying motion. I closed my eyes and breathed deeply, and then I hit the winch and broke through the surface and above, swinging from the crane in the warm Pacific breeze.

The only cameras waiting for us back at the marina belonged to the people who mattered: Mimi, Gracia, Josh's mom and Violet, the Sugars, and, of course, my parents. Mr. Alvarez was there as well, barking orders with Father Gonzales at crews of marine archaeologists from UCLA. The trawler docked at a spot closest to the street, where a nondescript moving truck idled, ready to take the Jaguar up to the father's team of restoration experts at the Getty Museum in Los Angeles.

"I never imagined being so proud of my daughter," Dad said, his delighted gaze bouncing back and forth between me and the Jaguar.

"I'll try not to let it go to my head."

My dad hugged me and lifted me off the ground, and he didn't let go until Mom tapped him on the shoulder.

"Bill," she said gently, and then, louder, "Bill!"

He released me, then wandered over to the Jaguar, which had been lowered onto the ground next to the truck and was somehow even more breathtaking in person than in my imagination. The tail was bent down and no longer poised like a whip, and the gold was gouged in places, but I could make out the deep ruby eyes and the razor-sharp green teeth of its openmouthed roar.

Dad put his hand up to the midsection and touched it, tenderly at first, as though he feared a burn, but then he rested both palms flat against its body. "It's beautiful."

"You want us to give you a moment alone?" Gracia said.

While everyone's attention was focused on the Jaguar, while they posed for pictures and generally freaked out about its awesomeness, Josh led me off to the side and kissed me. The treasure, the warm sun, the kiss from Josh that was somehow no longer surprising—it would have been hard to imagine my life getting better than that moment.

"We should do this more often," Josh whispered, motioning to the Jaguar.

"I guess I could get used to it."

He wrapped his good arm around my neck and pulled me close. "As long as you're the one who gets shot next time."

"Deal," I said. "As long as you promise to save us by being the most awesome diver in the history of the world."

"I liked you better when you were all mumbly and shy."

I elbowed him. "No you didn't."

"No." He gave me a squeeze and kissed me again. "No I didn't."

"Hey, you crazy kids," Gracia called out. She ran over and grabbed each of us by the arm. "Group picture before they load this kitty up."

I unzipped the wetsuit, ducked out of the upper body, and tied the arms around my waist, revealing the blue miracle fabric of Gracia's bikini.

"Finally," Mimi said.

Gracia raised her arms in praise. "Can I get an amen!"

"Amen!" Josh shouted. His mom and my parents exchanged a delightfully awkward glance.

With the Jaguar in the center, the rest of us fanned out in either direction, some touching the statue, others squatting down in front of it like in a soccer team photo. Father Gonzales held the camera and backed away until he got us all in the frame. "Everybody say 'treasure'!"

ACKNOWLEDGMENTS

I want to thank the insightful readers of the Antidote Workshop: Scott Repass, Casey Fleming, Rajnana Varghese, Irene Keliher, and Greg Oaks. Thanks also to the incredible team at Gigglin' Marlin dive shop in Houston: Joe Forneau for all his time and to my various instructors: Bill "Crash" Merrit (DPV & Equipment), Jeff Diamant (Nitrox), and Dan Bowen (Rescue Diver). The Parks Fellowship at Rice University helped me carve away the time to write. I will always be grateful to Edmundo Torres and his cute boat at Cha Cha Cha in Cozumel for all our dives together. Lisa Yoskowitz, Catherine Onder, and Ari Lewin handled an awesome tag-team editorial process, and Sara Crowe kept me focused what mattered. Finally, thanks to my family for their support—especially to Molly, the best dive buddy ever.